Love,
Courage,
and
Miracles

Love, Courage, and Miracles

A mother's journey and her daughter's
story living with cystic fibrosis and
a lung transplant

ROBIN MODLIN

atmosphere press

Published by Atmosphere Press

ISBN 979-8-89132-258-5

Cover design by Ronaldo Alves

Robinmodlin.com
Atmospherepress.com

For the individuals, families, and communities
living with cystic fibrosis and organ transplants.
Your love and courage are miracles to behold.

May this story of hope benefit all.

Table of Contents

Foreword

I met Anna and Robin Modlin when I directed the Cystic Fibrosis and Lung Transplant Program at Stanford University Medical Center, and, after a long medical career, it is natural that some patients remain front of mind, while others fade into the background. To be clear, in real time, everyone gets treated equally—at least that's the goal. They told us in medical school not to have favorites. But let me reveal a little secret: we physicians do, because we are human. Certain patients stand out. For me, one of those patients is Anna Modlin.

Like many young cystic fibrosis patients that I treated, Anna came with a team. And the captain of that team? Her mother, Robin Modlin.

If a common maternal trait is fierce protection of their children, or sacrifice for the familial good, or an abundance of empathy, Anna hit the jackpot with her mother. Robin was, and is, all of those things (dare I say, on steroids), but even more. She is smart, inquisitive, and totally vested in her daughter's journey, first through the CF maze and then the transplant gauntlet. I got to see the Modlins navigate both worlds: the one where a lung transplant was somewhere off in the future, something to be aware of if not totally engaged with, and then there was the second phase: the inevitable one when Anna was placed on our transplant waiting list at Stanford. Then our team took care of Anna for many years—that is, before she moved south, and I mean way south, to Australia.

What was that experience like for me, as head of the team that was charged with transplanting her safely and then keeping her well afterward?

Simple. It was a privilege. Anna was the kind of patient

that got us transplant folks out of bed in the morning without an alarm clock, eager to go to work to see what kind of miracle one of our patients demonstrated that day. With Anna, it was like she was manufactured in a place where perfect patients are made: smart (she must have inherited that from Robin and her father, Doug), athletic, relentlessly optimistic, and compliant with her complicated post-transplant regimen.

Except she wasn't "manufactured." She was emotional solid gold, providing not only comfort and mentorship to her fellow patients but also to the transplant team. When I saw her name on my list of hospitalized patients or on the clinic roster on any particular day, I raced to her room as quickly as I could. Yes, I wanted to help her get through whatever she was dealing with, but she gave me more than I ever gave her. She brightened the days when I needed it most—and some days, I really needed it.

And now comes *Love, Courage, and Miracles* by Robin Modlin, a beautiful, raw book about what it's like to walk this medical journey with a child, the laughter and the tears, the wins and the losses. In her beautifully written book, Robin lets us all take a look at what their family life has been like, told with grace, intelligence, and, most of all, honesty that could have only resulted from close introspection.

When Robin contacted me to tell me she was writing a book, she asked for my help. Before she got the question all the way out, I said yes. Then I read the words on the page, and I couldn't say anything. I could only marvel—at Anna, at Robin, and at this beautiful, messy thing we call transplantation. As they read these pages, patients and their families will find themselves nodding their heads, relating to the shared experiences that all sick patients have in common. But clinicians will find something in these pages, too: our "Why?"—the reason we leave our kids every day to take care of someone else's.

We don't get a chance to look at humanism this way very often, when it is up close and exposed. *Love, Courage, and Miracles* provides us that opportunity. Savor these pages.

David Weill, M.D.
Former Director, Stanford Lung Transplant Program
Author, Exhale: Hope, Healing, and A Life in Transplant

Preface

In January 2023, our family met in Kauai, Hawaii, for a vacation. It was a rare chance to be together and for me to share my writings with my daughters. I was writing about my journey as their mother and our family experience living with cystic fibrosis, CF. Anna, my first-born daughter, has CF and her life and disease set the stage for our family life. She is central to my story. My daughters, Anna and Sara, encouraged me to continue writing while they added their memories to my recollections.

While on the trip, we visited Lawai International Center, a historic park with eighty-eight miniature concrete shrines created over 100 years ago. Designed after a famous Japanese Buddhist pilgrimage, a path leads visitors up a steep, rocky hillside planted with orchids and ferns. Each shrine holds a different Buddha image or statue with offerings of flowers, stones, and other personal items left as prayers by the visitors.

When we arrived at Lawai, we felt how special it was. The director of the temple park told us the land was long recognized as a powerful healing place. She shared the magic of when she declared it was her life's purpose to be its guardian. She spoke about her intention to be the caretaker while inside an enclosed office with no open windows or doors when suddenly, from out of nowhere, she felt a wind magically swirling around her while lifting and scattering papers around the room. Believing the wind miraculously affirmed her desired role, she never wavered from her mission of caring for the grounds and shrines. The wind also accentuated her belief that Lawai was a special and spiritual place that could connect its visitors to their life purpose.

She told us this story while we sat under a lanai near the

temple walk when another mysterious wind suddenly blew as if from nowhere. It lifted our picnic paper plates into the air, hurling one at me and one at Anna. Mine landed directly on my chest over my heart. It was strange and mysterious and felt like a deliberate message and affirmation.

After finishing our lunch, we picked up tall walking sticks to walk the path of the shrines. The wind-blown plate landing over my heart and the symbolic walk reminded me of the story I wanted to tell of my mother-journey with its steep climb, rocky path, natural beauty, magic, and miracles. It felt as if I was being mysteriously encouraged to tell my story.

I had experienced a similar wind before. May 22, 2011, six months after Anna's double lung transplant due to CF. Our family had a garden party to celebrate her new life. After lunch was served and before the dessert of voluptuous cupcakes was devoured, a strong wind came up as a mischievous force. It lifted skirts, messed hairdos, and tossed paper plates with leftover salad in the air, marking a mysterious and unexpected interruption to the outdoor party. It was as if the universe was anointing everyone with a full blast of breath as a metaphor for Anna's life. The gust of wind symbolized her new breath carrying her into her miraculous new life.

Since that wind, Anna's life has unfolded in remarkable ways, and people who know her have suggested her story of hope and courage be shared. In the autumn of 2022, I saw a path to tell the story as mom and daughter. I have read amazing stories about people with cystic fibrosis and their families who love them. Still, ours is unique and includes the hope of her very successful lung transplant.

This story is about a mother challenged to accept her life as it is while entwined with her daughter's disease and a life of love, courage, and miracles. As the author, I believe the most complete and artful way to tell this tale is for both of our voices to be heard and folded into one beautiful origami.

Thank you, Anna Holyoak, for your heartfelt writings included next to mine.

"The spiritual journey involves going beyond hope and fear, stepping into unknown territory, continually moving forward. The most important aspect of being on the spiritual path may be just to keep moving."

Pema Chodron, *When Things Fall Apart: Heart Advice for Difficult Times*

The author, Lawai International Center temple walk. Kauai, Hawaii, 2023.

PART ONE

From the Beginning

a story of miracles

"Tune into the presence of miracles, and in an instant, life can be transformed into a dazzling experience, more wondrous and exciting than we could even imagine."

Deepak Chopra, *The Essential Spontaneous Fulfillment of Desire: The Essence of Harnessing the Infinite Power of Coincidence*

chapter one

A Wave of Her Hand

We were startled by the phone ringing before we climbed into bed for the night. Knowing we could get a call anytime that would change our lives, I answered, thinking this might be it. "Hello?"

It was Anna. "Mom, I got 'The Call.' I think it is going to happen this time."

I could feel my adrenaline rising to meet the moment. My body was preparing for the marathon I knew was ahead. Doug and I locked eyes, grounding us for what was to come. "OK, Anna, we will pull a few things together, and your dad and I will meet you at the hospital. I love you so much. This is what we have been waiting for," is all I could say.

I did not cry. I had been rehearsing for this moment for 119 days while she was waiting on the transplant list, or perhaps I had been rehearsing for her whole life. I knew what I needed to do as I shifted my gears from "wait" to "go," thinking of all the worried times, wanting this day to arrive. In our anticipation, we often said it would come soon. Soon was now. The evening's shift in direction gave the day a new meaning. Fate was taking our hands to witness either a new life beginning or our daughter's remarkable story ending.

Before midnight, our family arrived in spurts at the hospital from many locations to support Anna, including Anna's partner, John; her dear friends Isa, Ana, and Linda; her Aunt Sue; sister Sara; her father, Doug; and me, her mom. Leaving all our usual routines to offer hope and love as supporters and witnesses for this monumental event, we stepped into Anna's world, hoping for a miraculously successful lung transplant surgery and recovery.

It was 4:00 a.m. when the nurses from the surgical team came into our surreal scene of a family who had been up all night, sitting on the bed of a dying patient while drinking tea, talking, laughing, and nervously waiting for the possibility of her life being saved. I looked up. My eyes widened, recognizing that these nurses ready for surgery were not apparitions. They were really there.

It was time. The chatting stopped as Anna was addressed. "Are you Anna Modlin? We are part of your transplant team. Are you ready? We are a 'go.'"

We watched in hushed silence as Anna sat up and agreed. "I am ready. Let's go!"

Next, we found ourselves in a long, sterile corridor lit with a fluorescent glow. In front of us, a hospital gurney with our daughter, sister, niece, and friend was being pushed down the hallway toward the operating room. I looked at the top of her curly-haired head and wondered if this would be our last moment together.

Her loving supporters were all wearing matching navy shirts emblazoned with green saying, "Anna Banana's Bunch." We hoped we were officially on a winning team. The moment was exciting and felt like winning the lottery. Yet, our stride down the long corridor toward the surgical theater was measured. We knew the real prize, Anna's priceless gift of survival, was still to be had. The seriousness of what was about to happen came into exquisite focus as the gurney stopped, and our party went on hold at those swinging operating room doors.

The expected end of Anna's life was intersecting with the unexpected end of another's. Anna was twenty-nine years old, and without a lung transplant, her life was nearing completion. She was in the final chapter of her life after a long battle with cystic fibrosis, or CF, a genetic lung disease. Continual infections had ravaged Anna's lungs until little was left for her.

Bringing her close to my heart in a quick embrace meant to release her into the unknown; I had to fight back my tears while understanding this moment could be our last together. How could a singular moment as quick as it takes to breathe a few breaths, shed a tear, or even offer a comforting smile be infused with all that must be said? It was impossible to say the thousands of words of love and memories. Still, my faith, which had grown after being her mom for twenty-nine years, collecting blessings and miracles, accompanied me to those operating room doors.

Anna had successfully fought for her life before. In an instant, I remembered being back at the bedside of my one-and-a-half-year-old child with severe pneumonia. As her lungs were suctioned, long strings of mucus were removed, making it easier for her to breathe. She survived then, and I knew she could do it again. I truly believed it would all work out and she would survive and thrive because it was the only way to support Anna and cope with the potential of such a loss.

Meeting extraordinary challenges with extraordinary will and a bit of magic was what Anna did well. With all her built-in genetic challenges, my daughter always dove headfirst and came out the other side scathed, sometimes wounded, and always shinier. The hope and possibility of a new life she deserved with a gifted set of lungs was now only a transplant surgery away.

We sent our final kisses, our wishes for good luck, and a "We will see you with new lungs!" as the only way to say our wholly inadequate goodbyes. The two nurses dressed in blue scrubs driving her bed were now in charge as I released my clutch. A miracle was on order. We saw Anna's arm rise to wave goodbye as they wheeled her from us. She was confident, and yet I know she was scared, too.

Twenty-seven years before that walk down the corridor, our lives reached another turning point when we discovered Anna had CF. Its effects on our lives and threat upon our child's life made it our forever unwanted guest. Since her early childhood, I did not know how long her life would be. I became skilled in accepting each day and its new challenges. I could either live in denial or fear of all we had to face, or I could live with gratitude and accept the unease of living in the unknown while enjoying life and finding blessings around us.

Finding my spiritual footing became a motivating force. Learning how to cope and accept the fate I was given opened my heart and deepened my search for meaning. It also helped me recognize that life is chronically miraculous even while living with this chronically devastating disease.

Our family came together to fight for Anna's life. Waiting by her side for this moment of all moments was an opportunity rare and precious. When those OR doors opened, and she made her final wave, we stood there watching as she disappeared. Mixed with emotions, including a strong dose of fear and a bigger one of hope, we returned to the room where we had been waiting with Anna. After gathering our coats and belongings from the top of her ruffled bed, we occupied another space with upholstered chairs and coffee tables called The North Intensive Care Unit Waiting Room to reconvene the wait. She was now in the hands of destiny and surgeons.

chapter two

Before the Storm Rolled In

Outside my second-story bedroom at the home we moved into when I was nine, I could see the top of a grapefruit tree shaped like an umbrella. Under that umbrella, with its large hanging yellow balls of fruit, was a perfect limb for my perch. Sometimes, I would climb to sit in my private world, pondering why life was the way it was. For as long as I can remember, I have been very introspective.

As a child, I considered myself shy and afraid of standing out, yet I was curious about the world and who I was. My earliest memories take me to moments standing close to my mother's skirt, feeling very attached to the safety of her love. My father was always there for me to hug. He would play with me in the living room, teaching me how to fall off a horse safely and patiently listening to my forever wishes that he would gift one to me. My parents' love was my safety net.

I also remember closing the door to my room and wanting to be alone. I had two active older brothers and a baby sister born when I was five. I enjoyed time with my phonograph records, listening to stories about The Lone Ranger or Roy Rogers, being lost in my fantasy, climbing on my horse, and riding along. I loved my red tasseled cowgirl skirt, fringed vest, and hat that proved I was one of the posse.

Alice, an imaginary friend, was my earliest and very best companion. I was not shy with Alice. She had long braids and wore a blue dress. Alice sat with me and listened to my phonograph adventures. She was always there when I wanted her.

Mom supported my creative fantasies and ensured a chair was always at the table if Alice wanted to join us. After a while, Alice simply was not there. Still, my memory of her never left, nor did my mother's support to be a creative inward thinker and seeker.

I grew from a teenager into adulthood in the '60s and '70s, when the world was filled with anti-war political protests, peace marches, and evolving cultural norms. My parents organized outings to San Francisco, where we held signs about peace for the world and walked in unison with thousands of others. Women were burning their bras and finding their power with *Roe v. Wade*'s groundbreaking ruling.

A new influx of spiritual ideas, including meditation practices, was also coming ashore from the East. Spiritual teachers and their American students offered retreats and workshops to share new ways to view ourselves. It all intrigued me as it spoke to my desire to look inward. I had an opportunity to learn about this new Eastern view when I was twenty.

It was winter and cold while I waited outside the graduate student housing complex of mobile homes at Western Washington State University. I was carrying flowers, fruit, and a white handkerchief as offerings for a humble altar that was supposed to be inside. A young man, conservatively dressed, met me. He was my initiator for the program called Transcendental Meditation, TM, and invited me into his mobile home. I stepped in, noticing how the metal box had been transformed into a warm, comfortable space. Directed to enter a small room, I placed my offerings on an altar adorned with silky orange drapes, a picture of an Indian guru, Maharishi Mahesh Yogi, bowls of fruit, cups of water, and burning incense.

My initiator sat with me on a cushion in front of the altar. My eyes were closed as he gently gave me a word sound, my mantra. My mind and heart opened. I was told to sit and silently say my mantra for twenty minutes and told it was specially selected to be mine. Part of the condition of its magic was that I was never to share it with anyone.

In my meditation, I felt as though a veil was lifted. I went to a place I had never known, even though I had not moved from my seat. It was like I flew into a space of peace and well-being with a ladle to drink it in. The smell of incense reminded me that this ritual was not from my culture but from an Eastern place, taking me even deeper.

Soon, a gentle gong told me the time was done. It came too quickly. I felt it had only been seconds, not minutes, since I had begun the mantra recitation within my mind. Following my initiation and instructions on practicing this meditation twenty minutes twice daily, I stepped back onto campus as just another of the many students. Yet, deep inside, I was now gifted with a door into a whole new inner world. Everything changed color and shape. Life was now transcendent and magical.

I was a psychology major and completed my studies while TM expanded my spiritual interests. My reading list began to include writings about mystery schools, parapsychology, spirituality, and Eastern thought. This material and my meditation practice fed the deep hunger I had harbored since childhood to enter my inner world and understand my life. As a child, I was naturally curious about my world, where I came from, and where I was headed. As a young adult, my personal growth was primarily important to me. I wanted, most of all, to find meaning in my life.

In September 1975, I moved home to the Bay Area in California with my boyfriend, Bob. We arrived at my parents' home in Woodside. A studio above the garage became a new temporary home for us, but something inside me said this was wrong. Walking alone only two weeks after we had arrived, I heard an internal scream—"Bob is not the one for you. You have to break up and send him home!" Ouch!

I said goodbye to my dear friend after a difficult, heartbreaking talk. He took a train back to Seattle, where he settled before moving to Alaska. I became a young woman unattached to a relationship. It was freeing.

I loved being whole and comfortable with myself to create a world and life just for me. My spiritual pursuits and interests were at the top of my list as paths I wanted to follow, but I had to have a job. I had to find a way to be in the temporal world as a spiritual seeker. Still, the truth was I could go in any direction I chose and took a little time being on unemployment to stretch out my new feeling of freedom.

It was only a short time until a real paycheck was needed, and I became a chiropractic assistant. I had been a medical assistant at a federally funded medical center for Native Americans on Lummi Island in Washington before I traveled home. This job was familiar in some ways. I wore a clinical white pantsuit, taking the history and blood pressure of the patients who came for adjustments. This job only lasted for about six months.

Next, I became a temporary worker for a local electronics company, leading to a permanent job in the Human Resources department. There, I met a lifelong friend and fellow spiritual traveler, Wendy. She and I met at breaks and discussed the mundane "nowhere-ness" of the "snail farm" where we worked. We would then escape into a world of tarot cards behind the closed door of her office. Besides finding my dear friend, there was nothing else for me in that job. My interest in spirituality and healing was still calling me.

My interest in the healing arts also expanded into other esoteric realms, including energy healing. In the nearby home of a retired man, Bob Mahaney, I joined a group of exciting people using pendulum energy detectors. Gold-plated eight-inch tubes holding right-angled rods were our energy tools. As we asked questions about the where and why of ailments and disturbances, the rods would spin in their casings. The energy explorers were fascinated with how our minds could connect to a tool offering mysterious information that sometimes was from imagined past lives.

My dad and I went to these meetings together. It was fascinating, fun, and a bit too woo-woo for us in the end. Still, at these meetings, I made another new friend, Lita. She was a chemist at the Stanford Research Institute. Being a PhD scientist and energy healer made her a very interesting friend.

It was only a short time until Lita introduced me to a new young man, Doug. About eight months after my breakup with Bob, I was invited to meet Doug at a "let's get them to meet" dinner at the house of Lita and her partner, Chris. Doug was a graduate student in electrical engineering at Stanford, and Chris worked in the same lab. Lita and Chris were our matchmakers.

I was the first to arrive at Lita and Chris's house. Doug arrived in a classic white 1962 Plymouth Valiant. His hair was dark and curly like mine. He was tall, 5'11" and about two inches taller than me, with a dark, well-shaped beard and glasses. He looked intelligent and interesting as he walked into the house. I was immediately aware Doug was someone special.

It is a strange way to describe it, but I felt I saw myself when I looked at him. It was as if, in his face and eyes, I saw a reflection that mirrored my sense of who I was with all my faults, childhood history, and dreams for the future. I had never met anyone like him or had an experience like that. I was taken off guard. I did not expect or want to find someone to enter into another serious relationship with.

Our first date was to hear a talk on the mind-body connection at the home of a friend of Doug's mentor at Stanford. This was a subject we shared an interest in. In getting to know each other, we also discovered that our family backgrounds were very different; he had divorced parents, and mine were forever married, but we were both born in San Francisco and felt a connection to the city. Most importantly, we were attracted to each other and respected that we were both inner seekers looking for more understanding of who we were.

In my early twenties, I began a personal study of metaphysics, esoteric studies, and spirituality with a passion. I was devouring books on these subjects and wanted my life dedicated to understanding my spiritual self. I knew I would never be a monk or live in a monastery, but the idea of that type of commitment was quite romantic. I wanted to find a spiritual path to follow. Doug was interested, too, but his goals were different. He was an engineer and scientist and had to be focused on finishing his PhD program.

As our relationship and friendship grew, I drew away. I did not feel ready for another long-term relationship so soon after my breakup with Bob. It had been only a couple of weeks since I distanced myself from Doug when we ran into each other in downtown Palo Alto. The attraction was so strong we resumed our relationship. This time, I could no longer resist that inner voice telling me Doug was the one. I wanted to be a mother one day and knew I could still pursue my interests and explore my spiritual identity with Doug as my partner. He was the engineer scientist, and I was the spiritual seeker and artist. Two sides that made a whole.

We were both twenty-four. Ten months after our first meeting, we were married on March 20, 1977, under a blue sky in Portola Valley, California. Standing in a circle with family and friends surrounded by oak trees and two hawks flying overhead, Doug and I held hands as a rabbi officiated our country wedding.

I had a white shirt with billowy sleeves made for Doug; with it, he wore a blue tie with butterflies. My long white dress was handmade of eyelet with old-fashioned sleeves and a piece of antique lace at the top of the bodice. The lace had a butterfly covering my chest. We wore these beautiful butterfly symbols, not knowing what change or metamorphosis they represented for our relationship or the future. Now, I know they foretold how we continued to hold hands, supporting each other through the most profound and transformative challenge in our marriage a few years later.

Doug would be a dedicated graduate student for years to come, so I decided to leave my job in the electronic industry and enrolled in a graduate program, too. I was immersed in a master's program in East/West Psychology at the California Institute of Integral Studies, CIIS, in San Francisco, a private graduate school of psychology. This program was perfect for me and my interests, and I decided on a new career focus. I wanted to become either a therapist or a college professor one day.

In the morning, before heading off to my graduate program, I worked part-time in the neonatology department of Stanford Medical Center as a research clerk. My routine included riding my bike to Stanford from our little cottage in Menlo Park and returning home after noon to jump in my car for the forty-five-minute ride to San Francisco and CIIS in Noe Valley. Doug was deeply engaged in his engineering passion, and I was diving deeper into mine. I loved my classes and felt I was on the right track.

After four years of marriage and in the second year of my program, I discovered I was pregnant. I had let my guard down, thinking it was a good time to be pregnant and a mom alongside my newly pregnant friend, Wendy. When I discovered she was expecting, I was jealous, telling her, "Wait! You cannot do that without me, too!" Not thinking it would happen so fast, I just as quickly changed my mind. I wanted to wait on having a baby to first pursue a PhD. But it was too late. Fate was knocking at my door.

I went to classes in my second year of the program with a growing belly and my quest for spiritual knowledge, mystical experiences, and psychological understanding. What I did not realize was that my pregnancy and the birth of my child were to be the beginning of a PhD program in the life experience of psychology and spirituality that could never be matched.

About six months into the pregnancy, I was enrolled in a water exercise class for pregnant women. One morning, I arrived for the course at the popular Palo Alto Midtown YMCA athletic center as one of the pregnant women whose tummy bumps were as visible as mine. Holding on to the railing of the pool entry steps, I noticed another mother with her small child not far from me. It was easy to recognize that the child had Down syndrome with her telltale facial characteristics.

I stood transfixed while knee-deep in the pool, watching the woman beaming with love for her child. Hearing giggles from the gentle swirls made by twirling her daughter around in circles, her love was so clear to me. The mother's happy coos and loving words showered her child. I found myself coveting her circumstances. It was as if this scene was created for me to witness. Something inside me knew this not-normal child with distinct differences and health issues offered something more: a greater love, a more significant commitment, a more extraordinary teaching about life for this woman.

As I watched them, I knew she must have had grief and moments of sadness and worry, though what I witnessed was pure love and joy. I was coveting this experience and was taken by surprise. I recognized the unique and special bond between this mother and child that would be a teaching of life and love that part of me craved. I wondered if that was a path to more spiritual understanding.

It wasn't that my thoughts and coveting could cause my daughter to have special medical needs, but this was a check of my attitude about that type of mothering. It was as if the universe was giving me a preview and a hint that mothering a child with challenges was special and filled with extraordinary love. There was something that felt very serendipitous about seeing her.

When this unexpected message was delivered, I did not know that the child I held in my womb was also a child with medical challenges and a forecast of many storms of illness rolling onto our horizon that would eventually lead us to release her at the operating room doors.

chapter three

The Diagnosis

I was in active labor when my water broke. The nurses thought it held too much vernix, the waxy substance covering a newborn, which could have been a sign of distress. I was moved from the family birth room into the delivery room theater in case of any issues. As it turned out, that excursion down the hall was not necessary, and all went well. Anna Lark was born July 13, 1981, at Stanford Hospital in Palo Alto, California, on a hot summer day near noon. She was six pounds and one ounce, petite, and apparently healthy. Anna, Doug, and I were returned to our birthing room for my recovery. Not long after, Mom and Dad came by the hospital to meet Anna, and my mom promised me dinner when I returned home.

The hospital required that all mothers stay for at least six hours post-delivery. Six hours elapsed, and I requested release. "Sorry," the nurses told me. All the orderlies were delivering meals, and there was no one to properly wheel me out of the hospital. I had to wait, and it could be two hours before they could get to me. Holding my baby swaddled in a blue-striped cotton hospital blanket, I was having none of that. I was hungry and wanted to go home. I could smell my kitchen from miles away and knew my mother was preparing a wonderful dinner celebrating Anna's arrival.

We had signed all the release documents, so Doug and I picked up our things and, carrying our baby, walked out on our own. While in the elevator for one flight down, I felt a bit dizzy, reaching out to Doug to steady myself. It was a naive thing to do, but we were young and bold and got away with it.

When we got home, I looked out my back door, and in my little cosmos flower garden, among the tall stalks of purple daisy-like flowers, was one newly opened large white cosmos with a golden center. Seeing that flower felt like magic, and everything was perfect. We were so thrilled to have Anna. At that poignant moment, we could never have imagined the ride she would take us on being her parents.

When Anna was nine months old, I changed her diaper to find her regular bulky soft stool and felt worry creep in. After all of these months, her digestion had not changed. I was beginning to think that maybe there could be something wrong and wanted to find answers to my questions. I reached for "Dr. Spock" for reassurance and perhaps some answers to why her poop might look like this. I was also worried that Anna was so small, yet I told myself she was growing steadily. Still, this self-talk was not reassuring. I came from a family of tall and bigger-than-average people, and her small size was strange.

That morning, I found a reference to a rare disease called cystic fibrosis that matched some of her symptoms. I discussed it with Doug. He was getting ready to head off to classes and his lab at Stanford. I talked to him through the closed bathroom door, reading the description in my Dr. Spock book and wondering how he would react. He was quiet, and I imagined he was listening.

I continued speaking at the door separating us. "It is inherited, Doug. I don't know anyone in our families who had it. Do you?" His answer was "No."

Thinking of this now, I sense a "closed-door" metaphor that mirrors a blocked view or lack of recognition of this disease in children, causing many misdiagnoses. Symptoms can be explained as asthma, allergies, or digestive upsets, and few people know others in their families who have had children with it. It is as if a door needed to be opened to see the symptoms for what they were. Unfortunately, the many stories of children's diagnoses were missed because symptoms were not recognized as indicating CF and explained as something else. These missed cues caused late diagnoses, more significant illness, and sometimes death. CF was so severe and rare that no one wanted to see it behind the door.

Not long after that conversation, I took Anna to one of her well-child appointments with our pediatrician. I entered the waiting room with my nine-month-old Anna on one hip and, for balance, her diaper bag hanging on my other shoulder. As I sat down, I was unsure if I should mention my curiosity about cystic fibrosis to Dr. Martin. It was a topic Doug and I decided we would drop because we had no family history of this inherited condition, and it seemed so far-fetched.

Still, a nagging feeling churning within me told me that maybe something was wrong. I felt it most when I held Anna. She was just a little peanut. Having a child in the fifth percentile never seemed fitting when I was always near the hundredth. For reassurance, Doug's aunt told me his cousins were all small babies. That was supposed to ease my concerns, but it never really did. I desperately hoped that if I told Dr. Martin, she could reassure me that Anna did not have CF. My inner chatter would be quieted, and all would be OK.

After being screened for temperature, weight, and height and exchanging a few pleasantries, my churning mind came out with it rather bluntly: "Dr. Martin, could Anna have cystic fibrosis? I read about it in my Dr. Spock book. I am concerned about her small size, but I know she is growing on the curve, and I shouldn't worry. I also notice she has soft stools and an on-and-off cough."

"Is she eating well? How is her demeanor?" she asked.

I hesitated, not wanting to show all of my cards. The truth was, I was afraid. As she explored this with me, she was also dismissive about the possibility, telling me she had recently diagnosed CF in a child the same age as Anna. She implied it was statistically out of the question that she could have two with CF of the same age in her practice. I clung to this and told myself, "See, it can't be."

Later, I came to regret that she negated my inquiry. What seemed to be an impossible chance occurrence that two of her patients of precisely the same age would have this rare disease was not reason enough not to look further at Anna and her symptoms. Strange things happen. With the information I received that day, being young and naive and not wanting to believe Anna had this disease, I tucked the concern away (mostly).

As Anna grew toward toddlerhood, she developed deep coughs from her baby cold viruses that came and went. She seemed more congested than what would be expected in a small child. I was so unsure of what was expected and what was not. But my mom was noticing and let me know she was concerned.

We went to Carmel with my parents one weekend when Anna was about fourteen months old. This was the first time we had stayed under one roof together for a whole weekend since Anna was born. Mom had not had the daily chore of changing Anna's diapers until then. Sitting on the sand outside the house, Anna played with a plastic shovel and bucket. I was so glad to have time with my parents and sat close to my mom as we played with our little girl.

Playing with us as we built a pile of sand, Mom said, "Robin, I wonder why Anna's stools are so bulky with that very particular smell. I have never seen that in a baby."

I tried to ignore her. The power of denial is strong when you are new at something and a little competitive with your mother. I know that weekend together made me uncomfortable, and Mom was suspicious that something could be wrong. So, on my own, not saying anything to others, I wondered if milk products could cause it. After all, Doug and I had ruled out cystic fibrosis.

I tried oat milk and other alternative foods purchased at the local natural food store. A new friend in our neighborhood also taught me how to make it myself. This was a good out-let since I was interested in natural foods and new-age heal-ing. I wanted to learn more about non-dairy substitutes. Anna continued to be extraordinarily hungry, eating everything I offered her. I did not realize this was a sign of CF, as she was not getting the necessary nutrients from her food.

CF blocks the release of digestive enzymes from the pancreas, prohibiting the necessary absorption of nutrients and calories, resulting in bulky stools and sometimes failure to thrive. Still, overall, she seemed happy and was growing and not losing weight. Staying at the forever small but steady fifth percentile was apparently her normal. Still, if I was honest, the worries of my mother and the continued symptoms I had read about in Dr. Spock's book haunted me, and I knew something was off, and things were coming to a head.

Then, when Anna was eighteen months old, I took her to see Dr. Martin with a severe cold, causing a deep and lasting cough. She was diagnosed with pneumonia, and we were sent home with antibiotics. Wondering if this was a routine event in the life of young children while being so new at mothering, I decided it would all be OK, and she would recover soon.

After we got home, our landlady, Mrs. Darknell, greeted us outside on the gravel driveway. I told her the doctor said Anna had pneumonia. She gave me a look of concern. In her old-fashioned way, she tried to convince me not to be passive. "Hmm, pneumonia is not good. That is a worry. Keep her warm and inside. I'll come by to check in on you."

She was practical and, because of her years, knew our danger was real. Being an elder, she stepped quickly into her role of truth-seer. I felt the naivete of my youth and did not know yet about the danger and significance of what was visiting us. I was just a young mom who was determined everything would be OK. I did not know any better, and I did not have the experience she had, but I knew and appreciated Mrs. Darknell's down-to-earth style and wisdom.

When Saturday arrived, Anna had been coughing deep,

productive coughs that were racking her little body. Looking into her crib, where she was sleeping far more than usual, I saw a blue cast on her skin. I asked Doug if he could see it, too. He did.

I called the medical office with dread and serious concern in my tightening belly. The receptionist answered, and I told her in a desperate tone, "Hello, can I please talk with Dr. Martin? My baby was in on Wednesday, and I was told she had pneumonia. I think she is turning blue and not doing well."

The receptionist answered calmly, "It is the weekend, and we have only a few doctors for the clinic. Dr. Martin is not in, but I can have another doctor return your call."

My hand was shaking, and it was hard to put the phone down. I wanted help right then. I wondered how I could wait for the doctor's return call without going crazy. Doug was at home working on his research data. We nervously waited together for that return call. Time slowed, and I must have paced around our little house what felt like a million laps before the phone rang. "Hello, this is Dr. Lloyd. Tell me what is going on with Anna."

I told him the same as I had told the receptionist, and he replied with concern, "I only have a few more patients to see, so after I do, I will swing by your house and see how Anna is doing. I don't want you to have to come in." Thanking him, I agreed and put down the phone the second time with a sigh of relief that help was on the way. But we still had to wait.

It felt like another eternity, but after an hour or so, looking through our front door window a million times like the million paces inside my little house, I could finally see Dr. Lloyd's sports car drive up to park. I watched this handsomely dressed after-hours doctor hero in a tweed jacket and casual jeans walk up our neatly raked gravel driveway carrying his little black bag. I opened the door, eager for him to enter our little cottage. Inviting him in, I led him to Anna's crib, where she'd slept most of the day. It was even more clear that her complexion was blue. Urging us to take her to the hospital for "a little oxygen" in the ER, Dr. Lloyd drove me and Anna to the hospital in his sports car, and Doug followed in our car.

Dr. Lloyd and I pulled up to the emergency room, parking in a "for physicians only" parking space. Having a doctor engage with us to determine what was happening with Anna was a comfort. Together, we entered the ER with its waiting room chairs filled with people with illnesses and injuries of unknown origins. Before Doug arrived, Dr. Lloyd quickly whisked Anna away to be evaluated. It was only a short time until Doug walked through the ER doors, looking as lost as I was. After registering Anna for the ER visit, we held hands on the lonely ER chairs, not knowing what awful news would soon befall us.

We were stunned and scared and realized we needed family support. I used the pay phone down the hall, putting in a few coins to call my sister. It was January 29, 1983, and my father's birthday. Mom and Dad were in Sausalito with my sister and her partner, celebrating at their house. I hated having to call with this news in the first place, and even more so because it was my dad's birthday dinner.

I returned to my anxious husband in the ER waiting room, overwhelmed with worry. Soon, Dr. Lloyd appeared behind closed doors, where Anna was taken to be examined. "Anna's blood gasses are alarming. It was good we got her here. She needs to be admitted and intubated." He continued to explain what that meant. "She cannot process enough oxygen because of her infection and congestion. We must insert a tube down her throat to help her breathe. This is very serious, but with a little time on a ventilator for the infection to pass, her lungs can rest, and she should heal."

We were two distraught parents in the ER waiting room, hoping for good news, who were given bad news. As a couple, we both were tall with similar dark, curly hair, wearing our usual jeans. I had my favorite oversized black winter sweater jacket thrown on to brace against the chilly January, and Doug had on his regular zip-up brown suede jacket that he wore when I first fell in love with him. On the outside, we looked like our twenty-nine-year-old selves, but on the inside, we were lost in a fog of worry and fear we had never known. We were now parents of a child whose life was on the line.

That first night was devastating. It was so hard to gather my wits to know how to feel and what to do. Doug and I had to find ways to cope if we could even understand what we felt in this lost and strange new place. This life-altering episode began to shape our style of supporting each other. My way became more emotional. It was easier for me to cry and get upset. Doug's was to find the facts, understand what was going on, and make a plan. He balanced us. Our support structure has gotten us through the most challenging times. Still, there was little to know in those early moments and days except that our child was very ill. We did not know why.

Doug and I did not sleep that night. We were offered a parent room with chairs and pillows to rest on, but I only wanted to be next to our Anna. We did not know yet what caused this severe illness. When we arrived in her ICU private room, and they were ready to intubate her, Anna cried for me, "Mommy, no, Mommy, no." Her plea is still a vivid haunt.

This was the first time I could not help her. I could not make it stop and lost all of my maternal control. The pain in my heart was excruciating. Anna's circumstances prevented me from doing what was integral to being a mom: saving my child from her pain and her separation from me.

Curare, a drug that temporarily paralyzes, quieted Anna's little body. It calmed the scene and stopped her heartbreaking pleas. She could not flail her arms or be defiant with her ICU care. My darling, feisty child, my little one, had to lie still for these machines to help her breathe. She could not tug on the tubes or resist the continual treatments.

My parents came to the hospital in the morning after

Anna was outfitted with tubes and lines, monitors, alarms, and beeps while also being kept alive with attendants suctioning thick strings of mucus from her lungs. I had not yet been able to find the ground under my feet. It was hard for my parents, but I could not see them immediately. They had to wait downstairs for a while and sit with their feelings of horror about what was happening to their grandchild and daughter.

Knowing my parents wanted to be with us, I also knew I could not be the holder of all of our emotions. I knew how difficult it would be to see Anna this way, especially for my mother. I adored my mother, yet she was a deep-feeling and emotional woman who could use her emotions to distance herself or involve herself in my life. So many times, I had difficulty finding the boundary between her and me. Still, this experience gave me no wiggle room. I had to have a strong container for my grief and fear to be with hers too.

When we felt ready, Doug and I went downstairs to find them in a waiting room. As I walked toward them, exhausted and still in the same clothes I had arrived in the night before, Mom looked at me with pained eyes and did not get up right away to greet us. From her chair, she said, "You do not want to see us," and turned her head. Clearly, she felt slighted.

I could not hold her grief and mine at the same time. The pain, sorrow, and fear I held was genuinely overwhelming. I am so sorry this hurt my mom. It was a turning point in my adulthood. I had been given the biggest challenge of my life, and I only had enough bandwidth to contain my feelings.

It did not take long for her to gather her emotions. We all hugged in the mire of the upset feelings, and Doug and I took them upstairs to see Anna. The image of their little granddaughter lying on a bed in such a vulnerable state was difficult. It added more tension to the cloud of emotions that hung over and between my mother and me.

I sat by Anna's side every day, only going home to sleep. The room we were given to sleep in with chairs and pillows was insufficient for the rest we needed. The nurses let me bathe her with warm cloths and resume some maternal caregiving. My mom and dad visited daily to see how we were doing. One day, my eldest brother, Mike, came to see me. Walking down the hall to greet him, I fainted in his arms. He was there to catch me. It was all too much.

Days passed into weeks. I sat on a metal chair with a padded vinyl seat in her private ICU room or on an upholstered couch in the hallway to pass the time. Postured like a lioness at the entrance of her den protecting her own, I was beginning to learn the "do not touch my child unless I agree and understand" attitude that mothers of chronically ill children adopt.

While waiting for Anna to heal, I also focused on sewing a needlepoint design to hang in her room when she recovered. It was a little yellow duckling with pink flowers and a simple white background appropriate for a two-year-old child. The thought that she would have this needlepoint framed in her room as she grew up kept me sane and gave me hope. The quiet stitching of one thread pulled and then another was a meditation. Sitting in this vigil was the hardest thing I had ever done. The intense emotions, the loss of control, the not knowing why, and the not knowing how this would turn out were rearranging my thoughts about who I was.

Before this crisis, I was sure there was a spiritual dimension to life. But when my child's life was threatened, all remnants of those spiritual beliefs and mystical ideas died. I fell into what I believed to be a "dark night of the soul," relying only on the power of modern medical technology, pushing away any magical thinking or feelings about spiritual realities. It was the medical technology that was going to save my daughter. It was what had already saved her. It was the only thing that would bring her back to me.

In my young and newly formed beliefs about spirituality, I could not see how a baby nearly dying and the material reality of medicine to save her could be part of the universe of multi-dimensions, mysticism, and spirituality. I had yet to learn that all of life was imbued with spirit, even illness, the tubes, oxygen, and medicines keeping Anna alive. Because my understanding of my spirituality had not yet gelled, I was confused about how terrible things could come into our lives and cause such havoc.

Anna's diagnosis came about two weeks after her ER admission, and the specialists proclaimed loudly about this and that, never finding the correct conclusion. The most prominent idea was that this was a virulent virus of unknown origin. We were also told Anna might have cystic fibrosis. When she was off the ventilator and recovering, they would test her, but the diagnosis did not matter as her care would be the same. After days, it became two weeks with no change, no answers, and lots of frustration. Doug demanded that Anna have the CF test. He wanted all possibilities to be explored and could not accept the premise that her care would not change no matter what was found. Dr. Martin ordered a CF test, but she had to pull political strings to get it done.

A technician arrived from the children's hospital laboratory across the street, where the tests for CF were usually performed. Dr. Martin told us it was a struggle with hospital politics to get permission for a technician to perform the test in a different location. They suggested Anna be moved there to have the test. Finally, they were told that was impossible as she was critically ill and intubated in the ICU, and permission was granted.

An area on Anna's leg just above her ankle was chosen to inject a substance under her skin. The technician then wrapped a small strap around the site with a tiny electrical current to warm the area and make her skin sweat. Tiny sweat droplets were collected on a patch under the strap. Next, the sample was taken to a lab where the relative amount of salt in her sweat would be measured. The diagnosis would be cystic fibrosis if it was a high enough concentration. CF is a dysfunction of the chloride channel in the cells, causing too much salt to be released. We would not know the answer until the following day.

We guessed the results since we were invited to meet with the head of pulmonology at the children's hospital the following morning. Doug and I were led into a room without windows and a long table with chairs for our doctor-parent conference. As we sat anticipating the arrival of the pulmonary team and the test results, a big, burly man dressed in a pullover knit sweater covering his Santa-like belly knocked and entered the room. "Hello, I am Dr. Lewiston, the head of the pulmonary department. I am here with our social worker and Dr. Moss, who I understand you already know." They joined us at the table.

The anxiety Doug and I showed must have been familiar to this team. We could not escape the truth now. We wanted to know, but as a parent in a care conference such as this, I also did not want to know. It was so easy to feel the walls close in on me as now there was no escaping. The impulse to bolt was real. This was a scene made for a movie, not my life.

Part of the strangeness of that meeting included the appearance of Dr. Moss, who had been our friend for nearly two years. The coincidence was stunning. We'd met him while attending a childbirth class together. Our obstetrician who delivered Anna was the same doctor Dr. Moss and his wife, Jill, saw for the care and delivery of their son, Jacob, only a week before. After meeting, we saw each other socially as we raised our babies and celebrated their first birthdays in a park at a picnic table not far from where we were now sitting.

We knew Rick, Dr. Moss, was a physician at the children's hospital but did not know who his patients were. When Anna was admitted, we called him. He visited us but could not tell us what was wrong with Anna until that meeting. They confirmed Anna had CF. Our friend we had known as Rick was now to be known more formally as Dr. Moss, a pediatric infectious disease pulmonologist and Anna's CF specialist. His being there to tell us our bad news was an oddly comforting gift. It was uncanny that we serendipitously knew the physician who would be caring for Anna and guiding us in this frightening new world. That was if she could get off the ventilator and come home.

The information we received that day about CF sent us reeling. Dr. Lewiston told us, "Children like Anna are not expected to live into adulthood. We do not know if she will ever be able to get off of the ventilator, but we will try." When you receive news like this, other words, even those critical to understanding the whole picture, can blow away like leaves in a windstorm. We would have to be given this information more than once to absorb and process everything we needed to know.

Lost and stunned after receiving the formal diagnosis and the possibility that she may never heal enough to get off the ventilator, Doug and I left the room to go outside to our car. That was the only place where we could have privacy.

Sitting on the passenger seat with my window rolled up and nowhere to go, I screamed a full-throated scream with the sound of crumbling motherhood dreams. Doug felt relief, now knowing what was happening to our daughter, even though his heart was broken. Frightened by what we did not yet understand, he worried whether we could financially handle this situation and if we had enough medical insurance coverage. The CF diagnosis gave us some information but also lingering questions. All of it had jagged edges that were tearing at our hearts.

What I wanted most and aspired to was to be a mom. The other dressings of graduate school I was pursuing were secondary. Allowing the truth of this new information that we were the carriers of a gene that allowed our child to have a terrible and deadly disease opened floodgates of loss. Dreams for our future family would not be fulfilled, and we probably would never have another child.

I could not believe I was destined to mother my child into her passing, not witnessing her growth and accomplishments and never being a grandmother to her child one day. It was a vision for our lives that we had not expected. The ripping away of our young parental dreams left a gaping hole, and we had no idea how to fill it. That day and diagnosis moment truly changed our world and how we were to have our life together. It was a portal never to leave our memories.

We decided to tell my parents about Anna's diagnosis the next day. First, we needed a little time overnight to process our new reality by ourselves. That evening, after our care conference and after we touched down on the earth of our new reality, I called their house, and Mom answered the phone.

"Mom. Doug and I want to talk with you and Dad. Is it OK if we come to see you and have coffee in the morning?"

She said, "Yes, come on up," not knowing the real reason why we were coming.

In the morning, we drove to Woodside and my parents' home, nestled near a group of tall redwoods across the street from the elementary school and tennis courts. This was not the home where I grew up. It was their after-retirement home, but it was considered the family home nonetheless. It was perfect for my mother: Cape Cod-style, white stucco with a wood shake roof and dark green shutters like our little cottage. Mom loved old houses; she had beautiful taste and a collection of antiques that made it warm, interesting, and attractive.

We drove up, parking in the driveway, and, as usual, instead of entering through the front door, we walked up the four red brick steps that led to a side door into the laundry. Mom stepped from the adjacent kitchen doorway, greeting us in her familiar flower print cooking apron. She was never seen at work in the kitchen without one.

Stepping into the kitchen with the smell of freshly brewed

coffee and her favorite burnt toast, before we could barely say "Hello," she told us what she thought to be the real reason we were there to see them. With a familiar body language showing hesitation and an unsure smile, she said what she could no longer contain. Her thoughts about our morning coffee date must have been brewing all night. "I know why you are here, Robin. You do not want us to come by the hospital anymore. You have come to tell us this."

I was stopped in my tracks but should have known we might be greeted with this insecurity from Mom again. The stress and tension of the moment with Anna being so ill was tough on her. I knew that what she was most concerned about in her relationships with her four children was that she did not interfere. She was terrified of being an interfering mother and that I would not want to have her near me. The funny thing about this was her intense desire not to interfere actually was what interfered.

I quickly dismissed this judgment call on her part to say, "Oh, no, Mom. That is not why we are here. We came to tell you the results of Anna's sweat test. She has cystic fibrosis."

As those words spilled out of me and the truth of why we came was clear, I could not hold up any more boundaries and cried. This was what I was terrified of: my baby's severe illness. We discussed what this might mean, including Anna not coming off the ventilator. Even if she did, she would most likely not live into adulthood. Mom and Dad comforted us by listening.

It was hard for me to know how to support Mom and her feelings of insecurity while on this family journey. Still, I needed her support more than ever. There was always a juggling of both of our feelings. Our relationship was complex, although it was founded on love and respect, and we needed each other. My relationship with Dad was very different. He was my warm, wonderful father and, many times, friend.

With the advent of her diagnosis, Anna's treatment did

change even though we had been told it would not. But, thank goodness, after five weeks, she could finally be taken off the ventilator and breathe independently. Anna had what seemed to be a miraculous recovery with the help of the miracle drug prednisone. Rarely did children present their CF condition in such a severe way as she did and survive. Her case was well known and discussed in the hospital for a long time afterward. She was considered a fortunate child, but still had this very nasty disease. We were buoyed by her recovery, resilience, and courage. Our love for our daughter was unwavering, and we accepted our situation. In the years to come, we saw Anna meet her continued challenges by overcoming unfavorable odds repeatedly. How she did that and who she was becoming was a marvel.

Our lives were forever changed. Doug had to complete the final details for his PhD and would graduate in June, about three months after we were starting this new life. I was now a mother of a special needs child. This had been foretold when I saw the mother and child in the pool during my pregnancy, but it was unexpected. The significance of this change in our lives was profound. My constant quest for spiritual understanding and identity was particularly challenged as my circumstances caused me to grow up. I realized the day-to-day responsibilities of caring for this child were the most important and hardest things I would ever do. I did not yet understand that this was a powerful path for a spiritual life.

chapter four

Becoming a CF Family

On a spring day in 1983, shortly after her release from the hospital, I was walking with Anna in a stroller, enjoying the beautiful sunny weather in the unfamiliar neighborhood of mid-century homes where we had just relocated. Anna's body was healing from the severe pneumonia that could have taken her. She had lost so much muscle strength that she could not walk independently due to weeks in the hospital bed.

No longer listening to the constant beeps of lifesaving machines or hanging on to every word for clues to tell me if she would ever come home, I was beginning a new normal that was far from normal for a young mother. I was forever changed. My new understanding that life can dramatically change in a moment colored my world, and grief complicated my life in ways I never expected.

Mindfully stepping down the street one foot after the other, I pushed the blue umbrella stroller carrying my complicated child. It was time to catch my breath and find secure footing in my changing world with new expectations of how I was to be a mother. Questions of who I now was were whirling in my head. After walking a few blocks, I slowed my pace to a halt with tears for losing my life as I knew it. Looking around to see if I was alone and no one else could hear me, I asked out loud, "How can I do this? How can I be a mother of a child who will die within a few years?"

Asking this question to my deepest inner places, soul, spirit, and the whole neighborhood, I received a remarkably clear answer. A voice responded within hearing distance of my inner mind. "If she lives a short life, there will be many blessings. If she lives a long life, there will be many blessings. They are both the same."

The words resonated profoundly, but how could they both be the same? I knew then this parenting journey would be the teaching of a lifetime. Here was the most precarious path we could be on. Doug and I loved caring for our precious daughter, who had miraculously survived a terrible onslaught of illness, but it was not over. The journey had just begun. We had to live, not knowing what further winds and storms would blow through our lives. The message was clear: to survive, I had to take each step not knowing what was to be, while looking for the positive and finding gifts of spirit.

We moved to Sunnyvale, close to Doug's work, just days before my encounter with this crucial inner message. I was relieved not to feel isolated. If something went wrong, I had the support I needed within minutes. That was a blessing I could count on.

We were nervous and unsure about our new charter to parent a young child with little hope for a future. With no time to get ready, we had to immediately begin the regimen that all CF families had to participate in if there was any hope of staving off more of its ravages.

I had bottles of pills lined up on the kitchen counter, medicines in the refrigerator, and vials of bronchodilators ready for every respiratory treatment. I was starting this new path with so much to learn and this new inner guidance telling me that there would be blessings no matter what. It was up to me to get the job done to care for Anna and to carve out a life of meaning and hope in what first appeared to be a family life of exhaustion and fear.

Our mornings began with a routine meant to clear Anna's lungs of mucus. We had pillows and toys on the living room floor, and an air compressor was turned on to aerosolize medications, adding to the cacophony of morning sounds. The mist from the nebulizers was key to opening airways.

After about fifteen minutes of inhaling medicinal mist from a plastic tube, filling Anna's lungs, and making a small cloud around her, she would sit in front of us while we reached over her shoulders, tapping on her upper chest that held the upper lobes of her lungs. After a minute or two of tapping, we would press our fingers and vibrate the area three times, asking her to breathe deeply.

Next, Anna would cough. Her cough was always productive, so she spit in a plastic vial or tissues. This was chest physical therapy, or CPT, done in twelve positions up and down, front and back, on the pile of pillows. Our hands pounded all areas of her chest, back, and sides. Cookie Monster, Grover, Big Bird, and dear Mr. Rogers were our guests to witness the drumming. Later in the day, we had other videos to watch during our sessions. TV was our friend and helped to make the time of "treatments" fun.

In those first few months, we performed CPT three to four times per day, loosening the thick mucus in her lungs so that the bacteria that had nearly overwhelmed her would not have the perfect site to take up as home again. The treatments were an intimate and strange prescription for a mother, father, and child. Our house sounded like a drumming clinic with a mechanical mist machine accented by coughing and spitting. It was quite a melody and became familiar morning and night in our home as the telltale sign and anthem of CF, our unwanted guest.

And all of this was rearranging my sense of self. I was exhausted by the weeks of Anna's hospitalization, adjusting to our new reality and implementing our time-consuming routines. Who was I now, after all? Was I the woman I always was? Of course, I knew I was not. Still, something inside me wanted to revert to being the teenager or the woman I was before this happened, or even someone different without care and worries. Grief is complicated with confusion as it settles the losses, and I found myself behaving in a way I came to understand as a rebellion. I needed to rebel in some way. Thank goodness I caught it when it was still an innocent behavior that did not grow into something I could not handle.

Sitting outside on the cold concrete patio ground with my back braced against the outside of the house, I woke up to my strange new habit. Sitting there, taking a break from my reality while Anna was napping and Doug was at work, I was smoking a cigarette. I was smoking, for heaven's sake.

I had been secretly doing so for a couple of weeks. Like waking from a dream, I realized this would not work. I had a child with a severe lung disease. Was I to be a mother who would escape her life by grabbing a pack to smoke secretly? Would I take up other habits to numb my pain? What was I getting out of this? I loved smoking when I was sixteen to twenty years old. It comforted me. It calmed me. It is a strange thing to like, except it is an addiction.

It took me two years of abstinence to get the craving out of me in my younger twenties. Now I was taking it up again? Craziness and the workings of grief appeared this way as I settled into being Anna's mom. I had to move forward with healthy behaviors, not just for me but for my daughter. Those cigarettes went quickly into the trash.

We had so much to learn. To help us assimilate into our new world, we joined a group of other families in a local organization that fundraised for medical research, Cystic Fibrosis Research Inc, CFRI (years later, the name was changed to Cystic Fibrosis Research Institute). The community was a group of wonderful, intelligent, committed parents whose company we enjoyed. The children with CF we came to know had differing levels of severity of the disease, but they all were bright and engaging.

As it turned out, we learned about CFRI from the family whose child our pediatrician told us was diagnosed with CF before I told her about my concern in her office. A day or two after Anna was diagnosed while she was still in critical condition, Dr. Martin suggested we meet them. Although nervous to meet another family facing similar challenges, we made a date to go to the house of Jeff, Marlene, and Nina.

Not far from the Stanford campus, we arrived and knocked on the door of the first CF family we would meet. Our daughters were nearly the same age, yet the difference between them was stark. Anna was in the hospital on a ventilator, and their daughter was safe at home with them. Marlene warmly greeted us at the door with Nina cradled on her hip. Jeff looked professorial, dressed in a cardigan sweater with his balding head and trim beard. Jeff shook our hands as we walked through the entry, saying, "So glad to meet you."

Marlene introduced us to nineteen-month-old Nina with her smiling blue eyes and blonde hair. I wondered how she and my little curly-top daughter could have the same deadly genetic disease. As we entered their home, the stress we had been under made us feel out of place. I missed being a mom who could also introduce my daughter to them.

Offering us tea and a sweet treat, they were warm and concerned, understanding Anna's life was still in a delicate balance. As we visited, I suddenly remembered meeting Marlene before. The image of her holding Nina in a swaddle immediately came to me. It was quite strange, but we'd met when our babies were newborns before we knew anything about CF.

We had been at a graduation party a few weeks after Anna was born. I slipped away to nurse Anna when I met another mom with her baby. Little did I know that meeting with Marlene would become profound with both of our daughters having CF.

I put my teacup on the side table, startled by my sudden memory. "Marlene, do you remember meeting at that graduation party when our girls were first born? We sat together with our babies. I had hoped I would meet you again, but not in this way."

"Oh, yes, Robin. I do! It is remarkable that we met and did

not know we were holding babies with far more in common than we realized," replied Marlene.

Doug and Jeff had also met at the party, so we reminded them of our meeting a year and a half before. That familiar feeling of serendipity rose as shivers in my back. Pieces of our story seemed to be strangely connected to a larger story. It was odd that we were brought together to meet when we were so innocent, and now we were sharing a part of our lives that all four of us wished would disappear in the night like a bad dream. But now, this bond as parents of these children would give us a friendship that would last forever.

Like us, CF was changing their lives significantly. Jeff was a professor at Stanford who decided to change his lifelong research to study cystic fibrosis. This was a big thing to do as he had established prestige in his academic career, but having a daughter with this disease made him stop and review what was most important to him. Putting his resources, time, and talent into finding a cure for CF was the most important thing he could do, and he founded The Cystic Fibrosis Research Laboratory at Stanford. Dr. Jeff Wine has made many significant contributions to the CF research world.

After Anna survived her hospitalization and came home, my parents agreed to stay with her so that we could attend our first CFRI meeting. It was in a humble and aging conference room on the second floor of a building in San Jose, about twenty minutes from where we were living. I walked up the metal stairs outside the building while holding the railing with Doug ahead of me. We were about to enter another part of our new world and meet people we were unsure we wanted to meet. I didn't want to walk through yet another door into this world of dying children and grieving parents.

We were met with warm welcomes. These people became our tribe with their experiences and harrowing stories about their children. A few had lost their children to CF, but they had not given up the fight to find a cure for the next generation, including Anna and Nina. This group of lovely people had earned their medals for courage and compassion years before.

I relaxed as I found this group less scary than I feared. This blessing of community was a gift that nurtured and held us while we raised Anna. This was our extended CF family. I served as president and a general board member of CFRI for many years. Doug was an original Research Advisory Committee (RAC) member and head, still serves on the RAC, and is also a board member.

As parents in this organization, we shared an important characteristic. We all had one copy of the recessive CF gene, but our affected children had two, one from each parent. Created by nature to help our species find balance in a world with many diseases, one copy of this gene is believed to be an evolutionary attempt to help humankind survive the scourge of diarrheal illnesses that devastated ancient villages. These environmental scourges were highly contagious and deadly. Nature tried to solve the problem with this genetic mutation and natural selection.

If you have one copy of CF's genetic mutation, it helps you survive the loss of fluids. Those with one gene, such as Doug and me, are called heterozygotes or carriers. If carriers have a baby with another carrier like we did, there is a 25% chance of having a baby with two copies of the mutation, thus causing the disease cystic fibrosis. Historically, these were small and weak babies and did not survive long due to this condition. It was in the 1930s that CF was identified and given a name. In all of her compassion, Mother Nature must not have considered this. Or perhaps it was part of our evolutionary plan.

CF is not contagious but makes one more vulnerable to nature's obscure and infectious diseases. Hence, our species' evolution and nature's trial and error. We are born with what we are born with because it is what nature intended. Our new group of friends hit the 25% jackpot without prior knowledge of our collective genetic makeup. Anna, Nina, and others were born with CF, dramatically affecting their lives.

With the support of our community, we learned by listening to others far more experienced. We were also hopeful for new treatments and, someday, a cure. Until that miracle came, we had to deal with the many concerns of caring for a child with CF. Nutrition was a significant concern because of the involvement of the pancreas. Digestive pancreatic enzymes are blocked in CF individuals due to the sticky mucus, making it hard for them to digest their food properly. Supplemental enzymes are taken at all meals, especially when there are fats. CF patients have difficulty gaining weight, and Anna had to eat extra calories.

The lung disease, poor pancreas, and digestive system dysfunctions in a child with CF require double the calories for average growth and development. Sometimes, when a child with CF cannot gain weight, they must have a gastrointestinal tube to add extra calories by pouring high-calorie liquids directly into the gut. Eating well, taking prescribed medications, and having digestive enzymes at every meal were part of the routine, along with the respiratory treatments.

Anna was a typical toddler with normal resistance to parental requests. She just happened to have this condition with all of its requirements that we had to navigate. When we started this journey, Anna was nearly two, the age that says NO! The regimen for CF care took time away from playing, exploring, and regular activities. It was a definite challenge to always comply with a feisty two-year-old and her developmental needs while sticking with the rigor of the routine, but we did.

We had firsthand knowledge about what an exacerbation of pneumonia could look like if we did not. No way did we want to go through that again, but we had the terrible twos visit our house. At the same time, it was as if Anna understood that too much rebellion was not a good thing. She may have been particularly sensitive to our cues of concern when she did not comply.

To digest her food and take her medications, Anna had

her pills stirred into applesauce to be swallowed. This led her to eventually learn the magic trick of disappearing a handful of pills that would scare any adult by popping them in her mouth with one big swallow.

Still, I remember when she refused her food spiked with extra butter, cream, and any other way I could add calories, and her father intervened. Exasperated by her refusal to eat and our fears of this disease getting its way with her, Doug decided to take a new tack. We sat at our dining table together, and Doug told our defiant two-year-old, "Anna, from now on, I don't want you to eat anymore. Do not touch that food."

He was about to take away her plate when she defied him and gobbled what was in front of her. We made a breakthrough with some reverse psychology. I also decided the caloric extras did not make the food taste as good. She ate better without the added fats, so we offered her the same diet as we had but with encouragement to eat as much as possible. That also worked much better.

In time, Anna found other ways to use her sense of humor and food to provoke us. Sitting in her chair eating the food in front of her on a summer day, a cob of corn was raised high by a little hand as a toddler experiment in food etiquette. It ended on the top of her head. "Anna, what are you doing? That cob belongs in your mouth. Now, eat that corn," Doug said.

Knowing there can be tricks played with food, as we had done with her, the corn remained. With her little hand, she rubbed her head with a corn cob scrub brush. "Anna!" a stern voice called out. She looked at us with a trickster stare and continued the corn scrub as we fell into laughter that was hard to stop. This humor retaliation helped to lighten our home of its heavy responsibility. It was an early portrait of our Anna's personality forming with cheeky humor, frequently putting us into stitches with laughter.

This was a glimpse of what would be revealed over time as part of her delightful personality. Sometimes, her attempts at humor might overtake her, like when she would climb on the dining table and shake her little butt at us. When this behavior or entertaining with off-color noises of bodily functions would fill the room for the attention she was seeking, I would have to say under my breath, "Who is this child? She is so different from me!" Her humor took us off guard and into hysterics.

When she was older, she would use her humor at medical appointments. After seeing other patients in the busy clinic, Dr. Moss would enter the room in his white coat and head to the sink but had to make way for Anna in her "car." She sat on his rolling stool as if she were driving a car, pulling it up to the sink while pretending the pedals underneath were for brakes and accelerations.

If I was worried or disturbed, her antics would quickly shake me out of a depressed mood and into healing laughter. I am sure it helped her carry the heavy anxiety that must have visited her little self so many times. And, of course, it must have given Dr. Moss a bit of levity as each clinic room he visited held another problem, sick child, or heavy-hearted mom. It was a good, positive, and healthy way to cope. As the years went on, she told many jokes to the doctors and nurses who would expect a visit with Anna to be entertaining. She was well-loved.

When Anna was very little, and we were at the beginning of this parental challenge, I realized that I also had to do some of the opposite parenting other families with healthy children were into. For example, I had wished I could have a no-TV household, but that was not to be. It became part of our skillful means. Quickly, we developed a routine that was working. Anna was thriving. We were now CF parents, and we knew that we would, within reason, use any tricks we could to save our daughter.

This desire to find the best for Anna led us in many directions to discover healers, potions, and treatments to help Anna and ourselves. As it turned out, these alternative ways, combined with our traditional allopathic medical care, became vital in our lives, adding to the incredible adventure that Anna and CF were taking us on.

I was beginning to understand the meaning of the poignant teaching by that unknown voice that had talked to me when she was first diagnosed: "If she has a short life, there will be many blessings. If she has a long life, there will be many blessings. They are both the same." I was learning they were the same because every day was special with our Anna as we collected our promised blessings and continued the journey. Motherhood as a spiritual path seemed to be making sense.

The memory of the mother with the Down syndrome child also accompanied me. She was a goddess in my mind. Her image stuck with me as a goddess of love and acceptance with her special needs child. I loved having a goddess I could relate to.

If we had spent our days only wondering how it was all to turn out, we might have missed the joy right in front of us. Worries and concerns would rise and fall and never leave altogether. Still, I trusted that the source of the voice and the teaching of my goddess would stay with me, guiding the way as Anna grew and we faced new challenges.

The miracles I hoped for, which included a long life, were not imaginable through the medical care available then. The idea or possibility of a future transplant to save her life was not yet a dream. We were walking on a ledge with a visible, very steep drop. The real danger was known to us, and we needed the posture necessary to balance it all.

chapter five

Lama Gangha

The phone rang at about nine in the morning. Mom would usually call at this time to see how we were doing. "Hi, Mom," I answered.

She immediately told me, "Robin, I want you to know that I called your friend, Barbara Petty, to tell her what has been happening with you. I woke up this morning and felt she needed to know about Anna and what a difficult time you have been having. She was very concerned and told me about a Tibetan lama now living with her. She asked if it was OK for him to pray for you and Anna. I told her that I would call to ask you."

"Thanks, Mom," was my immediate response as a feeling of hope tingling inside told me this might be an extraordinary opportunity. "I will call her and see how we can visit."

Barbara Petty was a new friend. I'd introduced Mom to her when she came with me to Barbara's house in nearby Los Altos Hills before Anna became ill. She was the caretaker of a Tibetan meditation center. I met her because I planned to write about San Francisco Bay Area Buddhist families, their spiritual practices, and how they incorporated these practices into their daily lives for my master's thesis. To do so, I had to identify nearby Buddhist meditation centers, and this Kagyu center was one of them. Barbara was intriguing, and my mom connected with her. She had traveled widely with many highly realized lamas throughout India, Nepal, and the United States.

After hanging up from Mom's call, I thought maybe the intensity of my life was beginning to shift. I imagined I could get back on track with a lama blessing and renew my master's research. My wounds from the past months were deep. It would take a long time to integrate all I had been through with Anna, but I was beginning to rise to the surface. I called Barbara, accepting her offer, and asking, "Do you think Anna and I could come and meet this lama, Barbara?"

Barbara told me, "Robin, Lama Gangha is very special. As a young man, he lived in a cave in the Himalayas for twelve years and escaped Tibet to Nepal and India. We are fortunate to have him stay here for a while as he goes on a worldwide tour to teach for the Kagyu lineage. He is sweet and kind, and I know he would enjoy a visit."

I was thrilled and told Anna, "Hey, we get to meet a very special man who will give us healing. We are so lucky to be able to meet him." As I told her this, I am sure she was playing house with her baby dolls and unaware of our unique opportunity. I knew this could be one of the greatest blessings I would gather from the earlier promise made to me and my heart.

We drove only fifteen minutes to Los Altos Hills, which became our Shangri-la, our Tibetan healing place. Arriving at Barbara's house in the heart of Silicon Valley, we were coming to meet a person with a profound yet humble distinction. When we arrived, we were introduced to Lama Gangha. He was slightly taller than me with a shaved monk's head and wore a maroon and golden yellow Tibetan robe. His face was round, and he had a slight smile. He reached out his hand in a gesture of welcome. Not speaking English, he did not say anything. I greeted him with my hands in a gesture of prayer and a slight bow.

I had already been to this house on a hill settled into oak trees when I interviewed Barbara for my graduate work. Still, I was given another tour of Barbara's place, now considered a Tibetan meditation center, with Lama Gangha beside us. Her garage had been repurposed into a meditation room with maroon cushions on the floor set in rows to hold a few students, a foreign altar of the Tibetan tradition draped with maroon- and saffron-colored cloths, offering bowls, rice, incense, statues, and thangkas of Tibetan deities. I did not understand the symbolisms and had yet to experience Tibetan practices. Still, it felt right to be there with my daughter.

Since Lama Gangha did not speak English, we communicated with our eyes and gestures. Another much younger lama was there to help host him. Lama Dudjom spoke both English and Tibetan and served as a translator. After being directed to a particular room in Barbara's house, Anna and I entered a private space with this kind man dressed in his lama robes with his interpreter in a similar dress. Anna gave no resistance to being there and came along as a happy, compliant almost two-year-old holding my hand.

I could tell that he had prepared for our visit. He asked about Anna's condition, and I sensed he understood that her lungs and tummy were in trouble. I think he also understood that she had nearly lost her life. I don't think he ever understood that this was a genetic disease, and that we had Western medical routines and drugs we would have to give her forever. I am unsure about that, but I was sure he knew what he had to do from his tradition. Lama Dudjom left the room, and we sat on the floor with Anna in my lap.

Lama-la, a name of endearment, began his ritual. He chanted Tibetan prayers, moved his hands and fingers into mudras, offering rice kernels, and snapped his fingers. Toward the end of these recitations, he put up a mirror in front of Anna and me. While still chanting his prayers, he poured saffron-colored water onto the mirror. The golden water washed down our reflections and landed in a bowl.

Finally, when the ritual was done, he reached out to Anna to lay his hands on her belly with a bit more chanting. We were blessed with this ancient and intriguing healing ritual two or three times per week for many weeks. I cannot remember how many, but I knew I was getting stronger with each ritual. When we first started seeing Lama Gangha, the pressure, sadness, grief, and trauma I had been through during Anna's illness made me feel that any spirituality I had believed in had forsaken me. I came to question if there even was a spiritual universe. But my woundedness was changing, my heart was healing, and I was open to this ritual.

As weeks passed, we came for our healing pujas regularly. During our visits, Barbara's stories about supporting the Tibetans worldwide continued to intrigue me. When she told me about some of her travels to India, I wanted to ask her if she had ever met a swami named Sai Baba.

I was curious because I had what I thought was an "imaginary" relationship with Sai Baba through secret conversations with him. I had never told anyone about these conversations. I had read a book, *The Holy Man and the Psychiatrist*, about a sage who lived in India with a large following. The book was written by a psychiatrist who was trying to explain phenomena that this popular holy man displayed. He simply manifested things out of thin air and teleported himself to appear in multiple locations simultaneously, or so it seemed. I loved this idea and assumed it was true, piquing my curiosity and sense of humor.

My dad also read the book, and we decided we could ask Sai Baba for things we needed. Dad had experiences of finding stuff he asked for, like wood, for his art projects. I will never forget the childlike grin on my 6'1" father, born in Wyoming and raised on an Oklahoma farm, feeling blessed by this holy man who lived in India and must have heard his wish. His call to him for a particular piece of wood to complete a project appeared as if by magic, lying by a dumpster nearby. We had fun with this idea that there was such a person in the world who could hear our thoughts and answer our requests.

When Sai Baba would meet his followers in a group darshan, a giving of blessings, at his ashram, he would manifest vibhuti, a sacred ash substance used for healing. He would place it in people's hands. I thought, "So why must I go there for the vibhuti? If he is so magical, why can't he just manifest some next to me while I meditate?"

Every day that I meditated, I would first ask Sai Baba to put a little pile of vibhuti next to me so that it would be there when I opened my eyes. After my meditations, I would look and see no vibhuti. It was my game, and I thought it was silly but fun. I never told anyone about it.

I was in Barbara's living room with Anna, eating a cookie as she did after our healing sessions, and asked Barbara, "When you were in India, did you ever see Sai Baba?" Without my saying anything more, she stopped, looked me in the eyes, and said, "Wait a minute, I have something for you," and left to retrieve something from her bedroom.

When she returned, she handed me a small white paper that had been folded into a thin, perfect envelope. She said, "I have been keeping this for over ten years now, knowing it was for someone I would meet one day. Now I know it is for you!" I was stunned. She continued, "This was given to me in my hand by Sai Baba when I was at his ashram receiving his darshan. It is vibhuti, and it is for you."

My heart stopped. What had just happened? This was incredible, and it was real. The requests I had made over and over and over before my meditations were fulfilled by the swami who heard my plea through the ethers and around the world. My relationship with him was not imaginary after all. Could that really be so? It was, and I could feel it in my heart. The gift of that small white folded envelope and the vibhuti inside was so precious and profound that it is hard, if not impossible, to explain what it meant to me.

I had just been through a horrible trial with my daughter's illness and was in a very dark place. Now, a Tibetan lama was offering prayers for us, and there was this incredible miracle. This told me I was in the right place, and since then, my belief in something other and bigger, the mystical, the magical, and amazing, has not waned. Receiving that gift healed me in a remarkable way.

It led me to take refuge with Lama Gangha and take a Boddhisattva vow to delay my enlightenment until all beings are enlightened before me. I found a spiritual path in the Tibetan Buddhist teachings. Sai Baba and Lama Gangha became significant to the foundation of my developing spiritual identity. I needed this grounding of spiritual practice and a Buddhist community to make it through CF and have something uniquely mine.

At home, I had a small room to practice my meditations in that also served as my art room. My two practices of art-making and meditation started to meld together for me. I began creating Buddhist wall hangings with quilting techniques and my sewing machine. It gave me joy and a feeling of accomplishment separate from my life as a CF mom. I was also Robin, the artist and spiritual practitioner.

We continued to visit Lama Gangha while Anna, too, was healing. She was getting stronger and healthier, and we hoped her recovery would continue and she would grow to be an active little girl. Whenever it was time to travel to our "Shangri-la," Anna would run to get dressed, find something to bring to Lama Gangha, and, when we arrived, greet him with a hug.

Lama-la took to Anna, too. He delighted in her little girl's antics, laughter, and curly hair, offering her sweets and cookies that she loved. When he would leave for a while to fulfill his teaching commitments, he always returned with small yet thoughtful gifts for his students, including Anna. Among them was a small coin purse. It was brown plastic vinyl with a metal closure at the top and decorated with two shiny blue budgies. For some reason, I immediately wondered what the blue budgie meant, thinking it had some significance. I never forgot about my wondering. After Anna played with it for a while, I put it away as a treasure, always remembering how all his gifts made me feel. They were precious and magic. Years later, we again visited the magic of the blue budgie coin purse.

Lama-la also wanted Anna to heal with dutsi, a Tibetan

herb. These herbs are cooked and baked with an ancient recipe that includes the chanted prayers of lamas whose vibrations and intentions are part of the mixture. This was a magical dose of conscious intention as an ingredient similar to my coveted vibhuti. At first, she hesitated to put these small black pills and herbal brown morsels in her mouth, but we quickly gave them a name: Lama Gangha nummy nums. They were a treat from her healer to help cleanse her karma and the obstacles causing her illness, preventing her from having a full life, and she loved them.

These herbal remedies do not make all adversity disappear when ingested. It is understood that we all live with challenges, yet we can receive blessings, healing, and help along the way. Anna was two years old and loved her Lama Gangha nummy nums, never leaving Barbara's place without them. For me, they were a special remedy for our early hopelessness.

Meeting Lama Gangha so many years ago, along with his herbal gifts and Tibetan medicine, is still revered by Anna as part of the necessary ingredients for her lifelong healing strength, just like receiving the vibhuti was for me. Our healing journey led me to these experiences that were deeper and more personally profound than any classroom learning I could have had in my master's program. My little Anna and her condition of CF became my teacher.

Even though these healing rituals were powerful, we never expected Anna's disease to be cured or taken away. CF continued to progress, perhaps at not as rapid a rate as it would have if she did not have this type of care, but it certainly strengthened her spirit and our hope and joy. This was the beginning of how we were to be with our lives with CF, compliant with our Western medical routines while also looking for the mysterious, magical, miraculous, open perspectives and treatment alternatives for her care.

These additions of the supernatural sort gave richness to the mundane and repetitive routines she had to endure every day. We knew the daily treatment of aerosols, CPT, a high-calorie diet, and compliance with her medications were vital to her health, but so were dutsi and the magic of a friend like Lama-la. The magical miracles we found and looked for daily to make us smile and feel hopeful gave quality and meaning to living this life we had to accept.

In the years of having this extraordinary lama in our lives, we were moved by the great fortune of spending time with him and finding serendipity in our relationship. One day, a couple of years after we met, I learned he had the same birthday as Anna. "Really, Lama-la?" I said, sitting by him, incredulous. He pulled out his ID, nodding his head yes with a big grin. It said he was born July 13, 1931, exactly fifty years before Anna. So many questions arose. It was another layer of magic. Was this a sign that their relationship was meant to happen in the way it did and was not random? Was Anna karmically contracted with this particular lama to receive these healing pujas? Were unseen forces in our lives more powerful than we could ever imagine?

The probability of connecting with a man from Tibet who spent twelve years meditating in a cave in the Himalayas was already hard to fathom. Not only that, though; it was through meeting him that Sai Baba's gift was fulfilled and confirmed for my mind and heart that magic existed. Knowing this other improbable connection of shared birthdays made their relationship even more magical and poetic, cementing an even deeper connection with him. It was a remarkable coincidence.

When Lama Gangha visited or stayed at the meditation center, his students made chai. The tea was poured from a Chinese porcelain pot smelling of cinnamon, cardamom, and other spices. At one of these visits, Anna did not come with me. She had another cold and was very congested. Lama-la looked at me with a tilt of his head and a quizzical look. He saw I was feeling down, and I told him I was worried.

After our tea, I returned the teacups to the kitchen. Lama-la followed and turned to me. By this time, he had learned some English. He looked directly at me and said, "No worry. No worry. All OK. All OK. She OK." As he told me these words, it felt that he meant them beyond that day, week, or year. I broke protocol and hugged him. I loved embracing that wonderful maroon-clothed man. But, my doubting voice said, "He does not know what he says. A child with cystic fibrosis is never going to be OK. Anna will die early. We don't know when this early death will be, but how can his words be true?" Only the future could hold the truth.

Embroidering the story of Lama Gangha into our lives in an even deeper way, I believe he also helped me with the healthy birth of Sara. After Anna turned five, I wanted another child, one without the burden of cystic fibrosis. We had a 25% chance of a second child presenting with this disease. If our second child had CF, we would know early in the pregnancy because science had advanced far enough in the late '80s to discover the genetic markers for CF. Prenatal testing would tell us if our second child had this terrible disease. The odds were in our favor, but taking the chance with possible serious consequences was frightening.

I told Lama Gangha I wanted to get pregnant again and desperately wanted a healthy child. He immediately responded by giving me a paper amulet with prayers written in Tibetan, folded into a small square, and wrapped with multicolored threads. I was to wear it every day. It reminded me of the power of dutsi with its intentional energies and vibrations, a part of the ingredients necessary and common in Tibetan medicine. He also gave me a daily mantra practice. My dedication to this path instructed me to be faithful to his direction. After months of wearing the amulet and reciting the mantra, I did not get pregnant until after I had two visions.

First, I was at a nearby Buddhist event at the local high school, where I meditated with a large group. Sitting quietly in my theater seat, I saw in my mind's eye a bassinet adorned with colorful fabrics. It was waiting for a baby. Then, shortly after, I had a powerful dream.

Walking up a hill in a mountainous environment with open vistas, I arrived at a stone house. As I stepped inside, two lamas were waiting for me. I handed them an amulet, and they said, "Within ten months, you will have a child with a healthy and happy rebirth." I instantly awoke. I knew it was more than a regular dream. The images were vivid and felt real. I discovered I was pregnant a few weeks later. Sara was born precisely ten months later, arriving eighteen days past her due date.

Early in the pregnancy, my baby was tested to see if she had CF. The thought of having another child with this terrible disease was overwhelming. On the day I received the results, my father happened to come by for a visit. I was pouring grounds into a paper cone in my little galley kitchen to make Dad coffee when the phone rang. I answered and heard, "Hello. This is UCSF genetic counseling. Can I speak with Robin Modlin?"

Being so glad Dad was there with me, I replied, "This is Robin."

The call continued, "I am calling to tell you your results have returned to our office. Your fetus does not have CF but is a carrier." I reached for Dad, grabbing his arm while taking a huge breath of relief. The caller continued, "Do you want to know the gender?"

I could not contain my emotions, and tears were beginning to fill my eyes. I did not know what gender Anna was before she was born. We saved that for a surprise, but wanted to know this time. Even though Doug was not there, I knew he would have said it was OK to say yes. "Oh, thank you, thank you, yes, we want to know."

The caller said, "You are going to have a girl."

I was ecstatic. Thanking the caller, I hung up, dove for a hug, put my arms around Dad, and blubbered with tears, "It is a girl! I am going to have another daughter! And she will not have CF!" Dad held me. As my dream vision foretold, Doug and I were to have a healthy child.

We only knew Lama Gangha for five years. He died just before Sara, our second daughter, was born, but I knew his blessings were also a part of my new baby's life. Lama-la went on a trip to Tibet in 1988 with other lamas of his lineage for a short visit. He was very excited to return to his home. We learned that he had passed unexpectedly while in Tibet. He was almost fifty-seven and died of a malignant tumor in his neck. To die in his homeland was poetically right, even though we felt a significant loss.

Memories of the beginning of our CF journey and the healing comfort and blessings of Lama Gangha sit gently inside me. I remember Lama-la as a dear friend, mystic, and enlightened man. He dedicated his mind and heart for the benefit of all beings and devoted his life with a generosity, helping others in ways I could never truly understand.

Lama Gangha offered us a transmission of healing, opening our minds with his presence, rituals, and saffron water. It changed the course of our suffering, and I am so grateful. In my fantasies at that time, I wondered if he excised our negative karma and dissolved it as he transitioned into his afterlife with a magical and mystical formula. Perhaps, but now I ask, was it he who took away our negative karma, or was it our change of mind toward the positive that he skillfully directed us toward? It was likely the latter. Nonetheless, the memory of him and the power of his generosity lives with us always.

These stories of our family and Lama Gangha were not freely shared with others at the time. They were deeply personal and laid essential grounding for accepting life's mysteries, magic, and miracles. Alongside our faith in science, research, and modern medicine, they were woven into our attitudes as we coped with CF. I was learning we were on a remarkable adventure that was unique and good despite the difficulty, Anna's suffering, and our fear of loss.

chapter six

Our Healing Journey

In our first year with CF, there were other potent experiences in our healing journey. We began to explore other complementary therapies that we did not keep private and openly shared with her CF team. Dr. Moss accepted our experimentation as long as we complied with the regimen he prescribed for Anna. There were no cures for Anna's disease. Knowing CF was relentless, Dr. Moss supported whatever could be done, even if unusual, as long as the added treatments were not harmful.

In the summer of 1983, after meeting Lama Gangha, I took Anna to see Dr. Yat Ki Lai, an acupuncturist and herbal specialist in San Francisco's Chinatown. Barbara Bernie, a family friend involved in the legislative adoption and certification of acupuncture in California, referred us. She was a dear friend of my mother's and a friend of Dr. Lai. Barbara was miraculously healed with Chinese medicine when her cancer was cured after a lengthy hospital stay in a Chinese hospital while treated with herbs and acupuncture. This led her to study Chinese medicine and become involved in its politics. I had some knowledge of Chinese medicine through my graduate program, so it was familiar to me.

After Barbara Bernie made an appointment for us with Dr. Lai, we traveled fifty minutes north to San Francisco's Chinatown every other week. Sometimes, we stopped to pick up Mom, and she rode along for support and to be in the city. Mom was a San Franciscan, having lived there as a child and later meeting and marrying Dad in the city. She loved helping us navigate the busy streets of Chinatown with its open vegetable markets, smells of fresh fish, and curio shops brimming over with trinkets serving as tempting eye candy for our two-year-old.

Arriving at our destination, we noticed the office window decorated with Chinese lettering, and underneath in English, "Dr. Yat Ki Lai, Acupuncture and Herbs." We reached for the antique brass door handle to enter Dr. Lai's office. As we opened the door, a string was pulled to make a bell ring, announcing our arrival. There were no receptionists to check us in. We heard a man's voice say in a strong Chinese accent, "Come in, come in. Just sit over here."

We introduced ourselves as Barbara's friends, and Dr. Lai knew we were coming. He greeted us with a bright smile, using his hands to direct us to the back rooms. He was about forty years old, slender, cheerful, and kind.

Holding Anna in my arms with Mom in tow, we walked through the foreign doctor's office with its musty smell of herbs. On our left were stacks of shelves holding jars of visible but unknown substances that looked like roots, fungi, and dried leaves. Stalks of dried plants and herbs were secured with string hung from the ceiling.

Cubicles for Dr. Lai's patients were made with white cotton sheets hung as four walls for privacy. We entered one of these small rooms and sat beside an exam table. There were chairs for both Mom and me. We trusted we were in good hands as Barbara would never steer us wrong. We were committed to this healing journey for Anna, which included Tibetan medicine and now Chinese medicine for another tool in our toolbox.

It was amazing to think we did not have to travel far to find these approaches to healing. Tibet and China were right at our doorstep. For this new experience of Chinese medicine, Anna sat on my lap. Dr. Lai talked to her kindly and asked me to hold her hand while he felt her wrists as part of her diagnosis. At first, Anna was unsure, as any two-year-old would be, but she cooperated with my encouragement.

Dr. Lai explained, "At this age, we do not set acupuncture needles because it is too difficult for children to sit still long enough. We do it differently. You hold her."

He took a long, micro-thin needle to the inside of her hand, rapidly poking the skin on the two joints on each of the four fingers of both hands. A small bead of red blood or yellow liquid formed from the needle prick. Anna was startled and cried, but not defiantly.

Poking her skin was a treatment and form of diagnosis. Dr. Lai explained he was looking at how much yellow fluid appeared. The feel of the pulses, the color of the skin, a coat on the tongue, or the color of fluid that appeared at the needle's prick were all used to determine Anna's health. According to the tradition of Chinese diagnosis, Dr. Lai decided if she was too "wet" or "dry" or which acupuncture energy meridian lines were blocked. The information he gathered told him how to treat her. I was not learned enough to understand what he saw from this initial diagnostic treatment. Still, he let us know he was primarily treating her digestive system.

Next, Dr. Lai gathered a specific herbal concoction for Anna. There were leaves, sticks, tree bark, what looked like dried mushrooms, and other strange objects that you would rake up in the park on an autumn day. My instructions were to place them in a ceramic pot he gave me, cover them with water, and boil them down to half a cup, making a tea. I was then to have Anna drink it.

Holding Anna's hand, I looked at my mom skeptically, saying, "Can you believe this? For a two-year-old?"

She returned a look, raising her eyebrows with a gesture that said, "I know." Sensing we were unsure how this would work, Dr. Lai suggested adding a dose of honey, which might help Anna accept the herbal tea.

Each herbal concoction was in a small lunch-size brown bag, and each would be boiled twice. We did not know the names of the herbs or where they came from, but assumed they all had been imported from China. With our instructions and herbs in hand, we left to the ring and jingle of the door's hanging bell back onto the busy street of Chinatown, committed to doing everything we could to help Anna. I had never drunk tea like this, but I knew others who had. I heard the flavor was quite strong and disgusting. We thought our attempt to offer this tea to our little two-year-old could surely fail. Still, after buying a Chinatown trinket, we drove back down the peninsula to try it.

Anna surprised us at every turn. This child of mine took to Dr. Lai's dark black herbal tea and drank it daily! Every day, the steam and apothecary smells filled my kitchen. I sweetened it with honey, and after it cooled, I put the tea in a small blue or yellow plastic baby bottle with a nipple. After her respiratory treatments, Anna would suck on it while watching her favorite *Sesame Street*. She never refused the tea and drank it for years.

I was inspired to try other remedies suggested by Chinese medicine. When we visited Dr. Lai, I bought frog legs in a Chinese market and took them home for Anna, sautéing them in oil and garlic. The theory was that frogs have stored energy in their legs that is available when ingested. It was a fanciful idea that carried no potential harm. Anna needed energy for her healing, and she loved her frog legs, of course.

When we first saw Dr. Lai, Anna's digestion was not great even after taking the enzymes prescribed for her CF digestive issues. Our exotic treatment was supposed to help, and I was able to objectively measure if things improved by observing her bowel movements. One day, after a visit to Dr. Lai, her stool changed to normal. The next day, it changed back to its bulky character. Still, with the timing of the visits to San Francisco and the lessening of the yellow fluid from her tiny fingers, her stools progressively became more normal. The changes directly correlated with our visits.

This treatment was helping her, and I shared the information with her CF medical team. It was so encouraging, and we continued the regimen. Eventually, we stopped driving to San Francisco after we found another Chinese doctor closer to home in Palo Alto.

My mom was one of our behind-the-scenes guides on our healing journey with her intuitions on how to help Anna by first calling the two Barbaras. Otherwise, we may not have met Lama Gangha or Dr. Lai. It meant so much for her to see her granddaughter, Anna, surviving, thriving, and being willing to participate in her healing journey. It was a precious family affair of three generations.

Anna accepted all of the treatments we introduced to her. It was also clear that Chinese food was her favorite, and we regularly got Chinese food to go as my child, who needed to eat, would eat a large quantity. The high salt content was also good for her. All we could say was, "Who is this child?" And what was this foe of ours, cystic fibrosis, leading us on this journey with remarkable experiences?

As the years marched forward, Anna's indomitable spirit and willingness to do what had to be done, including her complementary therapies, respiratory treatments, medicines, tests, doctor appointments, later hospitalizations, and home IV care, continued to inspire us. And hope was growing in our community for the development of new treatments resulting from new and exciting medical research, the growing field of transplantation and its miracles, and the increasing longevity of patients. We were driving our life forward toward Anna's unknowable future.

We were fortunate and had remarkable opportunities with the best of all worlds. Still, Anna's CF was not cured or curable. Symptoms improved with various treatment modalities, and she was stable for relatively long periods, yet her disease progressed. It was slow and hard to see in the day-to-day bustle of life, but the effects would show themselves over time when lung exacerbations appeared.

Even though her physical body reacted to her disease process with what felt like a slow progression, we suspected and hoped it was also positively affected by the various alternative and mystical complementary treatments we found. We would never know whether or how much they helped her, but what was sure was that our experiences helped our spirits. They made the disease and its many difficulties also a journey of discovery. Our faith and hope grew with the acceptance of our circumstances. We loved our life, felt the stress and worry, and marveled at the magic surrounding Anna.

Sometimes, we could only feel the fear and worry. After clinic appointments, when her pulmonary function, PFT, was in decline, Doug and I would dig each other out with bits of our mystical and magical hope, remembering Lama-la's messages that she would be OK or adding a new herb to her concoction. New medical advances like the aerosol drug Pulmozyme thinned her mucus, causing her treatments to be more productive, making us feel even better therapies might be around the corner. We lived with it all in our pockets, which was our winning combination. Our pockets were bulging, and we felt abundant, hopeful, and realistic. My universe was putting me through a graduate education like no other. I was on one big, never-ending field trip working toward that PhD.

chapter seven

Miracle Collecting

In the course of a few years, from the time Anna was released from the hospital at less than two years old to when she was nearly eight, we moved four times—from Menlo Park to Sunnyvale to Mountain View to midtown Palo Alto and finally to the Greenmeadow neighborhood in south Palo Alto. At each stop, our homes changed to meet our needs. Anna was doing well, attending public school, and had shown us her miraculous spirit many times over. We were engaged in our local CF community and adopted the routines and attitudes we needed to live with CF.

Before we made the move to Greenmeadow in 1989, we lived in a little house in midtown Palo Alto that we'd just finished remodeling. Sara was a baby. Spring arrived, and I awoke Sunday morning to hear Doug saying, "It is time to move! I had a dream, and it is time to move!"

This did not sit well with me. I am a homebody and nester. I can be very happy in one place for a long time, and we had so many moves and changes in such a short amount of time. I was not ready to do that again. My wifely response to Doug was, "No! You are crazy!"

He was insistent. "It is time to move!"

That Sunday was a warm and beautiful day, and the swim club we had joined two years earlier was open for the season that weekend. We dressed the girls to go to the pool for the day. Sara was about eight months old, and I put her in a sunbonnet and sleeveless jumper. Anna, then seven years old, was in her green Greenmeadow swim team speedo suit. We had to make a short drive to get there.

When we arrived and walked through the entry gate, a sparkling blue pool welcomed Anna to dive in. This was her favorite place where she enjoyed friends and had good old-fashioned fun. The day was crystal clear; golden poppies and pink plum blossoms were everywhere. Other friends gathered at the pool and agreed to watch Anna as we took Sara for a walk.

Pushing the stroller across the pool parking lot and then across the street, we walked with our little Sara, enjoying the springtime. We saw a for-sale sign announcing an open house about half a block up. Doug said, "Let's go in."

I hesitated, wanting to continue walking, saying, "I don't know, Doug." I remembered what he said when he woke up that morning but reassured myself that no one goes and buys the first house they see.

We went in. It was in a neighborhood built in the 1950s by the famous architect, Eichler. All the homes were one-level mid-century modern homes with big windows and protected gardens perfect for California living. This one had five bedrooms and three baths and had been modestly remodeled. It did not take Doug long to say, "Robin, we are buying this house. I told you I had a dream that said it was time to move. This is the house. The pool and a wonderful park are just down the street, and we must live here with the girls. Can't you see? We must have a consensus about this."

When Doug decided on something, his mind would not change. My resistance could also be stubborn. "Are you kidding me, Doug? I have to pack up again after remodeling my cute kitchen, and our elementary school is just around the corner from our house?" And I gave him a big "NO!"

Well, as usual, that did not move him. He was determined and knew it was the best thing for us to do. It was as if his dream foretold a great fortune staring at him. We walked away, and yet he could not leave it behind.

The next day, we were told two offers were being presented for the house. We met with our realtor, I relented, and we put one in, too. I could see the potential to make the house my own with new landscaping. I envisioned apple trees, Japanese maples, climbing roses, a vegetable garden with snap peas for the girls to munch on, and there was the perfect limb in the almond tree for a rope swing. And that mature grapefruit tree in its umbrella stance was right outside the sliding door from the living room. It reminded me of my favorite tree as a child.

We offered one thousand dollars over the asking price and got it! After that, I was forever afraid of what the next dream vision might tell Doug to do. But now we had a house with rooms for all of us. The girls each had a bedroom and bathroom. There was an office for Doug and a sewing/meditation room for me. Still, if we had not gone to the pool that day or Doug had not had the vision in his dream life, we might never have lived in Greenmeadow, which proved to be the best place for our girls' happiness, Anna's health, and us, the parents.

As it turned out, buying that house inspired by a miraculous dream and the effort on Doug's part to make it happen created a feeling of magic for us. While living there, we often would remark what a blessing it was to have that great home, community, and pool for our girls to grow up with.

Two years before buying the Greenmeadow house, we learned the significance of having a swimming pool for Anna's overall health. She was five years old when I needed to check on her one night because I did not hear her usual nightly coughing spell. I was awake in anticipation of our in-the-middle-of-the-night routine. I tiptoed into her bedroom and saw she was deep asleep with her blanket, Bluey, and the ragged lovies she laid her head on.

This was unusual as we would get up and do a nighttime treatment every night, turning on the air compressor's aerosol mist and mechanical hum while snuggling on pillows, tapping and pounding our cupped hands on her front and back.

She would cough, spit up sputum, and return to bed with a warm glass of milk. But that night, she slept through, and I had to check to be sure she was breathing.

The day before, I had taken her to a public swimming pool, and it was the first time she learned to go underwater, hold her breath, and swim. It made her cough each time she came up for air, but she loved it. I had difficulty getting her out of the pool to go home. It was remarkable that this activity helped clear her lungs so well that she did not wake up that night. Her playful antics going up and down and under the water while loving the pool time proved to be a step toward another discovery about who she was.

In earlier times, before much was known about CF, children were told not to be active. They were overprotected and lived with mist tents to deliver aerosols and help loosen the mucus. Most children died very young. When Anna was little, it was newly believed that active exercise was good for CF kids. They were inherently strong and able children who happened to have this defect in their system that interfered with their life expectancy. They needed regular activity and exercise.

As Anna's parents, we were charged with keeping her as healthy as possible until the research findings and medical miracles we were waiting for finally came through to give her more years. Now, with this experience, we understood that vigorous exercise like swimming was a prescription that made a difference for Anna.

Shortly after learning the healing power of swimming for Anna, we joined a private swim club in the Greenmeadow neighborhood in Palo Alto. It was one of our medical interventions and our family's joyful place. The pool oasis was a lifesaver, and we learned that Anna was a natural athlete. She immediately took to the water, and we enrolled her in the swim team. Swim practice demanded hard work, swimming laps, and perfecting strokes.

I knew it was hard for her, so we offered incentives to keep her going. Even so, when Anna dove into that pool, it was as if she skimmed on the top with much less effort than other children her age. She had a natural talent that took after Doug's mother, her grandmother, TuTu, who was a champion golfer and athletic woman. We later learned to say Anna was gifted with TuTu's physical prowess.

Anna recognized that power in her TuTu. Through the years, TuTu made it clear that athleticism was essential to her life whenever we visited her in Tahoe or Reno. Anna loved her energy and sparkling style of diamond bling tennis bracelets and bright, colorful clothing. Her TV was always on sports channels; you could never escape it.

Once, while visiting, Anna watched a weight lifter hoist hundreds of pounds above his head and said to her fit grandmother, "TuTu, I want to be a weight lifter."

My protective mom response was to poo-poo that notion with some dismissive remark, but TuTu would not have it. "Anna, you can be whoever you want to be," she said. "Of course you can be a weight lifter."

My hackles stood up. How could she dare say that to this little girl with a lung disease that would take her strength away? I did not dare defy TuTu. I just cringed inside with the cracks in my heart about Anna's prognosis of a short life that I was sure would never include athletic prowess. But I was found to be wrong about that.

Anna began to show her talented athleticism by swimming on the swim team in the six and under age group. She would fly to the other side of the pool at Saturday swim meets, leaving the others in her powerful wake. Doug and I would look at each other and again repeat, "Who is this child?" Who does this? A child so close to death as a toddler fighting a chronic lung disease had grown to be a competitive swimmer at six years old. And then we might say, "Of course! She is her grandmother's granddaughter!" TuTu was so proud, as were my parents.

At weekend swim meets, we would let go of our fears and worries and enjoy yelling, "Go, Anna, go, go, Anna, go," as she raced with perfect form, whether freestyle, backstroke, or butterfly. In some races, Anna would make it to the finish and have time to get out of the pool, stand on the deck, and cheer on the others on her team to their finish line. It was remarkable, and her physical ability and talent were breathtaking. It was as if she won the Olympic trials every weekend.

Our swim team belonged to a league that had an annual championship meet. The summer Sara was born, 1988, was Anna's second year entering. The meet was scheduled two days after I gave birth to Sara. I could not go, so Doug filmed the events for me to see and feel the excitement.

I suspected how it would go at the meet, but I loved seeing each event on video. In her true form, Anna climbed the starting blocks at the top of her lane with a confident swagger, loving the attention of grandstands filled with swim team moms and dads, brothers and sisters, and other competitors. She would clap her hands as if to wake up the energies around her, owning the pool with its smell of chlorine elixir as she posed for the starting leap. She was so cool in her tight-fitting green speedo and Greenmeadow swim cap, ready for that starting horn to launch her in the perfect dive.

After entering the water, Anna rose with committed arms in beautiful form. It was gorgeous! Her best and favored stroke was the butterfly, which was notoriously challenging but beautiful to watch. She looked like a butterfly with wings rising in an arc from the water, or like a swan with majestic wings gliding onto a lake. Anna won all her races that day with thunderous applause from her team.

Next, our sassy child, with her strength and love of the race, was the only girl on the relay team with three other boys: John, Aaron, and Justin. They were hotshots. Even though they all had little bodies, those four kids had power and talent. In the medley relay, Anna was the butterflier. Watching her take off after the first swimmer touched the side, we'd see her fly off the blocks and push through to make up for lagging distances. The crowd went crazy as she gained speed in the wake of her competitors, overtaking their lead. "Go, go, go, go, go!" I could hear Doug screaming on the video.

It was so exciting, a magical thrill filling us with ecstatic joy. They won. Those little kids hugged and clapped and celebrated their victory at the side of the pool as each got out of the water.

That year, our Greenmeadow team swept many races against eight teams, winning the event and the high point championship trophy. Anna also won her individual high point championship trophy and earned the title of a true swim champion. She was our little athlete with a severe lung disease who had the gumption, courage, and spirit it took to practice and compete to make that happen. It was a miracle!

Mom and Dad came over the next day. They arrived at our dining table displaying a beautiful ice cream cake, flowers, blue ribbons, medals, and a gigantic golden trophy with the figure of a girl in a diving position on the top. The face plate read "High Point" and below, "The Junipero Serra Swim League, 1988." Anna's name needed to be added in an engraving. Being almost half her height, it was a task for her to hold. It was a time of magic and joy. Mom and Dad understood the magnitude of what had happened that day but could only say, "Well, Anna, you won your trophy. We are so proud!" There were no words for the miracle we all knew had happened.

And not only that; we had Sara, Anna's three-day-old sister, with us. Anna and Sara were our miraculous daughters. The joys of welcoming another healthy daughter into our family and Anna showing us her talent and physical accomplishments were beyond dreams.

During Anna's swim career, she won her high point again the next year and set a pool record for the butterfly that stood for over twenty years. We already knew we had a daughter with what it takes to beat the odds and survive. Still, she wowed us even more with her natural talent, power, and strength.

Those incredible experiences of physical strength and the magic of winning gave her a deep inner confidence. She overcame so much and knew she had the discipline and power within her to meet her challenges. Later, Anna wore a T-shirt that said, "Don't Let Your Fears Stand in the Way of Your Dreams." She embodied that saying, and I still have the image of that shirt folded in my memories and the actual T-shirt in a safe place.

Anna's CF continued to progress through her childhood, as that is what CF does. It was obvious that the swimming was good for her overall health and must have staved off a faster progression. Still, her swim career as the champion waned with her worsening lung disease. It was harder and harder for her to do the workouts necessary. That moment of magic and winning was only a point in time, but one we never forgot with its tingle of joy and incredulous memories.

A few years later, when Anna was eight or nine, she would swim, her strokes still beautiful and natural, but after swimming a lap or two, she would have to stop. Hanging onto the side of the pool, she would cough vigorously, leaving her breathless for a few minutes before she could continue her laps. She did not have the energy she had in those early magical years. From being a phenom to an average swimmer due to her disease, Anna felt like her worsened CF had stolen swimming from her. It was a heartbreak. Still, her love of the pool and her friendly personality kept her there, where she grew to become a lifeguard, swim coach, and instructor. Sara followed in her sister's footsteps. She too was an excellent swimmer, on swim team and as a lifeguard.

Buying the house in Greenmeadow during the swimming magic was like receiving a greater helping of the miraculous. It made it possible for Anna to have continual access to the pool. Even though I was the reluctant one initially, I had to quickly admit it was an inspired and right thing to buy that house for all of us. Anna's storied swim team career was short, but hanging out with the other kids and lifeguards around the pool as she and Sara grew up gave them a community of children of all ages that was safe and healthy.

But what was this idea of a miracle that we felt we were experiencing many times over? A miracle is first defined in the Google Oxford Languages Dictionary as "a surprising and welcome event that is not explicable by natural or scientific laws and is therefore considered to be the work of a divine agency." Its second definition is "a highly improbable or extraordinary event, development, or accomplishment that brings very welcome consequences." It is this second definition that is preferred by me and defines the miracles of our collection.

I am unsure that there is a divine agency outside ourselves in deciding on events and whether or how they happen. Even so, it can feel that way. Yet, I believe there are extraordinary people and events in life and nature that are unexpected, surprising, unexplainable, and feel miraculous. When miracles happen, it might take your breath away while knowing something more significant or grander than usual has happened. Experiencing that so many times increased my faith that our CF world was not only a difficult challenge but also positive and magical.

It's natural for people to want miracles to happen in their lives. If you want them, it is essential to actively look for them. Sometimes, they can be hidden, simply not recognized, or require extra effort or extraordinary faith to create the opportunity for them to occur. The most extraordinary miracles that involved Anna resulted from her determination, courage, and talent.

People have many opinions about miracles and whether to say if they believe in them. I love the perspective of Oprah Winfrey, who said, "I for sure believe in miracles. For me, a miracle is seeing the world with light in your eyes. It's knowing there's always hope and possibility where none seems to exist. Many people are so closed to miracles that even when one is boldly staring them in the face, they label it coincidence or serendipity. I call it like I see it." (*What I Know for Sure, Macmillan*, 2014.)

We placed our first conscious order for a miracle that Anna would survive her first hospitalization. Her chance for recovery was slight. When she came home, we felt something extraordinary happened with the best outcome we could have imagined. It was a miracle to us, just like our meeting Lama Gangha, Sai Baba's vibhuti, Sara being born without CF, Doug's dream foretelling of a family home, and Anna's swimming championship. These events made us feel that we were living a fortunate and miraculous life.

Beyond the personal magic and miracles in our family lives, we were also encouraged by the development of CF research in the 1980s and '90s which, for the first time, opened the possibility of lifesaving miracles in the lives of all of the families in our CF community. The prognosis for our children was improving. Their life expectancy was increasing. It was a hopeful time for us all.

The growth of CF research was partly due to Dr. Paul Quinton's groundbreaking work. Initially supported by CFRI, he provided the key to understanding CF as a chloride channel dysfunction. Inexplicably, Dr. Quinton has CF himself and is a living miracle. His work has led to an explosion of findings viewed as more than miraculous. These breakthroughs have extended the life expectancy of those born with CF today well into their middle age. He is just one example of a miraculous person creating the miraculous in our CF community.

When Anna was a little girl, we were hopeful that this emerging knowledge and good timing would play a role in the intervention of her health trajectory, bringing her that type of miracle. It was a race against time as CF's destructive force played havoc on not only Anna but all of the children in our community. We knew a growing list of wonderful children and adults who were dying.

It was a struggle for Anna to live with CF and for us to be confident about her future. Dreams of our daughter having an independent adult life and a child of her own were miracles I believed and accepted that I would never collect. But I was also learning that miracles happen unexpectedly and in ways you would never imagine. Anna's life had become so much more than we ever bargained for. We did not realize then that the future could offer what we would never allow ourselves to dream of. But we never would have believed she would be a swim champion when she first came home with her terrible diagnosis. Miracles were clearly happening in our lives and we were looking out for more.

chapter eight

Our Chronic Sorrow

The whir of coffee beans in the grinder was the first sound of the morning. I made fresh coffee every morning for myself. In my girls' rooms, they could hear the sound as a wake-up call. Always much earlier than most other kids, Anna wandered out of her room to get ready for school. In her baggy flannels and T-shirt, she would pick up three nebulizers from the kitchen counter. I filled them with albuterol, Pulmozyme, and hypertonic saline. Sometimes, there would be a fourth, Toby (tobramycin), the aerosolized antibiotic used every other month.

She also had English Breakfast tea with milk on the ready to help open her eyes. Every morning of every day began with a treatment. What that looked like evolved over the years with different mechanical devices developed to help expel the mucus in her lungs.

In her younger years, I was the one pounding with CPT on her before school. Later, she had the Vest that made her independent. The Vest was a mechanical device she would strap on during her nebulizer treatments. It shook her torso to loosen up the secretions stuck after a whole night's sleep or an active day. She could do all the shaking with the mechanical percussion blasts of air, squeezes, and jiggling of her chest to make her cough. Until the Vest, I thought we would be forever tied with the task of pounding, as I knew she could not easily have a day without it. The Vest was revolutionary for families who could be freed up to care for their other kids.

The door to the family room with the TV was closed

behind her as Anna prepared for her treatment. Her TV watching evolved, too, from *Sesame Street* to *Friends* and other teen favorites. While in the kitchen having my coffee and watching the morning news on my mini TV, I could hear that telltale CF anthem sung by the nebulizer, air compressor, and Vest accentuated with huffing and coughing. We were used to these sounds, especially Sara. She was seven years younger, and it was what she always knew to be part of our environment and what Anna did.

One morning, when Anna was about ten and I had finished her CPT, pain seized my back. I could not get up off the floor. I could not move. "Anna, go get Dad," I yelled in pain.

I had to be helped up and hobbled with Doug as my crutch to our bed. All I could do was lie prone. My back "went out," as they say. It finally all caught up with me. The treatments, the medications, the worry, the responsibility of my job as a mother with the lifesaving duties, and the most pressing stressor being this was a lethal disease, and my child's life was always on the line. At any time, the wiles of illness could change our direction to a place we did not want to go. This took the rug from under my feet. My strength and control to keep it all together just needed a break, but my circumstances would not let me. I needed support and help.

After finding that I had a bulging disk in my back and rest was required, that was all I could do. My body had told me to stop, and I could not refuse. My family had to help me, and Doug had to step in to do more treatments. It was hard to be helpless and strange to not be in control of the flow of the family. Still, we got through it.

After I was strong again, I went to the track to start running. I loved a two-mile run and had not done so for a while. I found it released me. My trial run was not successful. As I started my laps, my leg muscles tightened, and I could not go faster than a walk. I had to hobble home in pain. Within a few days, chronic stiffness and pain began to interfere in my life.

When I got up in the morning, it was hard to move, and I felt like a very old woman, but I was just in my forties.

My leg muscles, shoulders, and neck were inflamed with polymyalgia. Ibuprofen became a daily staple in my diet. I could not change the fact that we had CF living with us with its nasty grip on my daughter, and my body felt it. I had to do something different. I knew that I could try to lessen my stress by my attitude and how I mentally held it. I decided I needed time off just to be and smell the roses, so I planned private retreats to rejuvenate when I became emotionally depleted.

When I got to the point where I knew I was becoming overwhelmed, impatient, and tired, Doug would take over so that I could drive north above San Francisco to Green Gulch Farm. It was an extension of the SF Zen Center, where they grew organic vegetables for the center and their restaurant in San Francisco, Greens. When I arrived, I felt the silence the meditation center offered, and the weight I was carrying quickly began to lift. I craved quiet, alone time, and being in this spiritual space.

My guest room was simple, perfectly Zen, and just for me. The meals were vegetarian, nourishing, and made by another. I could just be. Walking on a dirt path not far from the guest residence where the sky opened past the tall eucalyptus, there were gardens surrounded with rosebushes and other flowers. I visited benches placed in these areas for resting and napping. The ocean was not far, and the cool fog and salty breeze filled the gardens.

After a nap and a walk to visit the ocean shore and touch the sand, I would go to the bookstore, a converted outbuilding with a glass-paned door that opened into a world of words that spoke to me. I would search through the books written by Buddhist teachers, gardeners, and nature lovers. The retreat center store had small jizo statues, Japanese guardians of children, other Buddhas, candles, and incense. I immersed myself in the things that I loved. It restored me. I was creating my prescription, a personal spiritual elixir to heal my wounds.

I knew all would be OK at home with Doug, Anna, and Sara when I went on these times away. It was an important time for them to bond. Usually, they did that at the pet store. Most times, I came home happy and rested with the girls often introducing me to a new critter for our family to love. Over the years, we had a menagerie of fish, birds, rats, bunnies, hamsters, lizards, and newts. These small creatures lived with our dogs, Reggie, Charlie, and Tashi, and the cats, Miss Kitty and Mooey.

Keeping things normal and as equal as possible between the girls was important to Doug and me. The girls were seven years apart in age and at different developmental stages. Not only was Anna the center of attention due to her disease and all of those concerns, but she was also much older with different demands. We were always weighing any gifts at birthdays and other holidays so that both felt we were fair. I made sure Sara had time alone with me without her sister. Sara was sweet and smart, did not make waves, and wanted to become a doctor. She was an exceptionally kind and wonderful child, so we felt we did not have to worry about her. Then we learned about a syndrome that affects siblings of children with chronic, life-threatening diseases.

At CFRI's 2003 annual conference for families with children with CF, a speaker addressed what was termed Chronic Sorrow. I had never heard this terminology before. She talked about CF being a disease that creates this condition in families due to its progressive nature with no cure. Other acute diseases affecting children that can come to a resolution affect families differently. A disease with no cure like CF means that a family will always expect to experience the loss of a child one day. That possibility sind eventuality pervades the family culture. This is "Chronic Sorrow."

It explained what we had been going through with my physical symptoms of back pain and muscle inflammation.

The relentless worry, constant attention, and responsibility for treatments and medications that should never be missed were taking a toll on us as parents. The speaker, Dr. Susan Roos, also described the typical profile of a healthy sibling in a family with a CF child. As she described a kind and caring child who never made waves and had high hopes and goals for herself that included healing professions, Doug and I were dumbfounded that she was describing Sara. She explained that these model behaviors were a cover for their hidden grief. Underneath the calm exterior of these wonderful children was a reservoir of emotions and desires never verbalized. It made so much sense, and our eyes were opened.

Realizing that there were parts of Sara that she had not shown us, we shared this new knowledge with her, and there it was; she melted into tears. We had not addressed many emotional needs in our fifteen years of parenting her. She was lost in the drama of our saving Anna's life. It was an impossible sibling position in a family like ours. She had a sister who was seriously ill. That was not ever going to change. Anna would forever be on the center stage of the family.

We started to talk a lot about this as a family and saw the pattern. Having Anna as her sister was formative to who Sara was in ways I never guessed. I simply did not see it until we learned about chronic sorrow. Sometimes, it is still a struggle for Sara, even as an adult, to know what is most important to her. It can be hard for her to take the initiative to get what she needs as she constantly worries about not harming others, causing too much commotion, or feeling she does not deserve her happiness.

It breaks my heart that this disease was so painful and injurious for Sara. She often told me that her friends did not get it when she was stressed or sad about Anna. No other kids she knew well had siblings battling a terrible disease. It was lonely for her, but I hope she felt more supported as she started sharing more with us. We listened more intently and saw the pitfalls we had missed years before. Sara's desire to become a doctor was motivated by wanting to save her sister at some level, but also by her compassion, empathy, and understanding of illness in a family.

While in college in her freshman year, Sara wrote about her experience of chronic sorrow in her Feminism class.

Sara: "*Every family has their politics, but mine seemed to be a little different. My sister has cystic fibrosis, which is a fatal genetic lung disease. This horrible illness has shaped me more than any other factor in my life. My sister's serious illness has caused my whole family to have what is called chronic sorrow; Susan Roos states, 'The essence of chronic sorrow is a painful discrepancy between what is perceived as what is reality and what continues to be dreamed of. The loss is ongoing since the source of the loss continues to be present. The loss is a living loss.'*

For my whole life, my sister has been 'dying,' so where does that put me? I was cast into the role of the well child. I felt that my feelings were obsolete and, therefore, would lie about them. When I was angry, depressed, or even joyful, I could not admit my emotions. Adrienne Rich states that '...she may also tell herself a lie: that she is concerned with the other's feelings, not with her own. But the liar is concerned with her own feelings.' I thought that by lying about how I felt, I would save others the pain because there was already so much suffering in our family. My silence was the only way I could fight the pain. I thought that I was protecting everyone around me.

The pervasive element of our family's politics is chronic sorrow due to chronic illness. My role within this political paradigm as the healthy sibling resulted in an unconscious participation in the politics of chronic sorrow. This is characterized by a silence and an inability to express what is deeply held within. Susan Roos, PhD, describes the well sibling as having survivor guilt; she points out that the well sibling has beliefs such as; I don't have the right to be happy unless my parents and siblings are doing OK; it's wrong to complain; I should be grateful for everything I have; and be perfect, but don't be important.

My sophomore year of high school was one of the worst years for me. I was incredibly depressed and could not open up to anyone. I was unsure of myself and felt I could not talk to my friends or my parents. I was ashamed and did not know how to react to what I was feeling and thinking. I shut everyone out and used art to express my anguish. I poured my soul onto those pieces of paper and was able to feel validated for the first time. Although I still blocked people out, I learned how to tell people just enough so that they thought I had opened up, when in reality, there was a lot more going on underneath the surface. This is how the politics of my family affected me.

I came home from a trip that summer to be confronted by my parents about my lies. They had attended a cystic fibrosis conference and a talk on grief within the family. Their eyes were opened to how the well child takes on the pain of the entire family. Once they realized my pain, I was confronted and practically forced to say my feelings. I felt like my world was crashing down. Adrienne Rich also brings up the point that 'The liar lives in fear of losing control. She cannot even desire a relationship without manipulation, since to be vulnerable to another person means for her the loss of control.'

My silence was my power. I was forced into therapy to learn how to express my emotions. I did not want to be there, and I did not want to lose my control. I am still working on opening up, and I hope I get to a healthy point where I can express my emotions more fully."

Navigating the emotional landscape of our family and the issue of CF's seriousness and prognosis of a limited life was very difficult for us as parents. How and when to tell Anna and her sister that this disease would take her life was tricky. Age-appropriate information was important for both of them. Doug and I had help with this issue when Anna started to attend a CF summer camp at nine years old. It was only about an hour away in the coastal mountains.

At camp, kids did not worry about their parents, and the parents did not worry about their kids. It was a perfect combination that allowed the kids to be just kids, have big fun, and delve safely into the reality of what they faced. Many of the volunteers had been with the camp for a long time. Along with this history came a roster of children who had been to camp but no longer were there because they had died from CF. Every year, there was another who did not attend. The loss was real and felt by all who went to camp.

A memorial was held every year to honor the children who died, but only the older campers participated in the ceremony. Candles were lit, and stories were told about the friends they lost to the disease they shared. This is where these kids, including Anna, faced the reality of CF and its chronic sorrow with brutal honesty. Their friends died and were missed but never forgotten at camp.

The sensitive way losses were addressed was integral to how these kids accepted their own lives, yet loss was not the central focus of camp. Living well and having fun was the focus. Between skits, games in the pool, and being plain old goofy, the campers had educational sessions to learn about nutrition and staying healthy. As they got older, they participated in rap sessions where they could discuss anything in their hearts.

The sessions were led by mental health professionals who helped the campers share their feelings of loss, anger, love, and relationships. Nowhere else could these children find such total support for dealing with the burden they always had to carry. And most importantly, their parents were nowhere to be found, so they could be genuine and honest, not worrying if they offended or troubled their parents with their brutal honesty. This was key.

The big, fun activities, honesty, camaraderie, and loving

care at camp helped Anna and all the kids accept who they were and what CF was. It helped the parents be better parents and deal with complex issues while they permitted the kids to be who they were with all their feelings. The parents could never present life to their kids as the camp did. It was a gift beyond all measure for the whole family. Many campers said they would have died long before if they had never attended the camp. The camp gave them the courage and support to face their challenges and a level of joy and friendship with their tribe that made them feel not alone.

When the camp was over and Anna came home, she and all the campers started planning for the following year. It was a vital part of their lives. Camps like the one Anna attended existed in a bygone era with CF. After a few years of Anna's attendance, concerns about cross-infection considerably changed the CF community. The necessary adjustments in how the camp was to run to accommodate these concerns eventually caused it not to be offered.

Instead, an adult retreat grew under the auspices of CFRI. The kids who grew up with the summer camp continued with an adult retreat with added infection control guidelines. To this day, when they meet annually, they continue the memorial, never to forget the hundreds of children and adults with CF who have died in our community by lighting candles and telling stories.

As the years went on, these losses mounted for all of us. Sara grew up knowing many with CF, too. She could attend parts of the adult retreat and felt accepted and loved as part of the community. The number of friends Anna had to say good-bye to and the number of pews we sat in during those years of her childhood was far more than anyone else we knew. Dealing with death and understanding the concept of chronic sorrow is a big part of living with CF.

As a busy married couple, it was hard to find time to process the progression of Anna's disease and everything else affecting our family. Doug and I found that time during the only private moments we had in the early morning hours while in a cocoon of quilts and covers for our worried minds.

In our darkened room, with only the sound of quiet in the early hours before dawn, I confessed to Doug what I could not hold in any longer. This time allowed for truth-telling and the unveiling of our dread. The safe comfort of our bed became the confessional where the loudest voices in our minds or the most painful heartbreaks were revealed to each other.

For so many years, either holding his head to my chest, our hands clasped, or embracing each other, I would open a vault where my motherly worry lived. "Doug, I am afraid. Anna's lung function has gone down. Her sputum culture is showing new drug-resistant bacteria. Her cough has increased, and she is coming home with slight fevers. Maybe this is going to be it. Maybe this is when her descent into the clutches of CF will begin again."

It was there, cradled and safe with only Doug to hear me, that these thoughts of fear and dread could be said. I knew his response would be an embrace of thoughtful listening with measured and realistic steps to take. He would bring me back to where I could face the next day with newfound support and perspective. "Robin, I don't think things are as dire as you fear. Maybe she needs a new antibiotic, or we can increase her treatments," would be his type of response.

Sometimes, we would just stare into the darkness, sharing the same dreaded pain. But it always seemed we came to some kind of idea or resolution so that we could start the next day. We might remember a hopeful thing that happened, a spiritual moment that dissolved fears, or simply the comfort of our love and commitment to each other.

These reassurances and our exchange of thoughts and ideas were precious lovemaking that we both needed. It was how we coped best. It is hard to imagine doing this type of parenting alone without a partner, and I know many do. We were so lucky to have each other. Thoughts of those under-the-covers talks are fond memories of our connecting, intimacy, and parenting of our children.

chapter nine

A Different Kind of Mothering

I was still collecting the blessings and miracles of Anna's life as she entered her twenties. Walking the tightrope of being positive with each passing year was becoming more challenging, as we knew that eventually we would have to deal with Anna's death. It was, as I would remark, a different kind of mothering. The unknown fate of Anna's future was forever shrouded, yet I wanted to learn more about this aspect of life that loomed over our family.

I recognized that our culture pushes away talking about our ultimate reality. It is common that most people do not want to deal with the idea of death. Our family's uniqueness included focusing on sickness and death more than others. It seemed we were doing pretty well with it all, but still, the haunting ghost of its eventuality ate away at hopes and dreams, and affected so many choices we had to make.

This topic was what our CF community dealt with regularly, and it was such a blessing to meet with others with the same struggles. I held various positions in CFRI, from president, education coordinator, support group facilitator, and writer for the newsletter. That experience showed me how vital support for all CF families was. I thought my growing expertise about the ins and outs and the trauma of CF qualified me to be a mentor for new mothers. I enjoyed meeting new families and wanted to share what I was learning in a broader sense.

In 2001, a postcard addressed to me described an interfaith chaplaincy art-for-healing program in Berkeley. It seemed perfect. I was using creativity and art to heal myself, quilting Buddhist wall hangings and selling some of them. I understood the power of healing with art. I felt I could help other families with children who were very ill in the hospital.

The work would take me into rooms where people were dying. I felt called and wanted to be there as a compassionate participant. Being a chaplain was a spiritual persona that I was curious to put on. I was still looking for more pieces of my spiritual identity. Going through this program would give me an important spiritual education and practice in reaching out to vulnerable people from the perspective of being part of the clergy. I decided to try this career focus and do something more outside of our home.

To complete the certification, I had to work as a chaplain resident for at least nine months to a year in a hospital setting with a Clinical Pastoral Education Program. Accepted into a position at Stanford Hospital and Lucile Packard Children's Hospital, I was the chaplain resident assigned to the families whose children were waiting for liver and kidney transplants. I attended rounds with the doctors and learned about the world of transplantation as lung transplants became more successful for CF patients. At that time, we had an increased hope of a transplant for Anna. In this program, I could learn more about what we might experience as a family. I could also learn more about loss and comfort families and mothers like me.

One evening in the hospital, when I was on call and alone, I was asked to comfort a family whose teenage daughter was dying. I entered the room where the girl was lying on her bed with her mother curled beside her. Her father, siblings, and other family members were there and encircled the bed. I entered with my prayer book and assessed the moment. Asking the family to hold hands, I said a couple of prayers; we had a moment of silence together, and I asked the group to share whatever was on their hearts. I noticed the mother, her grief and tears. She held her daughter in her last moments of life, and I was struck by the sadness and the intimacy of the family.

After our ritual, I left the room to return to my office. I sat down and picked up my teacup waiting for me on my desk, and it hit me. That mom could so easily have been me. I could be that mother holding on to each moment and breath that was left. I fell apart at my desk. I was so glad it was after hours and I could be alone. At that moment, I wondered if this was the right line of work for me with my life situation. Even so, the time I spent as a chaplain was life-affirming. The love and acceptance I witnessed of terrible tragedies and the opportunity to offer support and compassion affirmed how I wanted to live with my CF mother challenge.

I instituted a hospital-wide art-for-healing project with individually created healing flags for an exhibit in the roof garden of the hospital. The flags were inspired by the traditional prayer flags flown by Tibetan Buddhists in the Himalayas. The Buddhist flags are created with prayers for peace and healing and the flags are hung so that the wind that blows through them carries the prayers around the world.

The healing flags project at the hospital invited families, patients, and medical staff to contribute by designing messages and prayers on pieces of cotton cloth. When hung, as in the Himalayas, the colorful collection was displayed outside in the roof garden, allowing the wind to carry its heartfelt messages. It was beautiful, inspiring, and uplifting for staff, patients, and families to view the display. With the completion of the project and my commitment to nine months of CPE, I returned to my full-time motherhood at home.

The success of the flag project opened the way for me to offer similar projects in many other settings, including The Ronald McDonald House at Stanford, memorials for friends who had died, and Prayer Flags for Sophia, a way to inspire a supportive community around a family in our neighbor-hood. The parents of Sophia, born with Niemann-Pick Type A, another devastating life-limiting genetic disease, welcomed "Prayer Flags for Sophia" and filled their home with hundreds of wishes of hope and love on pieces of colored cloth.

The project was honored by placing first in the 2004 Blair L. Sadler International Healing Arts Competition for participatory art-for-healing projects through The Society for the Arts in Healthcare. My involvement in art-for-healing evolved, giving me deep personal satisfaction while my work at home as mom in a CF family continued on its path of supporting my two daughters.

I watched Anna as she graduated from high school and then attended a local community college. She in turn watched her friends move to distant campuses for college life, but her CF kept her near for the care she received at Stanford and the support she needed at home. We were always looking for ways that Anna could experience life like her peers and gave her opportunities that made sense.

After two years, she transferred to nearby Santa Clara University. This was a significant opportunity for her to be a regular college student living in a dormitory. While there, Anna met a young man. We were so happy John was in her life. This meant so much for her to have someone to love, be loved by, and go places with.

Anna also loved college, studying psychology and excelling in her program. She had a deep intuitive understanding of human behavior. It was also clear that her chronic illness experiences gave her unique insight. When graduation came into view, she decided to continue with a master's program in counseling psychology. Anna thought this line of study would provide her with a career where she could succeed despite her disease. She could see clients part-time, not overwhelming her by working too many long hours. Even so, CF was taking its toll little by little.

Doug and I were so pleased that she wanted to continue her education. We were unsure of her future, and it was in our minds that she might only live to be twenty-five or qualify for a transplant by then. We could see the decline in her health and were worried that being in the workforce would be too much for her. But being home on the couch while her friends and peers were making their lives happen was a terrible option. Being at the university was the best choice for her, especially because she loved Santa Clara.

After graduating with her master's, Anna got a job in an afterschool program for high school students. She also began preparing for her internships to accumulate the many hours she needed to become a licensed counselor. Shortly after starting, her career life went on hold. She got a virus from exposure to the young people that caused a steep decline in her health. My daughter was twenty-six years old and unable to work or pursue the dream that she had prepared herself for. It was very disappointing, but Doug and I had expected this. It was what we had always feared and seen many times in our CF community.

CF takes lives, bends lives into disabilities, and creates loss and huge disappointments. Anna applied for disability, and because she was an active teen and employed as a lifeguard for a few years, along with a few other odd jobs, she qualified to receive a small sum. This was such a plus for her. I was so glad that she qualified because she had been able to work those few years at the pool.

With her new identity of being disabled and unable to work, we wanted to figure out how she could live independently as an adult. We did not want her to have to stay home under our wing. John was still in the picture, and they wanted to live together, so we found a way to purchase a condo so it could happen. Anna pinpointed an area that we could afford and had promising value. Together with her dad, they found a perfect condo.

The purchase opened up the exciting world of real estate to Anna, who toyed with the idea of becoming an agent. However, the reality of CF was still in her way to fulfill any career dreams. She was a full-time patient taking care of all the physical problems she had developed from her CF.

The blessing of this time was that with the purchase of the condo, Anna could have her own home while in an adult committed relationship. That was unexpected for Anna a few years earlier. We were also fortunate that due to her disability, our medical insurance through Doug's work was obligated to continue her coverage beyond the age of other dependent healthy children. She could be on his insurance policy for her lifetime if she was not married. This incredible gift offered security, but it made for a complicated relationship with John. Even so, it was a dream and a miracle come true that Anna was living an independent adult life. This was something that I never thought would be possible. If she was to have a short adult life, I wanted it to be full of good, normal experiences with their accompanying blessings.

As we watched Anna's decline, we were acutely aware of the hope of a double lung transplant. For many years, we watched other CF patients come to the end of their lives with CF but then be resurrected with the gift of new lungs. We also saw this fail and knew it was dangerous, not for sure or forever, but it was our hope.

There were other advances in research and potential treatments, but their promise was still very far in the future and primarily directed to younger patients with less involvement than Anna had. We knew these advancements would not be available in time to save Anna.

With her health declining, Anna spent weeks in the hospital at Stanford. I was a regular sleepover mate. Other mothers of twenty-some-year-old women were not still attached to the care of their children. My supportive mothering was still needed and continued long past the usual cutting of apron strings. Still, we were close, loved being together, and shared interests. Anna needed support, an advocate, and a go-to person. This was my job.

To this day, when I enter a hospital, I am reminded not only of the pain and breathlessness of Anna, the treatments, the doctors, and the therapists but also of the comforts of early morning coffee and oatmeal in the cafeteria, the walks outside touring Stanford University, and the gardens and flowers. I imagine most people do not have that combination of thoughts and memories of hospitals. It was my lifestyle for those years, and I had to make it the best I could.

My daughter and I were a team. As long as she fought to be well, I wanted to be there as long as it took. I was living a different kind of mothering than other women I knew. We all gave birth to our children, but I was the one who was told that, most likely, I would also care for my child into her passing. It was not the way a mother usually viewed her child with so much worry and fear. This disease complicated our relationship, requiring an acceptance and determination that deepened our mother-daughter connection.

It is common that CF parents have a very strong bond with their CF kids. It is not only the child whose life is affected, especially in the hospital, but the whole family, mostly the mother. We knew the future with this disease would continue to offer frequent interruptions in our lives until it was time for Anna's lungs to come to the end of the line for her. She would die, or they would be replaced with a gift of new lungs. We also knew that the average length of time that lung transplants would last was five years. Still, those years, however long or short, would be precious.

Once again, like how we started this journey, it would take a miracle for Anna to continue to walk the earth with us. That miracle was the hope of a lung transplant. As time went by, we lived each day as if that miracle would be her future. After my frequent overnights at Stanford, I loved my hospital coffee and oatmeal in the morning because it meant she was still with us. I could still care for her, love her, and be her mom.

To make it to transplant, we had to work diligently. After spending time in the hospital, Anna would leave with IV medications to be administrated at home. She and John worked together to ensure her medications were taken on time. I helped, too, as they had a lot to handle.

At least three doses of multiple IV antibiotics three times per day, eight hours apart, had to be administered along with percussion treatments, aerosols, handfuls of pills, and a diet of high-calorie healthy food to be eaten. Also, the house had to be kept up, groceries purchased, and food made. It was an exhausting and grueling schedule, particularly for someone with decreased lung function and little energy. To help them, I would wake at 5 a.m. at my home and drive about five miles to their condo. Sometimes, it would be chilly and dark outside before sunrise as I used my key to open the door while they slept.

When I walked in, I found a small table made clean and sanitized with alcohol. On it, there were syringes laid out for me after the last infusion only hours before. I found saline flushes, antibiotics in syringe pushes or balls, and heparin syringes to complete the infusions. After washing my hands at her kitchen sink, I would gather the first saline and antibiotic dose with alcohol pads and enter their bedroom. Anna and John would be sleeping.

As I kissed Anna on the head or touched her arm, she would move, waking as little as she had to for me to reach her port line dangling from her chest. "Good morning, Anna. It is Mom. I am here and will take care of you. Don't wake up."

It seemed inappropriate for me, her mother, to invade their bedroom space. I was given permission so they could have the sleep they needed and a small break from the routine that would last three weeks. I would give the first dose, leave her and John to sleep, and then step back into their kitchen to make coffee.

After twenty-minute intervals, I would return to flush the IV line again and deliver another dose. "Me again, Anna; this is your last dose. Next, I will give you the heparin," I would tell her.

When the doses were done, I prepared the tray for the next delivery of medications eight hours later by swabbing it with alcohol and precisely laying out the syringes and antibiotic bulbs that needed to warm up from the refrigerator. Anna would take care of those later in the day.

Between doses, I sat with my coffee and read the morning newspaper. I sat quietly and always with comfort and discomfort in my heart. The comfort was that I was able to do this. I was able to help my daughter and her partner in their fight for her life, but the discomfort was that I had to do this. I had to push drugs into my daughter's veins to save her life. I had to interrupt her bedroom with my presence to do this.

My quiet thoughts would lead me to questions like, what was this life I was living? It seemed so odd in many ways. Why did I have this life that made my heart ache? Was my life giving me enrichment or the desired spiritual lessons I was praying for? And sometimes, who is Anna? Why did she come into this life with so much difficulty?

Indeed, there was no enrichment when I saw her suffering. My job was to support her in this way from the time she was first ill and diagnosed with this terrible disease. It was what I had to do to save her. It was up to us in the intermittent moments, in the in-between times of exacerbations, when we could take a breath, dreaming of happier times.

But as her health declined in her twenties, those fanciful days became fewer and fewer. Our in-between moments became more defined as moments between treatments on a given day. In those moments, we would escape to watch an entertaining TV show or have tea until the next pounding on her chest or infusion of IV was required. We might also share our innermost thoughts while hugging on the sofa, my arms enveloping her body with that sweetness we had together.

Being Anna and Sara's mother included many painful, intense, and spiritually challenging times with many serendipities and miracles. These blessings gave me a rich and full life as their mother. Our lives were not ordinary, and this was a different kind of mothering for both of my daughters. Despite the challenges, Anna and Sara were simply our precious daughters. I loved them both with everything I had.

chapter ten

The Pieces Coming Together

Resting on the edge of a sprawling vineyard, a new residential neighborhood was in its final stages of development. Houses in a craftsman style with porches for outdoor potted succulents and chairs for sitting while sipping California wine were welcoming new homebuyers. Doug felt he could no longer commute from Palo Alto to his new workplace in Livermore, so once again, it was time for us to move. If we were going to move from the house where our daughters' childhood memories filled the rooms, it had to be to a special place. We always wanted more of a rural feel to where we lived, and this neighborhood that embraced the wine-grape agriculture gave us a sense of open space and a new life. We put in an offer, and it was accepted.

It was autumn 2009, and it seemed that things were calm and Anna was stable. We knew it was momentary, but those are the times you make changes if you can. We wanted to make this move closer to Doug's work, but with the move, I would be farther from Anna, and caring for her needs would be more complicated. Still, at this moment, she was stable, doing well, and had John.

We could make this decision because Doug and I had recently said goodbye to our mothers, who had been included among our primary concerns. Doug's mom, Renee, TuTu to the girls, passed from lymphoma in December 2008 while we were with her at her home in Reno, Nevada. My mother, who lived near us in Redwood City, passed away in April 2009. I was her primary caregiver-child as I, out of her four children, lived the closest to her. I had two hats during those final few years of my mom's life. I cared for a daughter who desperately wanted to live, yet was threatened by her disease and cared for my mother, who did not want to be on the planet any longer but could not find the doorway out. It was a dichotomy wrought with emotion. I had a juggle of the heart, Anna at twenty-eight wishing to live and Mom at eighty-five wanting to depart. She was never happy after the death of my father.

My dad was diagnosed with lung cancer in February 1997 and died in November of that year. Chemotherapy was not offered to him because of its advanced stage. He had some radiation to help reduce the tumors and give him more comfort. To emotionally deal with his bad prognosis, Dad fought his illness with Chinese medicine. He traveled to Oakland to another Chinese doctor our friend Barbara Bernie recommended.

My brother, Mike, who lived nearby, would meet and sit with Dad, encouraging him. Dad was so hopeful that the herb tea he drank daily, like Anna's concoction, would do the trick to save him. After ten months of trying to be positive and finding support with his Chinese medicine, he came down with pneumonia and landed in the hospital. It was clear his life was ending soon. The day before he was to be discharged, we were told he would come home on oxygen and with hospice care.

After going home for the evening that night, Mom felt that she had to see him and got in her car to drive back to Sequoia Hospital, about a fifteen-minute drive. She told us as she entered his room at about 8 p.m., he said gruffly, "What are you doing here, Elayne?"

She answered, "I just had to see you, Bill."

After a short exchange and a kiss, he told her to go home, and she did. Mom fell into such a deep sleep that she did not hear repeated phone calls from their doctor in the night. Later,

I received the call because he received no answer from her. "I am so sorry to tell you. Your father has passed. I have not been able to get in touch with your mother. It was so quick. When the nurses came to check on him, he was gone."

Dad was found sitting on the edge of his bed with his hands folded on the side table and his head resting and balanced so that his body stayed in that position. He simply left. His heart stopped. It was time for him to go. My dad would have hated us taking care of him at the end of his life. He was such a proud man. He was sorely missed.

My mother's exit began with a fall in her apartment and a broken hip. With this accident, Mom saw her light at the end of the tunnel, and it called to her. She broke her hip on a Tuesday. Deciding with conscious determination that it was her chance to escape this earthly home, she left us the following Saturday.

I knew my mother's wishes; she had made it clear to me so many times that she did not want to live any longer. She was done. She wanted to follow my dad's lead. Soon after arriving in the ER in the most terrible pain from her broken hip, Mom told me, "Tell them I don't want to live and if something happens during the hip surgery, to please let me go."

Imagine your mother telling you this. It would be tricky and embarrassing to talk this way to a surgeon. But, to be faithful to her, I did that. The orthopedic surgeon must have thought I was nuts or something much worse.

It was strangely simple. Somehow Mom saw her light at this unexpected time and, unafraid, desperately wanted to depart. The surgery required for her care to repair her broken hip was successful. Mom awoke the next day in a single room. My sister, Sue, had arrived that morning from Oregon, and as we approached her bed, Mom was propped up so that she could have her essential morning black coffee. We told her she was doing well. "Mom, you are looking good this morning. Your surgery went well. How are you doing?"

She told us in a loopy mental state loaded with painkillers, "I am fine. I finally have no pain, and my headaches are gone too." We were relieved.

Mom had been suffering from intense migraine headaches for at least a year and could not get relief from them. The news that she was no longer in pain was welcomed. We then told her, "Because the surgery went so well, they want you to get up and start your physical therapy immediately. It will take work, and you must be committed, but we will be with you to get stronger."

Her immediate reply was, "No!"

She did not want to get better. She wanted out! She was determined to leave this life on her own accord. We were incredulous at her will and determination. Still, Mom refused food and water after that final coffee, then willfully and quickly entered active dying the next day. This was the hospital where our father, the love of her life, had passed away twelve years before. She was never the same or happy without him; she just wanted to leave. I don't think she thought she would be with him again, but she thought it was just not fun living without him.

That night Mom drove to the hospital to see Dad, she must have known he was about to die and said her final goodbye. Now, she was ready to do the same and wanted us to say goodbye to her. It was poetic that they both would pass in the same hospital. My sister, Sue, and I sat with the palliative care team at Sequoia Hospital in a room down the hall from where our mom was supposed to recover. We told them the story of Dad's passing years before and her wishes. "Mom says no to the physical therapy and wants to pass on. We want her to have her wishes, and we know it is what she wants."

Remarkably, they understood and supported our mom, saying, "When an elderly relative falls and breaks a hip, the family usually will do everything they can. Even so, many patients will pass within six months, even with all the interventions."

Mom and Dad were very conscious about their choices concerning their deaths. In the 1970s, their close friends talked about death as a group. As friends, they supported each other with the idea that if they thought it was time to die, they would take control by simply refusing food and water until they were no longer. I am sure memories of that pact supported this path for Mom.

We followed her wishes and did not execute extraordinary measures to save her. It was sad that this moment had finally arrived. I had been preparing for her to depart for a few years, but it is true you never know when, how, or how you will feel when it comes. I trusted my mom and just wanted to love her and support her. While she was in her state of falling unconscious, her organs coming to a standstill, I told her we knew she wanted to go, and we were letting her with the support of the palliative care team.

When Mom heard this while in her disappearing act and with her eyes closed, she smiled at me in a wide, sincere grin that said thank you. I had not seen a smile like that on my mom for many years. I knew she was at peace with what was coming and running in that direction.

Sue and I sat most of the dying vigil with her. Sara sat with her grandmother too as she began to slip away. We went home for some sleep the first night we knew she was dying, but after a few hours of sleep, I returned in the wee hours of the following day. I did not want her to be alone. I sat with her with a small light on. I told her I was there and began chanting. I sang some Buddhist mantras. My mother was also an inner seeker and loved meditation and our dear Lama Gangha. I also read some of the *Tibetan Book of the Dead* out loud. It seemed only fitting to offer these sounds and spiritual words to uplift her and assist in her transition.

In the nighttime hours of the hospital, when there were no other visitors and all was quiet, I could feel her room fill with beings. It felt crowded sitting there in the dark, empty room with Mom. I did not know who these disincarnate beings were, but I could feel their movement and presence surrounding us. My chanting welcomed even more to be with us. I had constant chills on my arms and back.

A welcoming party was happening for Mom. It was an experience that gave me comfort even though it was a bit scary. I had an impulse to get up and leave, but stayed with my discomfort. The experience made me consider that there could be welcome parties like this for all of us in our time of passing.

I have told this story of how my mother found her exit and chose to go. Many who have heard this story do not believe me. I believe it demonstrates that the power of our minds and will to choose our life story's ending is possible. Mom showed this to us in her conscious and gentle passing.

Doug and I, Sara and Anna, and my sister and sister-in-law were there to wish her love as her spirit flew up and away from the binds holding her to our world. My eldest brother called on the phone at the moment of her final passing. I answered so he could also be a witness and there for her. "Mike, Mom is passing right now. You are here with her too," I told him as I saw Mom's eyes open wide and her chest lift with its final breath. It was remarkable. My mom got her wish to go, and she took it.

After retiring that hat of being my mother's caregiver and her wish being granted so lovingly, I wondered if my daughter's wish to stay would also be granted. I hoped the dichotomy of desires that tugged on my heart would turn into a joint granting of blessings for two of the most significant people I loved dearly. This was a turning point that allowed change in our lives. It took months for the transition to be completed, but it was then that Doug and I could start moving our home closer to his work.

Mom's influence on me and my caregiving and mothering of Anna was characterized by a strong and committed relationship. It was a significant loss to no longer have her in our lives. Anna and Sara would greatly miss their Grammy, but I also understood it was time for the change. Mom loved Anna and Sara so very much. She always saw how difficult this path was for me as a mother and did what she could to love her granddaughters and support me. So did my dad.

After Mom passed and when we thought things were calm for Anna, we moved across the bay to our new vineyard home in December 2009. We only had a short-lived peace before the CF dam broke again. Anna started a steep decline in her health.

Without knowing our move was timely, it was also auspicious to have made the change when we did. Doug was close to work, and our dog, Roxy, was with him. Anna's change in health shortly after we were settling in caused me to be the one traveling back and forth from each side of the bay. This had been the plan with our move, and I could do this as now I was wearing one hat instead of two, and Anna was my primary focus. It was early 2010 as we began a new stage in the evolution of her disease and how we would care for her.

After a few months, Anna's decline led her to be evaluated for a lung transplant, and after years of expecting this, the time had arrived. I never fully settled into our new home. Still, it was reassuring that Doug no longer needed to commute, as he was five minutes from the laboratory where he worked. Sara was graduating from UC Santa Cruz with a degree in molecular cellular biology and headed toward medical school. With our moms in peace and my other loves in a good place, I could focus on this intimate and delicate time with Anna as she was accepted into the transplant program at Stanford.

The waiting for new lungs involved working hard to keep her well enough for the surgery. Patients are accepted into the transplant program when their FEV1 lung function is only 30% or less. Usually, continuous oxygen is also needed. Patients are so ill that their prognosis is they do not have long to live (no one knows, but maybe six months to a year) but are strong enough to survive the grueling surgery. Anna was in that sweet spot. The time we never wanted to arrive did indeed arrive.

Another of the qualifications for being accepted into a transplant program is if the recipient has adequate support. We were Anna's team, and Doug and I, Sara, and Anna's partner, John, committed to caring for Anna before, during, and after the transplant. You must agree that three months post-transplant, the recipient will always have someone with them and that you reside within a reasonable distance to get to the ER quickly if there are complications.

Anna and John lived about fifteen minutes from Stanford, and Doug and I rented an apartment about a mile from their condo in Sunnyvale. The apartment was to serve as our family crash pad so that one of us was always close by. The apartment was a safe place for Anna to go to right after her release from the hospital. I would live with her and drive her to the many appointments, blood draws, etc. that would be required.

Before the transplant, during the waiting period, the apartment was to be a place for me to rest and restore during the week. I cared for Anna during the day by doing percussion treatments (she had three to four per day to help keep the mucus at bay), cooking for her and John, cleaning, and going to the market. When John came home from work, he would take over and do the fourth percussion treatment in the evening so I could go to the apartment and rest. I would return early in the morning to begin our routine again. On the weekends, I would go back to Livermore or our other country home about two hours away from Livermore in Murphys to be with Doug and Roxy. Sara was also available to help on the weekends.

The apartment was a welcoming place for Sara. She graduated from the University of California at Santa Cruz in June 2010 and kept her home in Santa Cruz. If we needed her, she could stay with us in the apartment.

As it turned out, Sara became part of the transplant process with a new job. She accepted a position working in the Cystic Fibrosis Research Laboratory at Stanford under Dr. Jeff Wine. This very fortunate position allowed her to be involved in CF research studies, studying the tracheas of CF lung transplant recipients. Her sister would be one of the participants in the study. It was another one of our serendipitous conditions, making this transplant experience seem strangely orchestrated. Sara was thrilled to have a job allowing her to have pre-medical school experience and a way to simultaneously be involved with this significant event in our family. Her experiences in this position were profound.

Since Sara was part of the research laboratory and her stated job description included visits to the operating room, she had a window into our new world of transplantation that was particularly unique. She held two views: one of a sister whose sibling was waiting for her lungs, and one of an eager student wanting to begin a medical career. As part of the job, she asked potential lung recipients for consent to use their tracheal tissues for research following their surgeries. She also witnessed recipients on the surgical table receiving their gifts of life. It was a profound experience, expanding her awareness of the miracles in science and medicine that saved lives.

To see and understand more of the process, Sara told me she was invited to go on an organ procurement with a team of doctors to retrieve a set of lungs for an impending transplant. She drove with the team in a van to another hospital in the SF Bay Area, seeing firsthand the team's importance so integral to the success of the surgery. They had to successfully transport donated lungs to the patient already in the OR being readied for their diseased lungs to be removed.

Sara told me about entering the room where the brain-dead donor lay as all the teams for the organs gifted to patients in the local area gathered. To begin, a representative from the organization Donate Life led a moment of silence for everyone. This ritual was meant to honor the donor with gratitude and recognize the miracle gift of life that was about to be given. It was a remarkable moment for Sara. She told us her heart filled with profound gratitude for being able to participate.

Then, the process began with the heart being clamped, removed, and whisked away by the heart transplant team. Next were the lungs, which went into a hand-carried cooler for transportation. Following that retrieval, Sara returned to Stanford and the waiting patient with her team.

It was truly unique and miraculous that Sara's research position was tailor-made just for her while her sister was waiting for her lungs. It could not have been more perfect. Things seemed to be in their place and continuing to unfold as we started our wait for Anna's new lungs. I loved having Sara and Anna's synchronicity play a song in our lives.

This poignant juncture was an intense time of working hard and keeping Anna well. Waiting for a donor amplified our feelings of being in the moment and part of a mysterious, miraculous, and unknown universe. We were hopeful, and I sought clues from my world to tell me whether Anna would survive. Among my collection of signs to keep me going was a message via a fortune I had received about nine months before.

In October 2009, shortly before our move and preparations for the transplant, I traveled to Japan with our dear friends Ana and Isa, who were filming a documentary about their lives with CF and lung transplants. They invited me to join them at the beginning of their adventure and to meet other CF mothers in Japan. While there, I visited a temple and prayed for Anna and our family. Afterward, I participated in a temple tradition to throw sticks for a fortune with my friends. My fortune was remarkable and foretold so much.

When spring comes,
Katsura tree flowers are in full bloom, smelling so well.
Your fortune will open wide when your season comes.
If you get the chance open, you will get fame and honor,
climbing the way to the top of the sky.
Also, you meet a great person with honor who helps you.
The moon in the dark sky will get bright again,
in the clear sky, you can meet the fortune soon.
"Your request will be granted.
The patient gets well soon."

Asakusa Kannon Temple, Tokyo, Japan

I took this magic home with me after my incredible trip. This was a positive sign from the universe for me, our family, and Anna. I wanted to believe that when we were at that point of transplant, it would be true: "Our request would be granted with the patient getting well soon." And, now, we were at the time of "our season." We hoped with all our hearts that the "moon in the dark sky would get bright again." Anna was being evaluated for this lifesaving surgery. It was a second chance at life that we never imagined possible when she was first diagnosed.

Medical care had grown, and the miracle world of transplantation had become possible for those whose lungs were ending with cystic fibrosis. Anna's life at the time of diagnosis began with the miracle of her survival. As her life with CF was ending, we hoped that she would be saved with another miracle gift: a double lung transplant. We were ready for this and more miracles to come.

PART TWO

Transplant and Recovery

a story of courage

"Although you may not always be able to avoid difficult situations,
you can modify the extent to which you can suffer
by how you choose to respond to the situation."

Dalai Lama XIV, *The Art of Happiness*

chapter eleven

Blogging

Every day while waiting for Anna's transplant miracle, I opened my computer to record my thoughts and share our experiences. We had friends from many areas of our lives who wanted updates on Anna's health status and to know when she would get "The Call." This is when the transplant surgeon would call Anna to tell her they had lungs for her.

Sitting with my morning coffee before heading to Anna's condo or my evening glass of wine, I wrote. While taking care of Anna, there was little time to spend with friends or even Doug to process my complex emotions. Blogging and writing was a way to not feel alone and process our journey. Anna also wrote when she had enough energy or something significant happened. We felt connected to our outer world by getting it on the screen and selecting "post."

Our collection of writings gave immediacy to our feelings and an invitation to whoever else wanted to travel with us. It was a window into that tender pre-transplant time when it was unknown if we were in for a sprint or a marathon before Anna's perfect lungs arrived. Anna and I decided to continue to blog no matter when that would be.

Anna began her lung transplant evaluation in June 2010. She had to undergo a week of testing in the first part of the process. It was grueling for someone with low oxygen levels. It felt in itself like a marathon to endure. Transplantation requires knowing the patient's overall health in fine detail. Each day, we would drive up to Stanford, and I would get one of the available wheelchairs for Anna so I could wheel her to each appointment in the rigorous schedule. We had to pre-serve as much of her energy as possible. It was exhausting for me, too.

Our evaluation week included lunches and strolls around the campus near the hospital between appointments. Once, I wheeled Anna to the art museum. It was closed, but outside was a permanent Rodin sculpture garden exhibit of his famous Gates of Hell, other human figures, and exaggerated body parts on pedestals. Our minds were overwhelmed with our tasks to get to transplant, so everything around us looked like an advertisement for organ donation. Looking over the field of artful carnage sent us into uproarious laughter, lightening our emotional weight. We imagined the heads, arms, hands, and torsos in the garden were waiting for recipients to finish their evaluations. We wished it could be so easy to simply pick our needed body parts out of the garden.

Lunches and dinners came from local restaurants, as we had no time to cook. Twice, we had Chinese food with fortune cookies that also lifted our spirits. One of the fortunes for Anna foretold, "Long life with the blessings of family and friends is yours." I told her, "You chose that cookie; it could have been mine, but no, it was yours." We both smiled, and she folded it safely into her wallet.

The week of testing ended with another Chinese dinner takeout eaten at Anna's so we could collapse. Before leaving for my apartment to spend the night, I chose one of three fortune cookies wrapped in their cellophane. It said, "You will soon witness a miracle." I stood there dumbfounded. My blog was called Miracle on Order. What better way to be told it was about to arrive than from the mail of a fortune cookie! At that point, Anna and I swore not to open any more fortune cookies. We were delighted to have these.

The unseen magical world that appeared to us in the fortune cookies seemed to be in order and our favor. Still, the importance of that week was about the physical world and Anna's body. That was all in order, too. She was in "the window." The window is where a patient is sick enough to need a transplant and well enough to heal from it and thrive. That is where Anna was, and there was nothing to disqualify her from the surgery. They knew everything about her body; there were no secrets left.

Selected Blog Posts
June – July 2010

June 17, 2010 – I Do Not Want To Do This – Robin

I do not want to do this. There is something inside of me that rebels. I just don't want to. I don't want to watch or be there while CF makes its final assault. It was so much better when it was in the future and not in the now. But here it is, and I cannot say no to being a witness and part of the infantry fighting back with all that we have, all that Anna has. Her strength and determination that swings at the obstacles and coughs out the polluting crud while trudging through the trenches is nothing but inspiring. The hope beckoning in the eyes of friends who have been here and now are living new lives is what we strive for every day.

I really do not want to do this. I do not want to see her exhaustion and the lack of vitality when, at twenty-nine, she should be eager to run out the door engaged in her life. It takes hours to prepare for the day, and a shower is a major event. I took care of her as a child. I was a devoted, stay-at-home mom loving every minute of it. CF lived with us, haunted us, challenged us, interrupted us, scared us, and exhausted us, but my little girl could run from the house into her life with energy and a giggle in those days. But this stay-at-home mom, in the prison of CF mom, in the never-ending fight against chronic lung disease mom, watching its clutches on the remnants of her lungs, is not what I want to do. This stay-at-home mom wants something else. We are fighting to get out of here, to run out the door.

I do not want to be here until I hear Anna say, "I cannot believe what it will be like to have so many more hours to my day without treatments. Just think of what I can do, and you can save the world in that time." That makes me want to be here. There is nothing I would rather do than what I do not want to do. To give it my all, to fight this damn disease to the final punch until the miracle we are ordering finally arrives and I can hang up my stay-at-home mom, fight-CF mom hat and run out of here with her hand in mine!

July 3, 2010 – *It's No Lollygagging Picnic* – Anna

Well done. Finished my week of tests for the transplant evaluation. Today, the magnitude of what I just accomplished hit me. Holy crap, did I really just do that? The thing that I was so scared of doing for years before this? The place I never wanted to be? The place I have been avoiding my entire life? Is it here???????

You don't get a transplant because you are doing well. You get a transplant because you are at the end of your life without the intervention. I am almost twenty-nine (in ten days) and am at the end of my life without this? Well then, BRING IT!!!! I have so much more to do. CF does not get to take that away. The future possibilities are where I get the strength to get through this.

July 4, 2010 – **Sunflowers Smile Even When You Cry** – Robin

I am home in Livermore now for the weekend. John is caring for Anna. It is good for me to be here with the garden, near the vineyards and the birds at the feeder because I am tired, so tired, bone tired. We all are. It is the physical exertion of going every minute that comes with caregiving. This tiredness comes from the worry about a very sick daughter, the concerns for the well daughter and husband, the missing of my home and the sweet dog who loves me, and the body no longer so young anymore. Yesterday, I noticed this tired, this feeling. What is this feeling? How can I describe it?

It is fatigue, I guess. There are aches and pains around my legs, and my stride is slowed. Taking a nap helps but does not get rid of it. I am not as resilient as before. And this is not over. We are in the thick of it. So, I think, of course you feel this way. It would be strange if you did not. Your daughter is fighting for her life. How could I feel any other way? I will be tired until we finish this job and then go on vacation.

Waiting in the cardio cath lab for Anna's final procedure, I could feel this malaise, this bone-tiredness. After a week of tests, this and that, and walking all over Stanford Hospital, I looked at her. Most of the time, I just see Anna, and sometimes I get another type of glimpse, and I cannot believe what I see. My beautiful daughter with plastic O2 tubing in her nose, without the vim and vigor that defined her cute personality, now with the constant persona of a sick girl. It is shocking when I see it. I stop, and it stares at me. It makes me sad, so sad. She is so vulnerable and sick that she needs a transplant. The concept overwhelms me. Then I think, but we have talked about this for years. This is the miracle that we have seen time and time again in many of our CF friends. But it is so poignant and intense that my mind must reconstruct a new sensory apparatus to decipher its complexity. That in itself is exhausting and haunting.

I know I must accept it all to do this work and get to the other side. I must look at the tiredness, the sadness, the feelings in my body, the potential loss, the present loss, the work ahead, the declining health, my own aging, all of it. That part is not as fun as finding the fortune cookie fortunes and the signs of hope and love surrounding us, but all of it is true. All of it is what we are experiencing. The release of joy cannot be genuinely felt without knowing its opposite. The recognition of a miracle can only happen by facing the truth of what is. We live in this world of all things: life, death, health, sickness, happiness, and sadness. Where we usually wish for the fun parts, we must also allow ourselves to befriend the un-fun parts.

A Buddhist teaching says it is all the same taste, the very same taste. It instructs us to open to all and feel all in each experience. When you are sad, you can reach into your heart. When you have joy, you also can reach into your heart. All experiences have ways to enter a deeper understanding of our circumstances. When you do, you sense the taste, the deep joy and miracles present despite the flavor of the moment that distract you with their coming and going, like my tiredness, hopefulness, happiness, and sadness. There is an ever-present love, an ever-present calm. The flowers bloom even though you are sad, the birds still sing and visit the feeder even though life is tough, and the seasons appear and disappear as will this moment.

It is all the same taste, the very same taste, and sunflowers smile even when you cry.

---

*July 12, 2010 – **The Miracle, the Magnitude** – Anna*

Today, I am feeling the magnitude of what is going to take place. The tears are rolling, not for myself, but for my future donor's family, the gift I will hopefully be given, and just simply for the opportunity I have even to get a shot at this. It is an amazing miracle. The 'why me' thoughts are beginning. The unfairness for others, the unfairness for me, the blessing for me, the opportunities, just simply the BANG that will happen when my life and my family intersect with the tragedy of another's. It is just HUGE. I am not sure why I am so lucky to be in this situation, but I am trying to BE in humble thankfulness and acceptance of what is.

chapter twelve

Listed:
The Countdown Begins

We made final preparations for the coming moment, focusing on personal details that needed to be cleaned up or readied. Our anticipation was high, and we were already tired of waiting, but the official wait had not really begun. Days passed into a few weeks before Anna was finally placed on the registry and listed for a donation of lungs. The unfinished tasks of ordering her medications, making medication lists, signing an advance directive, doing the laundry, and cleaning her patio were finally in order. All she needed to do was finish packing her bag before walking out the door. Her faith was strong, and she visualized her new lungs, saying loving-kindness meditations for her future donor and family.

She was as ready as she could be and, one night, dreamt that she pulled CF out of her lungs so she could breathe. We wanted to push the "go" button but still had to wait for the medical insurance approval.

In her readied anticipation, Anna wrote, *"Right now, I feel like the universe isn't in control. I can see my papers sitting on someone's desk at Blue Cross, collecting dust, forgotten and lost. Please don't forget me! I am ready to live, fight, and rock on. Now let's go!"*

The United Network of Organ Sharing, UNOS, listed Anna as a recipient for a double lung transplant after the evaluation and insurance approval on July 27, 2010. That became day one of our official wait. Our drama was about the age-old struggle of a family fighting for the life of a loved one and praying for intercession. We were waiting for the uncommon and unbe-lievable opportunity to entwine with another person whom we did not know to give us the greatest gift on earth: life for Anna.

To be a part of the transplant community, whether as a recipient, their family, or the donor family, you become part of an awe-inspiring reality of hope, joy, and grief. The ride there can be bumpy, scary, exhausting, and painful, but also encased with hope—the hope of a new start, even if for a short time. That was what we wanted for our Anna.

It took a positive life perspective, the love of our family and friends, and Anna's spirit, courage, dedication, and will to live for us to meet each day in the best way we could. Like we had for years before, we used metaphor, humor, honesty, the experience of serendipity, and a search for magic and the mys-tical to find hope and help with the waiting. We were waiting for a miracle, after all. Signs and messages revealed here and there kept our spirits strong and our vision forward.

In this spirit of waiting, Anna saw an energy healer to help clear the way for her gift of life. Wendy was my dear friend who worked with clients to help restore physical, emotional, and spiritual well-being using the Omnium Method. The work was used to dissolve misaligned beliefs and emotions by focusing on Anna's intention to receive a healthy pair of lungs that would fit easily into her body with no rejection issues. As part of the session, they imagined a pair of lungs that would be donated to Anna. Then they cleared the donor's lungs of imprints from her life so that they would become resonant with Anna, allowing her body to recognize them as her own. It was as if they created a template for healthy, clear lungs to fit and be free from the donor's experiences, beliefs, and emo-tions. Wendy and Anna continued to imagine and sense these clean, pure, Source-created lungs as she waited for them to arrive.

Selected Blog Posts
July – September 2010

July 27, 2010 – Day 1 – **Listed!** – Robin

I stop. I want to send love to the donor family. This is a serious moment as we travel into a confluence with many emotions and consequences. One tragedy will turn another tragedy into a triumph. One grief will turn to joy and hope, and one new grief and woe will begin for another. I take a moment to contemplate this. I take a moment to hold this gently, thoughtfully, consciously, gratefully, and respectfully. I take this moment and feel the rawness, the piercing emotions, the deep meaning, the profound opportunity.

----

*July 29, 2010 – Day 3 – **Warning: Profanity Below** – Anna*

Do you know what really chaps my ass? Ridiculous things that doctors say…

Wow, Anna, you are really stable. Five hours of treatments? Maintaining weight? Good blood sugars? Staying out of the hospital? No bowel blockages? Working on building your muscles? Keeping up with sinus rinses? Stable pulmonary function test?

YOU REALLY NEED TO BE WALKING TWENTY MINUTES IN THE MORNING AND TWENTY MINUTES AT NIGHT. AND GOING TO THE STORE AND WALKING AROUND THE HOUSE DO NOT COUNT!

WHISKY, TANGO, FOXTROT / WTF

I apologize for the vulgarity, but this really chaps my ass. I do EVERYTHING right. I walk when I CAN and have TIME…but honestly? Do I not finally get a break? I am SUPPOSEDLY dying. Isn't that why I am on the TRANSPLANT LIST? Isn't that the time when they finally don't have to pester me to do MORE than humanly possible? I understand that exercise is important, and we try to keep me moving as much as possible. Still, you can't ask someone to do that much. You can't ask someone with so little energy that they need their 'f'ing mom to make them food, help them clean, to go out twice a day, and walk around the park with their O2, on top of everything else. Do you know what exercise means to someone who can't breathe? It means doing the exercise for the given amount of time, resting for the same or more time, and feeling like absolute shit while doing it! THAT is what it means.

Readers, do YOU have time in YOUR lives to go out and walk twenty minutes twice a day? Probably, but I bet you don't do it. Do YOU have time to do five hours of treatments? NO. Imagine you are balancing a plate piled HIGH with spaghetti, and you are trying to keep your meatballs on without them rolling off...and someone comes and puts a big old piece of bread on top, and it all falls down. THAT is how I feel. That comment made me feel completely disrespected about where I am in my illness. Completely unseen by the doctor, who I would think out of everyone would understand. My lung function is at 28%. When I walk, I need six liters of oxygen. How do you fit that in on top of everything else? Isn't feeling good and being stable enough? It just chaps my ass.

––––––––––––––

August 16, 2010 – Day 21 – **Lama Gangha Nummy Nums** – Robin

Today Anna received a letter from a friend of mine.

Dear Anna,

You may not remember me, but I've known you since you were a very little girl. Today, I'm thinking of your efforts to obtain a lung transplant. I am sending you my hopes and very best wishes that your health insurance decides to cover it. You're on the prayer list at our Buddhist meditation center, so know that the community has you in their hearts and minds.

Enclosed are spiritual Dharma medicine pills, a few large, many small, that I've received from very high lamas called Rinpoches. You can take them any way you wish—one or more at a time, chewed or not chewed, just as long as your mind is focused on love and compassion for yourself and the world, with the idea that all who are sick may be healed or, if you want to be more specific, that all who suffer from CF find a cure that liberates them from their illness. Be sure to include yourself in these thoughts.

With fond regards, Judith

Judith's letter was timely; the last time Anna was in the hospital in May, I was pretty scared by how sick she was becoming. She was very vulnerable. After all these years, I remembered keeping a few Lama Gangha nummy nums in my ritual belongings. I brought them to her. She immediately wanted to ingest them and their positive energy, and she did. Still, she wanted to keep at least one for the day that she would need it the most, the day of her transplant. I had also been given other tiny pouches of vibhuti from the Hindu sage Sai Baba's community. We decided to keep it for that special day as well.

Today, I remembered that we wanted to keep these precious substances nearby for the transplant event, so I placed them in the "go to the hospital bag." And, today, of all the days, more arrived from Judith. We are well supplied. I feel a serendipitous coming-together of forces again with the corresponding gatherings of healing substances. It makes me wonder if the manifestation is near. Perhaps, but we know that time is relative. Thinking of these things and appreciating past magical events has given us strength and hope to help us.

August 17, 2010 – Day 22 – **Rituals** – Robin

Today, Anna and I did a little ritual with Judith's gift of blessing herbs, our nummy nums. What was important was that we allowed the time we used to be focused. We ceremoniously offered the special herbs to ourselves with conscious intention. We verbalized our gratitude and dedication of compassion out loud before placing the incense-tasting herb balls on our tongues. As they dissolved, we thought about the end of suffering for many other people. It was a lovely moment. We can all find time and ways to create rituals to accent significant events. It is a good and balancing thing to do that reminds us of what truly matters while quieting the mind.

August 22, 2010 – Day 27 – How Are You Doing? – Anna

I just want to write about how I am doing. Everything is relative, but I would assess my situation as good now. This is the longest I have stayed out of the hospital in a couple of years. I am going on my fourth month of inhaled antibiotics between hospitalizations. I am not even feeling like I am wearing down. I can feel some congestion in the left side when we bang and beat on it, so that is good.

I was able to walk around the park twice today, which, combined with walking there and back home, is about three quarters of a mile. So that is good. I am keeping up and staying strong. I say this with my fingers crossed because we all know how fast things can change. My GOAL is to keep out of the hospital until I get my new lungs, but I won't drive myself into the ground for that. It is a fun goal to see if they come soon enough!

Other than that, MENTALLY, I am doing well. I have my ups and downs and times when I think about the what-ifs, but I stay focused on the positive and visualize the things that I want to happen when I can breathe deeply. The waiting sometimes gets to me. But I know so many others on the list have been there so much longer and deserve their calls before I get mine (even though that is not how it works anymore). I still feel it should be somewhat first come, first serve.

----

*August 27, 2010 – Day 32 – **One Month** – Anna*

Today is August 27, which means today is officially one month on the T-list. Wow. I don't want to minimize the magnitude of my situation, as I am facing the biggest day of my life, but each day is just like every other day. I would have thought that living on the list was different than this. But honestly, it is easier than I ever anticipated. I have had my moments, but I trust and have faith that the right lungs will, in fact, come at the right time.

I am getting more and more ready for them. I have been working on opening my heart and energy to accept this unique gift I am waiting for. I have been trying to connect energetically with my future donor. I hope they live their lives to the fullest and enjoy their time with their family.

The one difficulty is knowing that the list continues to grow because there have been very few lung transplants this year. I hope there will be more transplants soon and the people who need their lungs most get them soon. I am healthy and stable now, but it won't last forever. I used to think my transplant would happen fast, but I no longer have that feeling. I have settled in, and I realize this is partly because I am not entirely emotionally ready. But I do hope it happens this year... I just hope my donor lives their life to the fullest with the time they have, and I continue to prepare for the biggest day in my life.

September 23, 2010 – Day 59 – He Has the Vibe – Robin

Recently, Anna requested to meet the surgical team, or at least a representative, at her next visit. She was promised that one of the surgeons would meet her at the clinic today. She had an excellent discussion about the surgery, what happens, how long it takes, and what happens if something goes wrong. Anna was able to ask all the questions she wanted. The regular questions opened up to the wild fantasy questions of "What if?" and these are my greatest fears.

Anna first asked what would happen if there was an earthquake. Answer: Unless it is over 8.5 or 9, then all would be fine. Question 2: If there was a "shooter with a gun" who shot the surgeon, what would happen? (I am not kidding.) Answer: In that case, the shooter probably would have to be a family member like her mom (he looked over at me with a wary eye), so it most likely would not happen. Question 3: What if the lungs are out and the new lungs don't arrive because of an accident? Answer: This was highly publicized in Michigan a few years ago. The lung recipient stayed alive on the heart-lung machine, with another set of new lungs arriving a few days later to save the patient's life. Anna was relieved. These have been questions swirling in her mind. She thought each of these seemingly unlikely situations could cause her not to survive the surgery and that she would die right away, but no, that is most likely not so, very relieving. Isn't it incredible you can have your lungs removed and live for about one week on the bypass machine? Amazing.

Then, toward the end of this conversation, we were startled. The surgeon revealed that today, they denied an offer of lungs made for Anna and turned them down because they needed to be better. It took our breath away. There is a blank space of memory after that news entered our minds. We could not hear anything else he had to say until our nerves were restored.

Anna could have been called today. We would never have known this if she had not gone to the clinic. It was amazing that he revealed this info. Wow, that made it so real. It also gave us restored hope. Waiting is very hard, and you do not know how long it can be. Now we know it can be so soon, just as we are simply going about our day. There is such an unreal part to living this drama. Today, this information makes it more real.

Next, we saw Dr. Weill. Yes, he confirmed, there has been a lack of donor organs this summer across the country. He said that it is changing now. He admitted the near call for Anna today and that her name had been discussed. He looked directly at Anna and said, "Be ready." He believes it can happen soon. October sounds likely to him. But how can he know? The thing is that this physician feels vibes, too. He is feeling the vibe. More organs are starting to be donated, and the climate is changing. Let's hope so.

The realm that everyone wants to go to and share is the vibe realm. It is more fun there. Talking stats is attractive to a point, but it is tantalizing when you are feeling the vibe. When your brilliant doctor goes there, you perk up and listen. He must know. This is his work, and I have new hope. He is feeling the vibe, and the moon is full.

September 29, 2010 – Day 65 – **Writing and You Are Helping Me** – Robin

Keep writing. Keep writing. It fills the space while I am waiting. Ho hummmm, impatience is arising. I know it can be contagious, and I could work it out on the page so that its viral arms do not grab anyone near me into its neurotic hold. It is a time of "let's get on with it already!" Last night, or rather early this morning, and at this minute, as I write, a double lung transplant is happening in the OR at Stanford. We have the inside scoop since Sara's job includes calling the OR multiple times daily, asking, "This is the CF Laboratory. Are there any lung transplants?" The nurse in the OR will say no or yes. Last night she said yes. Some lucky someone had the perfect match to end their waiting. Sara is surely up now and at least on her way to Stanford to retrieve the old lungs for the lab. She was so excited and loves her job. This is a good test for her if she really wants to be a doctor. I think she does more than ever.

As Sara said, this breaks the pattern. There have only been two transplants per month for the last few months. This now makes three for September. Good. Maybe the tide is turning, and there will be more. We are certainly hoping for October for Anna. Early on, when we all made our "predictions," Sara said October 3. That is coming up. Maybe, maybe. Even though I am getting antsy, I still feel all the good thoughts, positive prayers, and wonderful support. I just want to get this done. It is the control in me. It is the mom in me. It is me in me.

Breathe, let go. I have been trying to practice body movement regularly when I get up in the morning. If I let myself move as in a dance of tribal shaking and calisthenic stretches combined, I seem to do better. It loosens things up. I feel stuck sometimes. My body hurts and wants to break out of this holding pattern. I have been in a holding pattern for many years because of this disease. Will the new lungs change this? I wonder. I wonder if I will feel freer. Will the stiffness in the muscles and the pains from down deep open and release? I am looking forward to seeing if it will and experiencing it. I am ready to get on with it.

Movement and writing. These are my therapies, and I do the first alone and the second with you as a witness. One day, we will move together in dance and celebration that this is complete and successful. I look forward to that day and will continue to use my trusty computer to help me process and share this amazing experience and the coming fruition of a miracle on order. Thank you again for traveling with me.

chapter thirteen
The Dalai Lama

October and autumn arrived and more blessing magic came into our lives. We met a special visitor to Stanford University's Center on Compassion and Altruism Research and attended a private event for sick children and their families that we will never forget. October was truly special.

**Selected Blog Posts
October 2010**

October 3, 2010 – Day 69 – **An Orchid Sits By Me Smiling** – Robin

An orchid sits by me, with tight blooms waiting then opening. Is it a sign? Is the orchid smiling?

We think we know how our life should go or look like. Mine is not supposed to be like this for very long. It has been OK for a while, but I know myself. I am very patient, up to a point. Yes, I am a very patient person. My mom always told me that. But then, there is this point. When does the point arrive? When I have had enough, not when the event is ready for me, but when I am ready for the event. So, does this mean that I am patient? Or does this mean that truly I am a very impatient and controlling person who seeks to manipulate and barter with the universe to make things go my way in my timing? Makes one think about themselves.

That is what this is about: patience and faith. Virtues. This is about virtues. I guess I have a lot to learn here. We stretch to our limits and then find that we can stretch some more. I am stretching. The muscles sometimes resist and hurt where the stretching can go no further. Then I must accept the pain and move on with it. We are in week 11, and we are waiting.

----

*October 3, 2010 – Day 69 – **Not So Fun Sunday** – Anna*

The truth is that I am a sick person and not a healthy person, and I tend to forget this. Call it eternal optimism, naivete, or just plain denial, but I forget this sometimes. I often convince myself that it is a mistake that I am on the transplant list, but today, I feel it, and I just feel yucky.

My body detests when the weather starts to change from warm to cold. My joints ache, I am unable to get warm, I am lethargic, and I get cranky. I have no desire to do anything. My lungs hurt today, my airways are tight, and I feel a general malaise. This is a drastic change from yesterday. I had fun with my sister. We went out to lunch, sat in the sun, ran errands, and went out to dinner...it was a nice day. But I didn't sleep that well last night, and today, I woke up with the yuckies.

I am thankful that still, even listed, more days are good days than bad days...but on bad days like this (when I didn't do the dishes from Friday, John is cramming to get all his reading done, and it is cold outside), I just don't feel that great. It is days like this that I know I am ready for a change. I can't keep living like this, not pulling my weight in the household. Everything revolves around the sick girl. And to top it all off, I just dropped my Snickers bar on the floor, but I will eat it anyway because I haven't had my transplant yet ;).

I also realized the great tragedy that is my life today. I realized that I would never be "well." I might get a transplant and be able to have healthy lungs to go run and jump and swim with, but I will never not have a disease. I will live my entire life with this disease. I know that I should know this; it is genetic, but the absolute truth that I will never be healthy sank into my soul today.

Strong women always advise that you should never depend on a man. You should always make your own money to survive on your own. I will never be able to do this. I will always have dependency one step away from me. It is a very scary world, and I need support. I can't support myself. It is incredibly humbling that I will always need a doctor and my family. I will never be able to do it alone. Now, I need my donor to help me through this challenging time. The strongest I can be is to admit that I need help.

It just feels like I am letting the women's movement down. I am an educated woman who is in desperate need of support. Pretty pathetic if you ask me. But all I can do now is swallow my pride and keep going. I just have to keep on living. I am grateful for those who support me because I could never do it alone and would wither into non-existence. It is a hard reality.

But I am opening my arms to welcome my donor and their family into my life. I think I am truly ready for this gift. I need to make a change, and I can't keep living like this...

October 10, 2010 – Day 76 – **Flags of Hope** – Robin

Well, it must be another one of those encouraging gifts from the universe. My day on Friday was spent at Ronald McDonald House at Stanford. A Healing Flags for Hope project began in June and was ready to be hung. I created this project in 2007 by organizing the decorating of fabric flags with families staying at the House and then displaying hundreds of flags as a healing art exhibit. It stood for a couple of months in front of the House.

This new project was a sequel to the first and spurred by the upcoming visit of the Dalai Lama. My life did not allow much involvement in the project this time because I was caring for Anna. Still, I helped with getting it started and hanging the flags in preparation for the important visitor. Once again, the families and children of the House made inspiring and touching flags for the exhibit in preparation for the event.

Coming to the Ronald McDonald House is a special part of the Dalai Lama's trip to Stanford for a conference on consciousness and will include a group blessing of the children. The House is decorated with about 300 flags, a project inspired by Tibetan prayer flags from the spiritual traditions of His Holiness and Tibetan Buddhism. I was greatly honored that the House's executive director invited my project to be a part of the event. Not all flags were hung in the front of the House to greet his arrival. The internal gardens and patio also include strings of cotton messages about hope and prayer.

Today, I attended the House meeting where the families were told about the event, who the Dalai Lama was, and why this was to be so unique and special. Some people understood who he was and what a precious opportunity it was to participate in this event. Still, I could see that others did not.

I know that for everyone lucky enough to attend this blessing of the children, it will leave a lasting impression upon their hearts to be in His Holiness's presence. Anna and I hope to also be there on Wednesday.

During my June visit at the flag project kick-off, I met a ten-year-old girl from Washington State who had just had a double lung transplant. She was not a victim of CF but had another rare lung disease. It was very inspiring to meet her and her mom. This time, I had the gift of meeting another lung recipient with CF. He is seventeen years old and received his lungs three weeks ago. Both he and his beaming and exuberant mother were doing fantastic. It is just three weeks post-surgery, and he already walked four miles daily! His mother said he could not sit still and needed to move and feel his new lungs. His muscles are suffering with the exercise, and he needs to build strength, but his lungs are amazing. It is difficult for him to fully describe what it feels like to breathe deeply and normally.

Last week, I drove Anna from her condo to Murphy Street in downtown Sunnyvale. It is exactly two miles. I set a goal for us to walk there for lunch one day after the transplant. Returning home will make it four miles in total. It will be our first walking goal. She hesitated, saying, "Now, Mom, I won't be able to do this right away." It is hard for her to see that this utterly impossible task could be so easy when she has lungs that work. In a way, it does not compute. Meeting the boy at the House demonstrated that she could accomplish this soon after her transplant. I know she does not want to keep her hopes too high, and she knows that everyone has their own recovery story, but I see this for her.

I am so grateful to have met this teen and his mom at the House. It was a shot in the arm for me. He waited six months for his lungs. I hope we do not have to wait as long, but as his mom told me, "It happens when it is the right time." Yes, that is true, but a mother's heart wants so much for their child to be relieved of suffering immediately, with no wait. It is hard to suppress that desire, but it is true. It will happen at the right time.

---

*October 14, 2010 – Day 80 – **The Greatest Gift I Have Ever Received** – Anna*

Yesterday was a day to be savored and remembered for my entire life. It was a day where kindness and compassion led the way. It was a day I believe was "supposed to happen," and it felt like a destined journey. His Holiness, the Dalai Lama, personally blessed me.

Honestly, there are no words to describe the miraculous experience for me. No matter your religion or spiritual practice, there is no denying that the Dalai Lama is a powerful being. He emanated light, kindness, and hope. Every fiber of my being was lit up from simply watching him walk through the doors of the Ronald McDonald House. There was the hustle and bustle of the secret service, the accompanied camera paparazzi, his translator, and his fellow lamas. He had an entourage, but it didn't take away from the amazing grace this man exuded from his soul. He walked through the doors, and it felt like a burst of sunshine. EVERYONE's breath was taken away. We were in a room of children, and there was SILENCE, absolute silence. It was an awesome moment. Totally awesome.

He is memorable and famous, yet so familiar and safe. One of the kindest people I have ever met. Let me qualify; he is ONE of them ONLY because I have had other personal experiences with Tibetan lamas before this. Lamas are the kindest people you could ever meet. Their touch is soft and comforting, but firm with direction and intention. They have smiling faces and kind eyes, but are full of wisdom and depth. All the Tibetan lamas I have met have given me this experience. I can't quite quantify or explain the event yesterday, but the timing and the magnitude of the situation that unfolded were just so humbling and incomprehensible.

I have been gravely ill twice, NOW and when I was diagnosed with CF. My mom took me to Lama Gangha when I was diagnosed with CF. We spent many days together while he gave me blessings and honored me with herbs and special "Lama Gangha nummy-nums," as I called them. I had magical experiences, and Lama Gangha was my friend. I forgot about Lama Gangha after growing up and being a teen. The memories of our times together faded. But recently, it has all flooded back to me. The taste, the smells, the touch, the feelings, the healings. I need these memories.

The experience of needing a transplant forces you to dig deep inside yourself into a place you may never think you will go. Mentally, it is taxing and forces you to find peace and comfort. Many turn to their different faiths, and I have heard many stories of those who have found God. My understanding of this experience is that they happen when there is a karmic connection to these lamas. I can't explain the fortune bestowed upon me at this time in my life, in my greatest time of need, that the Dalai Lama would appear as Lama Gangha did. And I would be welcomed against all odds to have this auspicious experience.

I knew I needed to see him when I learned he was coming. But how could that be? Why should I be so lucky? Who am I to get this experience? I am not a practicing Buddhist. Those are the people, the people who know of his greatness and follow him, who should see him. Not me. How could I be worthy of this? But the little voice in my head told me I would be there.

It isn't a complete miracle that we were there, but it is in many ways. My mom orchestrated the Healing Flags project designed for the event. She was consulted for the project in honor of His Holiness. So we assumed that we would be able to attend. Well, as it turned out, decisions about attendance had to be made due to security and space availability. As a result, only the most significant financial contributors and the sick children from the House were invited. They were the obvious choices. So as of Tuesday, we believed there was no way we could attend. However, my mom's cell phone rang on Tuesday at 7 p.m. It was Honey, the executive director of the Ronald McDonald House. She had mulled it over, and it didn't feel right that I could not come. She told my mom, "Anna is so gravely ill and needs all the support she can get as she heads toward her transplant. It is just not right that she cannot attend. I am bending some rules to ensure you can come." We were allowed to go at the last minute! The necessary security paperwork needed to attend had already been filled out. My mom did so when she helped install the flags, hoping we might go. All barriers to attending were lifted. How awesome was that? Thanks, Mom!

This experience truly was the greatest gift I have ever received, as of now. The invitation to attend and the blessing I received were beyond expectations. When His Holiness entered the room, he touched many children on their heads or hands, asking what ailed them. One boy sitting in front of me with his father had liver cancer, and his surgery was scheduled for that day. His father explained that the doctors agreed to postpone it so he could be at the event and meet the Dalai Lama.

He spread healing and light to the whole room. He spoke for a few minutes about the sadness of children being ill. Still, it isn't sad if looked at from a new perspective. They can find other ways to look at it by suggesting they had the great fortune to be there at Stanford with the greatest medical care and food to eat and be loved by their parents. He also spoke about Tibetan medicine.

He traveled around the room, blessing the children and some parents there. The House provided white silk scarves for the blessing, traditionally known as khatas. I stood up and moved from my second-row seat to the front, where he could reach me when he came by.

Once he reached me, time stood still. He knew exactly what I needed. He went quickly to put the khata on my neck, took my hands in his, and realized I needed more than that. He stopped and looked me dead in the eye, staring. I don't know how long this was; my mom thinks it was about thirty seconds, but it felt like time had stopped. I looked back at him in the eyes with all hope and openness. I have not been this close to many people in my life. But this was close. He held my hands, looked into my eyes, and then kept looking and touching my face and hands again. When he finally let go, I could barely utter "thank you." It was the most intense experience of my life. It was such a personal experience I can't share all that I learned from it, and I will continue to learn as it settles in my body. But I can tell you that I heard my mind yell, "Woah, NOW I am ready."

His Holiness also held my mom's hand and offered her a blessing. This was such a tremendous gift for both of us. It was an acknowledgment of a life's work with art for healing through the healing flag display for my mom and for her project to be honored and seen by the Dalai Lama himself! WOW. I don't think she even understands the *magnitude of that, either.*

We were not allowed cameras, or I would have included a picture. But there were cameramen there, and the pics should be available at the House at some point, and we will get some, I am sure. I can't wait! But until then, I will leave you with this...

Om Mani Padme Hum

October 14, 2010 – Day 80 – **The Magical Mystery Tour** – Robin

It was all so surreal. Here we were in the presence of the Dalai Lama! Here we were, receiving blessings from the Dalai Lama! Wow, so special. At the same time, it felt ordinary, as if it was so natural that this was happening. We know this is not a commonplace event. A father that we met while there was from Nepal. He told us, with his blind son by his side, that this type of audience never happens in India and Nepal. This was very auspicious. We know this, and we are so grateful. The Healing Flags of Hope did their magic.

This evening, all we can do is integrate the power of the energy and blessings we received. It was so powerful. Anna says that she is "zapped." She knew she needed this blessing and healing energy he transmitted before her surgery. She now feels ready (for the transplant), more than ever before. The depth of this man and his spiritual power is so remarkable. We are humbled and in awe that this happened at all. It is one of the many miraculous, lucky, and magical events and circumstances that have come to us during this pre-transplant experience. All I can call it, for now, is the Magical Mystery Tour.

October 18, 2010 – Day 84 – **Hearing the Song of the Ancients** – Robin

Today, we rested and integrated. Our visit with His Holiness was transformative, and the afterglow stayed with us. It was as if we were still with a foot in another universe. Many times, we said to each other, "Did that happen?" Yes, it did, and it was real and so very special. The past few days, our conversations included philosophical thoughts and trying to verbalize what it all meant.

Most of all, one of the greatest teachings from the experience was how everything is interconnected and how the movement of our lives toward a transition can be seen all around us. The other thing I told Anna that is very, very important is, even though we are in this critical time with her health on edge, there is still this magic. As His Holiness said, it is sad when there is an illness, but there are so many facets to look at in one's life and find what to be grateful for and what is truly beautiful. This experience is a bit of everything. We experience danger, fear, hope, magic, sadness, laughter, love, friendship, loss, pain, confusion, and moments of clarity of thought.

When you have a severe illness threatening your life, you are challenged. You are also challenged when you are the mother of a child turned adult who has fought disease all her life with you always at her side. When the edge of the precipice is dangerously under your feet, a time comes after so many years of sickness and caregiving that you are so very tired of it all. Then, you begin to hear the ancients in your bones. They begin to sing to you and beckon you to listen deeper as you continue the tasks. The ancients know how you feel. They are the ones who, through all the ages, have fought illness, loved and cared for others, made beds, cooked soup, and held hands.

My experience meeting the Dalai Lama yesterday helped

me to hear these ancients, the "mothers of all time," more clearly. Being in his presence and touching his hand, I heard them sing to me through my bones. It is a song of heartfelt longing and sorrow with a sweetness that lulls you into a peaceful acceptance of what is. Their songs wrap you in wise threads and a familiar human melody about a path of caring and understanding. All you need is to listen. That was the teaching he gave to me.

chapter fourteen
The Call

November arrived, and we reached 100 days of waiting. Thanksgiving was approaching, and we hoped to be thankful for Anna's new lungs while eating our turkey.

Selected Blog Posts
November 2010

*November 12, 2010 – Day 109 – **The Dry Run** – Anna*

Well, as my mom said, I am having the FULL transplant experience, dry run and all! I guess I should take you through the whole "Call" experience to get everyone updated and on the same page.

I went to bed at about midnight, put the phone by my bed, turned off the light, hooked up my bi-pap, and played solitaire on the iPod Touch to fall asleep. John was watching Family Guy in the other room when I went to bed, so the lights were still on, and our house was not completely asleep. I had been asleep for about thirty minutes when the phone rang. I can't remember much, but I looked at the phone and didn't see it say "Stanford" or "private," so I was confused; but who else could it be at 12:42 a.m.?

I answered, "Hello?"

"Hi, is Anna there?"

"This is Anna, ummmm." There were some holy shits, holy craps, and "Wait, can you say that again?" because I was so confused from being woken up. I was wondering what John was doing, and he was listening on the other line in the hall. We were both dumbfounded

that "The Call" had actually come! We had been waiting for this for a long time, and it was here. How strange it is. My wonderful friend Ana told me on Wednesday, "No matter how much you know or prepare, nothing will prepare you for what it is really like." YUP. This is true, and I haven't gotten that far in the game yet.

Back to the call... He nicely and calmly told me that the donor was at Stanford and that more tests would be done in the morning to see if the donor was suitable. He said, "Now, get some rest and come in at 8 a.m." GET SOME REST? CRAP. If you get woken up from a dead sleep and try to fall back to sleep when Santa is coming...not really that possible.

I went completely numb all over my body. My hands were clammy. I realized because I had taken my bi-pap off to talk, I wasn't wearing my O2, and I figured that would be part of the tightness in my chest. I quickly put it back on once I figured it out. After we got off the phone, I looked at John, and we both looked shocked. NOW WHAT? Do I call my parents or wait because he told us to sleep? NO, CALL!!! So, I called them and informed them. They were shocked, too. They didn't sleep much, either. After talking to them, we decided I should call Sara instead of letting her sleep because she would be pissed if we kept it from her. Well, it turned out her phone was turned down low, and I called five times, and she didn't pick up. I texted and left her messages, but no answer. It was decided that in the morning my mom would drive to the apartment (where Sara was sleeping) at 6 a.m. to wake her.

We went back to sleep. John slept, and I lay there for a long time, finally falling asleep at about 3:30. We woke at 5:30 a.m. to do my "last treatment," get a shower, and head to the hospital. (It was not my last treatment; I am doing one as I write this.)

Despite all the planning, my brain flew out of the window when the call came. I was trying to decide what to bring. Luckily, I wrote a list I kept in my bag with all the necessary electronics, cords, phone, computer, etc. We began loading everything in the car to head off to the hospital. Luckily, Mom and Dad came over to help us load everything. John and I were overwhelmed. As many know, we are not morning people, and getting out the door takes a lot of work. I am glad we had the help.

Once we got there, I was worried because we were a little late, but the room wasn't even ready yet. I went to Admitting and said, "I am here for my transplant today." It was so surreal to say that. Once they checked me in, we sat in Admitting until the room was ready.

We quickly got to the room: Mom, Dad, Sara, John, and ME. As much as I wanted every person there, they were already calling our group a "party," so it just wasn't the place for large groups.

Anyway, back to the day's events... We got to the room, and I put on a hospital gown and got hooked to a heart monitor. I was placed in the intermediate ICU for cardiac patients and was treated as a heart patient. Kinda bizarre but fine.

I sat in bed for twenty minutes before the surgeon fellow (who called me) came in. He told us that he had bad news. The lungs were not good. He told us a lot, but I can't remember much of what he said. In my brain, I was already out the door. The donor was given a scan, and they found that even though the history didn't indicate it, the lungs had emphysema. So, I am happy they discovered that and did not give me the lungs. They did say that if I had been in dire straits, like on a ventilator, they would have accepted the lungs for me because their function was good despite this finding. It ended quickly, which I am thankful for. It wasn't a drawn-out process, and I didn't have to get any unnecessary pokes.

The doc told us they had been getting several offers, so I may soon get new lungs. I have a friend who got their REAL call the day after their Dry Run...so it could happen quickly. But for now, I would like to get a good night's sleep. I am off to bed early tonight. I worked hard to get a treatment in early. Gonna have some pumpkin pie, Mother's oatmeal cookies and milk, and head to bed!!!!

I am still thinking about the donor and their family's tragic loss. Hoping the family finds peace and their loved one has given new life to others.

I couldn't do it without your love and support, which has given me the strength I never knew I had. Having you all supporting and loving me and my family makes me elated and so humbled. Even though I can't respond to every text, email, comment, or Facebook message, know it means the world to my family and me. We feel and appreciate the love and can feel how much you care! THANK YOU! Now, I go back to the grindstone. Tomorrow is day 110 on the list.

November 15, 2010 – Day 112 – **Moving On** – Robin

It is the end of the day on Monday, another week. Next week is Thanksgiving, and I cannot believe it. The dry run had a more significant impact on us than we first realized. Doug and I were absolutely spent over the weekend. We rested, staying in bed Sunday morning until the afternoon. I have not done that since I was a teenager. I almost ordered popcorn to watch TV in bed, but the sun was shining, and I needed to get out in the beautiful air. After a walk, I slept some more.

I am feeling better today. We are picking it up and moving forward. Anna stays strong with her eye on the prize. Who knows when the next call will come or whether it will be another dry run? We will reserve some of our high energy until we get the final go-ahead.

Tomorrow is another pulmonary function test and a six-minute walk test to check Anna's O2 saturation. This will determine how much oxygen she should use during the day and night. Then, Thursday is another pre-transplant appointment. Again, we never thought she would get to this appointment. We thought lungs would have appeared by now. The transplant fellow in the hospital told us on Friday that an offer comes in for Anna every four days, but the main issue has been size. They are looking for the perfect match. Again, Anna reminded me today that is why she got on the list when she did. She wanted to be strong enough to be able to wait for the perfect lungs for her. If she had been very ill when these last lungs were offered, they might have had to take them to save her life. She does not want to be in that situation, ever.

I never liked roller coasters. Is it the heights that scare me the most, or is it the fast speed on a rickety track? They have always scared me, and I was never very attracted to them. Friday was like a roller coaster ride, but the emotional energy spent on the ride up and ever so quickly down was far more than I anticipated. Now, a roller coaster at a park doesn't seem such a big deal after all. I could survive it just fine. I wonder how many transplant dry runs it would take to wear me out totally. We all must carefully conserve our energy to make it on this journey. It is indeed a wild ride.

----

*November 21, 2010 – Day 118 – **I GOT THE CALL! AGAIN!** – Anna*

HEY ALL…I got "The Call" again, and this time, it felt real. Good old Dr. Steve Singh called, and they got lungs for me (sounds like they are YOUNG ones), a match in all the ways. They said to get there faster this time. So, I'm heading in right now, rushing to get ready. Doing my last hypertonic saline neb right now. PLEASE SEND GOOD VIBES. I feel it. Needing strength for myself and love for the donor and their family. I really feel this one is it.

It is when you least expect it. Love to all! Anna Banana

----

*November 22, 2010 – Day 119 – **Anna's Transplant** – Anna (Sara)*

Hello, all! This is Anna's little sister commandeering Anna's blog while she is unable to write. Wanted to give you all an update on the night so far.

Well, we got to the hospital a little after 11 p.m. tonight and went to Admitting. But, lo and behold, no one was there! After a few moments of "Uhhhhh, what do we do?" I did my usual daily ritual of calling the OR. We discovered where we were supposed to go and that her surgery was scheduled for 4 a.m.

We made our way down to E Ground and got settled in. Having gone to as many transplants as I've been to, I knew they were always pushed back. Somehow, the time went by, and those five hours zoomed past. This call felt much more real. It is going to happen...

Lots of love and kisses were given to Anna, and we all posed for a gazillion photos. Then, at 4:30 a.m., they walked in and told us it was time for her to go! All of our stomachs flipped. This is really it, and it is happening. This is the fastest transplant I have ever witnessed. Typically, they are scheduled for a particular time and then pushed back at least four hours. But not this time. Thankfully, we did not have to wait long, and now our waiting is over!

We went up to the second level with her to see her off. We walked up to those OR doors and gave our last kisses as we watched her wheel away, cracking jokes like our usual crazy Anna. The doctors don't know what a party they are in for. The nurses said everything was a go and Anna would be under and intubated within fifteen minutes.

We have settled into our new home on the second floor for the next seven-plus hours, waiting for news and being grateful for the donor and the donor's family. Thank you to this family that has been able to see outside their own grief and give this incredible gift to my sister. Please send good thoughts to them and Anna!

chapter fifteen

Miracle Delivered!

The north intensive care unit waiting room was all ours for the rest of the very early morning. We were camped out, our feet propped on coffee tables, exhausted heads bowed or resting on pillows with sweaters and blankets draped over us. Next to us were our computers with tops open and our bags spilling over with our personal items. The wait of 119 days was over, and a new wait had begun.

It would be hours spent in a hospital waking up to the morning shift and into midday before we would find out how Anna fared on the operating table after watching her make a final wave of goodbye to all of us. We had turned the bend on this marathon, but the finish line was still not yet in sight. We kept Anna on track, still strong for the surgery, and her will was very willing. Next, the success of her transplant would depend on how things went in the surgery and her recovery.

It was early morning, around 7 a.m., when Dr. Weill first entered our den in his white coat and usual comfortable style, telling us all was going well. A few more hours passed, and Dr. Weill again arrived with the best news: "Anna is in the ICU, and all went well. She can see you in an hour, but you can only go in two at a time."

We thanked him with a shower of gratitude that must be what he receives whenever he gives good news to families. It must feel like a reward to a doctor who has stood by his patient and family waiting for a lung transplant to see the relief on the faces of loved ones after such a long and stressful wait. The surgery fulfilled what Anna was promised by Dr.

Weill and his team. The next part of recovery that she would enter was another unknown journey, and we were relying on him to help guide us through.

By early afternoon, we all had a chance to see her. For a second round of visits, Sara and I saw her together. We were told it would not be long until her breathing tube was removed.

Feeling like we had just jumped over a mountain, we stood beside Anna in her ICU bed. Covered in wires, lines in her neck and arms, and tubes that led to drainage bags, Anna tried to communicate with us. We gave her a pencil and paper. This did not satisfy her, and she started writing a "W" and other letters. Trying to understand her message, Sara asked, "White? Are you white?" Then we said together, "Oh! Whiteboard!" And with that, she threw the pencil at me! Anna was back!

Only three hours after leaving the OR and having her lungs removed and another set sewn in, she was present with her spunky self. We forgot that she planned for us to have a whiteboard for her. She looked up at me with disgust at how I'd failed as a mother, and we fell apart with laughter. Anna was once again returning to run the show.

We assured her that John would be there soon with the whiteboard. Things were going so well that we did not have time for all the pieces of our post-transplant plan to be in place. To add to the high of the moment, Dr. Weill stopped by and, pleased with how things were going, said, "You will be surprised how fast we will be able to get her out of here." I wish it had turned out that way.

The next incredible moment came when I stood at the foot of her bed again, only hours after this monumental surgery. I watched in awe while the nurses released her from the breathing tube. My daughter, who had struggled to breathe, tethered with an O2 tube and cannula for so long, would be breathing independently. She took a big breath as the tube was quickly pulled from her throat and mouth. It seemed eyes everywhere had stopped to look and see this miracle.

I stood there with my mouth open, consciously taking a deep breath, filling my lungs as she did hers. As she settled and had some time to breathe more, the nurses asked if I wanted to hug her. Of course I did.

Gently, they helped Anna swing her legs to the side of the bed. Slippers were put on her feet, and a fluffy pillow was given to hold onto, protecting her chest. They moved and rearranged her tubing every which way and helped her stand on a box, making her taller so that we were near equal height when I came to hug her.

I moved closer and could feel the delicate care the nurses offered. They knew Anna and I needed to hug and connect in our new world of her fresh new breath. I reached around her and held her as my body began to shake with the need to cry. The power of what had just transpired could only be felt emotionally and spiritually. My daughter's life was saved. She was here, and we were together to make it through the next recovery challenge.

Through the afternoon, Anna continued to improve. We spent as much time as we could with her. She expressed her love for all of us, and when visiting with the surgeon, Dr. Steve Singh, she called him her hero. When she saw Dr. Weill checking in, she would smile and give a definite thumbs-up. Her sense of humor and deep concern for doing the right thing was also intact.

She told us she was ready to go home. The huge bolus of steroids hit her, and she thought she could do anything when riding high on pred. Usually, when she had to take prednisone, she would want to build houses for Habitat for Humanity. When she would say this, I would have to remind her that she did not have a hammer or a saw and that it was the pred talking.

This was the miracle we had on order that was delivered. We now understood when it would come—"soon" meant November 22. Doug and I had the unreal opportunity to have a child with a lethal disease come to the end of that journey and be blessed with a new life and a new journey. Even though her CF lungs were gone and Anna could breathe, CF would still share its presence in other ways. But CF's immediate threat to her life was mitigated. The magnitude of what had just happened was overwhelming, and we were so fortunate.

Doug stayed with Anna in the ICU by her bed that first night and caught a few winks of sleep slouched on two chairs in the hallway.

On the second day of her recovery, there was concern about her kidneys. We were told that she had very low blood pressure during the surgery, causing stress to her kidneys. We were also warned that their ability to function could get worse before they got better. The transplant team was considering starting her on kidney dialysis until they healed. Her strength and the continued progression at this early stage made us confident that she would recover from this, too.

On the third day after her transplant, Anna began dialysis. It was Thanksgiving, and our troupe celebrated in the cafeteria without Anna. We were exhausted, excited, and not knowing better, we had few worries as we ate our turkey. We believed all was improving and accepted the dialysis as a necessary addition to her recovery treatment plan.

Her recovery included breathing into a spirometer to help expand her lungs. It was fun to watch her do it because each time, she tried to breathe deeper and deeper, getting her number to go up higher. Every time it rose, her eyes got big, and she smiled. Sara asked her what it was like to breathe with her new lungs, and she said, "I don't feel anything. It's so weird. It's amazing. It's awesome!" She could no longer feel the restrictions and pain ever present with her CF lungs. She also told us, "I got really good lungs!" We all were breathing deeper. We were elated!

The next day, when we arrived in her room, Anna was more alert and sitting in her chair eating breakfast. I noticed a strange look in her eyes, and it was clear she was suffering from the effects of the super high dose of steroids given to all transplant patients. It can cause hallucinations and make patients appear a bit crazy. Before the surgery, Anna feared she would be significantly affected by it. That morning, she started having numerous hallucinations, seemed drunk with slurred speech, and dropped things. The doctors believed it was part of what was expected and due to the steroids.

I reminded Anna that she had told me how the scenario would go, saying, "I will have a rough time in the beginning, but once I get over the hump, all will go smoothly."

She repeated this many times while we were in the waiting game and acknowledged that she was right. She did not know the details and did not expect the kidney issues, but we went with her premonition that it would all resolve and we would move forward.

Throughout the day, Anna continued to be goofy, seeing blue tape on people's faces, green spoons on the floor, and little birds flying. It was hard not to be concerned. Sara volunteered to watch out for her sister and spent the night with her. We decided to take turns sleeping with Anna, as we did not want her alone in her mental confusion.

The next day, a big change in her mental status became obvious. I brought her a favorite dessert from the cafeteria, and she became suspicious when I offered it to her. "Hi, Anna. Dad and I just had lunch, and I saw this pumpkin pie downstairs. We also have this mochi from Ana and Isa. I thought you might enjoy one of them."

She responded, "No way am I going to be tricked, Mom. I will not eat those."

I thought she was kidding me, and it was one of Anna's jokes, but she was serious. She glared at me, saying she did not trust me. "Why would you do that, Mom? The jig is up!"

Shocked by this crazy reaction to me and what I heard her say, I could not convince her. "Anna, this is me. I wanted you to have a yummy dessert," I explained. She refused, looking at me in a way she never had before. The real crazies she had feared had begun and grown into full-blown paranoid psychosis. It was frightening.

Her hallucinations grew into stories about conspiracies against her and society. The doctors said her lack of sleep and being in the ICU was the main cause of ICU Delirium. Still, it was also the buildup of toxins in her blood, with low-functioning kidneys that could not cleanse her system. For a couple of days, she had running themes of "you cannot pray away the gay" or "education is the key," and she talked about a place called Cacapoopoopeepeeshire! It was worrisome but admittedly also very funny. Even so, she needed to be protected from herself, and we had to get the doctors to see this was now getting beyond little flying birdies.

On day seven, she ate a good breakfast. Then, as we walked in the unit, she displayed her new persona of suspicion and crazy, looking for proof of her mental conspiracies, including those surrounding Oprah. I gave her my "normal" perspective on what she was saying and a little personal care, like washing her hair, hoping this would bring her back to our world.

She continued to go without sleep for days, and we were sure this contributed to the growing insanity. Finally, there were some quiet moments when she slept soundly. Her new lungs were doing well, but she was scheduled to continue dialysis as her kidneys and mental status were not out of the woods yet.

It was my turn to stay with her for the night. We hoped she was finally going to have a full night's sleep. We had a room with a cot for me to sleep on. I tucked my daughter with a crazy mind into her bed, wishing her a good sleep. Before we drifted off, her nurse checked on us and turned on her bed alarm. Earlier in the evening, Anna had nearly fallen off the bed due to her crazy, erratic self, and the nurse wanted to know if that happened again. All seemed quiet and OK, and I was beyond exhausted. I tried to stay awake and watch her, but it seemed she was falling asleep. I could not resist the touch of my head on the pillow.

A loud alarm and a rush into the room awakened me. Anna was in crisis. I did not know why until I got up and looked at her. She was lying in a pool of deep red blood that was growing. The crash cart and a crowd of doctors were suddenly there. All I could do was curl up in a ball on my cot. I could hear their voices say that her central line stitched into her neck and her dialysis catheter had come out, and she was bleeding out of her jugular. The only way this could happen was if she pulled it out herself.

Being there on the sideline of the emergency, knowing her life was so dangerously close to ending, I was paralyzed. I could not believe that this would be the way that it would end. My mind was racing, yet I could not move from my fetal position curled up on my cot until a nurse put her hand on my back and told me I had to leave. Somehow finding the means to get up and out, I left the crowd of emergency workers there to save her life. When I finally made it out of the unit and sat in the waiting area, I called Doug, Sara, and John. "You have to come now to the hospital. Something has happened, and I need you."

Alarmed, they had to pull on their clothes with their bodies still craving sleep, jump into their cars, and race to be with me. I sat alone and in shock until they arrived. They arrived with a fast and determined stride coming up the hallway. All I could do was collapse into them and tell them through my tears what had happened. Not long after they arrived, we were told Anna was moved back to the ICU, and she would be OK.

The crisis was averted. Later, after healing in the ICU, Anna told us the story going on in her mind that caused her to pull out these vital lines, nearly costing her life. She remembered swimming with other transplanted friends and, in all seriousness, said, "We were swimming to Cacapoopoopeepeeshire when I felt this Post-it note on my neck. Realizing you cannot swim with a Post-it note on your neck, I had to remove it, so I did."

The absurdity of such a delusion juxtaposed with the grave seriousness of what had happened floored us. We laughed uncontrollably after she told us this story. The absurd humor of it all lasted for days and days, giving us a relief valve we needed to continue.

It took time—years, in fact—for me to get over the intense shock of that experience. Our lives finally came to this miraculous moment, and so quickly, in a moment of crazy, it almost ended. Anna could have slipped away while I was lying beside her, oblivious. Her life was saved because of the smart decision of the nurse to turn on that bed alarm. I am forever grateful and probably still healing from that experience. It could have been our story of Anna ending then and there in the hospital, but she survived due to good medical care, an angel on her shoulder, great good fortune, and the fulfillment of a life that had to be lived. As Anna would say, this was no lollygagging picnic, and we were still not out of the woods.

After her near disaster, Anna was cared for in the ICU with a particular psychiatric medication called DEX and finally slept about forty-eight hours straight. With more dialysis to help her body release toxins from her system, Anna was brought back to her good and stable mind. Doug and I took this time to sleep at the apartment and rest. It was a good sign when, after days of sleep, a nurse called me in the morning soon after I woke up, saying, "Hello, Mrs. Modlin? I am Anna's nurse, and she wonders when you will be in today."

The ICU visiting hours began at 10 a.m., and I promised I would be there. On the way, I picked up a berry smoothie and Hobee's coffee cake, her favorite breakfast treat. After arriving, I could see that her brain was much better, but she needed to tell me, "Mom, this is so hard, the hardest thing I have ever done."

"Anna, I wish there was a magic incantation to make it all

disappear," I replied, with my mom answer. It is unbearable to see your child suffer and to continue to endure. The best we could do was comfort, love, and allow the process to move forward. She agreed. But all we wanted was to close our eyes, fall asleep, and then wake up in about one month to find all the tough stuff over.

It helped to be able to wash her hair with a shampoo cap made just for hospital stays and then run my fingers through her cute curls, making sure there were no snarls. I also loved to help the nurses bring new warm blankets and attend to her comfort needs. Anna wanted to walk some, so we held hands, and I walked backward, and she stepped toward me like a dance across the room. After only a length or two, this waltz was tiring, but she could not stand being still in her bed for so long.

Anna left the ICU that day and went into the step-down unit. No more hidden conspiracies were lurking in the hallways. Anna's mind was clear, but she never forgot what her crazy mind manufactured. We tried to heal with laughter and hoped she would go home soon. We wanted to finally be in our protected space to find peace and our new normalcy. While we knew things were getting better, all the intricacies of being in a hospital and having tubes coming from every which way continued to interfere.

Life in a hospital is a series of events with no schedule that can be relied upon and often no sensitivity to the patient's needs. Things get done in an order that can feel chaotic and intrusive, making the hospital circus all too much to cope with after weeks in one of the main performance tents. That night, I returned to the apartment, ate three pieces of toast with butter and raspberry jam, a frozen dinner, wine, and chocolate, and concluded the world was nuts.

On day sixteen, Anna was released, and we finally went home. This did not last long, though. We committed to returning to the hospital for daily blood draws, dialysis three times per week until her kidneys healed, and clinic visits twice weekly. On the second morning home, she went back for a dialysis session, blood draws, and an X-ray due to her reports of discomfort with breathing.

An increase in fluid in her chest cavity was seen upon X-ray, so they decided to try to draw off the fluid. After dialysis, we went on to another procedure, a thoracentesis, where they tried to get the fluid to drain through a needle catheter. There was some success, but they were concerned more was needed. The conclusion was there was probably new and old blood between the new lungs and the chest wall, forming a membrane-like sheet that needed to be drawn off with a larger port.

After just two days at home, she was admitted again. Anna told me she was not scared about this; this was just one of those things that happened, and you have to take care of it. This complication occurs in CFers with a transplant. The old CF lungs adhere to the chest wall and cause a lot of abrasions. It takes a while for it to heal. So, extra bleeding can happen. Again, this amazing team of doctors was not worried and felt they could handle this.

We were back at it. Doug volunteered for night duty again. He was fantastic and enjoyed those late nights with Anna in the hospital, telling her, "We are with you and will never give up."

Since I am the early bird, it helped me to sleep and arrive around 7 a.m. to relieve him. Anna was so much more herself. It would not be long until she could spend the night without us, but for a while, it helped her to have support from one of us around the clock.

Anna's first release was just too soon. After her second admittance, she settled into a great new private room with a view, where we stayed for another two weeks. We were told it was the VIP suite, and we were happy it was ours. She had more chest tubes placed to help with her drainage and continued her dialysis. It was much more comforting to be there, even though that circus could erupt into its chaotic performances at any time. She needed this care I could never give her at home, and driving back and forth would have been too much.

As she grew stronger, she began to think about life after it all. On her twenty-third day post-transplant, she decided it was time to start her athletic training to prepare for competing in the transplant athletic games with her friends. To do this, we began to walk more briskly around the unit, increasing our "mileage." But then the training was cut short by the need for one more surgery to remove even more fluid from behind her left lung. They would also work on the chest wall to help improve lung adherence, and it was viewed as a final fix for her.

Managing her pain was challenging, and Anna had to recoup from the final surgery and pain overload. The courage, fortitude, good attitude, and general soldiering required much more than Anna imagined or expected from the transplant recovery period. Even so, her spirit was strong, and after this new trauma, she said she would just take a day off from her "athletic training." I assured her, "Every athlete takes a day off, which is an important part of the training."

The next day, we went for a walk to resume her exercise regimen. Anna walked a brisk five laps. Her nurse followed us closely, measuring her oxygen saturation. While exercising, Anna's oxygen saturations were 97, 98, and 99%! Tears were in my eyes. Before the transplant, during her "six-minute walk test," Anna walked with six liters of O2 and a saturation of 94%. This time, there was no O2, but she had the giant pink transplant mask over her mouth and nose, and she was at 99% while lugging IVs and drains! She was on her way to athletic performances, exotic adventures, and a life beyond anything we could ever dream of. We did not know it then, but more than once, our daughter would blow our minds with miracles we would not dare to imagine.

But before that, we still had to get home, so we dreamed of a Christmas miracle and got one. On December 22, a month after her transplant surgery, her body decided it no longer needed dialysis, and just like that, she was released. We had Christmas at home in our little apartment with a small green tinsel tree I found at Target and gifts for us all. That was our best Christmas ever.

A few days later, we visited Anna's old lungs to finish this intense recovery period before rehabilitation began. We went as a family to The Gross Room, as it is called at the Pathology Laboratory.

Her dried-up lungs were wheeled out to us on a small metal cart, lying on a green surgical cloth in a posture of "I'm done." They had been dissected for research, and the pieces had been reassembled for us. Wearing blue nitrile gloves, Anna picked them up and thanked them for all they did to get her to this point. It was time to say goodbye to this part of her that we all had clung to, shook, and beat on to clear its mucus. Her well-used lungs, seemingly with nothing left, kept her going until her transplant miracle could arrive.

chapter sixteen

She's Launched / Now On My Own

The truck carrying medical equipment arrived to retrieve liquid oxygen tanks that had become part of the furniture in Anna's home. No longer would the plastic tubing trace her steps from one room into another. The Vest used for her respiratory treatments was packed and in the closet. Other CF memorabilia that were no longer needed were simply dumped.

"New Life, New Lungs, New Breath" was the motto for moving forward. Anna still had other medications for her CF-related problems, including diabetes and digestive issues. She also had sleep apnea and wore a CPAP at night. But the most critical threat to her for her entire life, CF lungs, were gone. The next threat was being a transplant patient with all its issues and many drugs she had to take. Organ rejection or serious infection was to be a real threat now. Still, that was being managed by the medicines and close care she was being given. Our next three months of healing focused on protecting Anna and preparing for a future.

As Anna continued to heal, a few bumps on the road involved monitoring her medications. She started her Pulmonary Rehabilitation Program with the guidance of therapists and adherence to a routine of exercises. Her body got stronger, and her progress was helping us to begin the process of unwinding our lives from one another. My work being her mom will never be done, but this work of immediacy to save her life was now ending. We both had to figure out who we were independent of each other without CF lungs to bond us.

The transition meant more than me physically leaving the apartment and moving home. It was a huge shift in my emotional body, discovering a layer of grief barely under the surface. The new healthy ground we were on was not yet firm and had started to give way to what had happened in the past year. We had just fought to save Anna's life with singularly pointed determination and conviction. Not knowing what would come, we were willing to overturn all obstacles, including the haunting reality that under our pounding hands, Anna was dying.

Grief needed to be buried to get through, but with the beginning of our transition, it finally showed up in my tears as I recognized this was also my personal story as a mother. Working through my emotions and easy tears, I found vulnerable, tender spots. Since I can be tough on the exterior most of the time, I honored these moments. My toughness helped me get through our rough times, but it was healing to be softer and feel my grief.

Sitting on my kitchen table, waiting for me to act, was a letter of notice to vacate the apartment. It was almost twelve weeks post-transplant, and I wanted extra wiggle room of time, so I pushed that date up a bit to March 12 for our transition to launch. I was still attached to the safe house, being only a short distance from Anna, so I did not want to let go of my key or my closeness to her. Fear that another crisis could be around the corner made my hold even tighter. I had to believe Anna would continue to improve with no more obstacles, just healing, restoring us into a new spring.

Living without the everyday intensity as a lifesaver and mother hero alongside my daughter hero came with a loss of identity and purpose. I did not want the super focus on the moment we had to end. I clutched at time. The hands on my watch circled its face while those moments of strength as warriors were now changing. It was a withdrawal from adrenaline that so frequently coursed through our veins. I was now waking up to stillness and time.

Celebrating our launch from each other at PF Chang's, our favorite Chinese restaurant, was a way for us to finish loosening the knot that had held us so tightly. It was lunchtime, and after we sat in our seats, Anna reflected, "Mom, we have come full circle. Our journey started here. Remember during my transplant evaluation when we went to lunch, and you got that fortune?"

I remembered that fortune in early July that said, "You will soon witness a miracle."

"Wow, you are right, Anna. We swore we would not have another fortune cookie after that, but today, we should," I replied quickly.

After enjoying the famous lettuce wraps, hot and sour soup, and pot stickers, the check arrived on that ceremonial little black tray we knew so well. Two cellophane-wrapped fortune cookies were asking us to pick them. Anna chose hers, but I opened the other one first, and it said, "Good things come to those who wait." Perfect, I thought.

Anna's said, "You will travel to exotic places." At the time, it also seemed perfect for her. From her crippling pulmonary disability to being able to realistically dream of a tropical vacation, we felt the full circle. Miracle witnessed, miracle received, and now to be lived. Little did we know that the fortune foretold a truly exotic story of an unexpected life about to unfold with travel to far-off places and dreams never dared to come true.

On our next trip together, we sat on my mom's memorial bench in a native plant garden near her home in Woodside. Eating bakery cookies and sipping coffee, we wanted to tell Mom that Anna had made it. While I had sat on that bench since her transplant, Anna had not. Our hearts felt full, showing her Grammy the results of our challenging past year. As we sat, Anna said, "I have a feeling I will have these lungs for a very long time. They feel like they are at home inside me, and they are happy here." And she was launched!

Anna - *It was over three months since my transplant, waking up to an empty house with two kitties, one at my feet and the other attempting to snuggle my face, and I didn't have plans for the day. I was alone and tempted to find someone to hang out with, but I decided to spend time alone. I needed to get to know who I was without CF lungs.*

John was off snowboarding, and my mom had happily returned home with Dad. I sat on the couch, relaxing, drinking my coffee, and watching Million Dollar Listings *on* Bravo, *one of my guilty pleasures. There were no nebulizers, coughing, or pounding on my back, only the delicious sound of sipping my coffee and the musings of TV real estate agents. It was the beginning of my next chapter.*

I saw how I was a different person in so many ways. I was sipping coffee, for crying out loud. This early morning activity would have never happened before. I hated coffee. Did my donor love coffee? I was told after my surgery that my donor was a thirty-something woman, and this was all I knew about her. Was I learning more about her through the changes in me? Did she give me her preference so that I would never forget her? There were so many questions I wanted to answer as I moved forward in my life.

My new coffee habit started on Christmas, two days after leaving the hospital. We gave my dad an espresso maker for his present that morning. As he made the first few cups, the aroma filled the apartment. Sitting on my bed, uncomfortable and swollen, the coffee called me. In his flannel pajamas, Dad handed me a small porcelain coffee cup filled with a fresh brew, a pour of steamed milk, and a sprinkle of cinnamon. I held that cup like the greatest gift I had ever received. Precious and warm in my hand, it represented my life being saved and a celebratory toast to being alive.

I no longer had an O2 cannula in my nose and could smell the dark grind, feel the smooth steamed milk on my tongue, and taste the spice of cinnamon as it slipped down my throat. This sensual pleasure marked the beginning of a new journey in my life. I had made it through the greatest of challenges and defeated death. Strangely, that cup gave me a happiness that seemed to have hitchhiked a ride along with my new lungs. My daily cup still reminds me again and again of that moment. I will never tire of my coffee habit!

I was in such a new place that I didn't have much to report to my friends. Things were just simply good. I still had to deal with blood levels, small changes in medication doses, and wait for my scar to finish healing. I had a divot in my chest that I hoped would fill in, but never did. It reminds me of my vulnerability and power to overcome the odds.

My life changed dramatically in countless ways, including my medical identity. Some people think you are fine if you remove the diseased lungs, and life goes on. "Well, not exactly," I have to say. We transplant patients have so much to do, worry about, and take numerous medications, but it is so worth it! My life now has possibilities that were beyond my imagination.

At the beginning of my new freedom, I didn't know what to do with myself. I had lots of ideas. I wanted to help people, find a way to make money and live an exciting life. The ideas ranged from working with girls with eating disorders, getting into real estate, starting my signature program, making food for transplant families, or simply being a homemaker. I could see all of these possibilities and wanted to start moving in a direction. I never liked being stagnant without goals and reasons for moving forward. Even with my medical disabilities, I had proven myself by graduating from Santa Clara with two degrees and what I had just done, a successful lung transplant! I did not want to waste this chance to live fully. I knew it would take time for things to come to fruition, but I was impatient.

This chapter in my life was going to be about "playing

hard," but it had been so long since I felt well that I didn't know how to initiate adventures. I had a mental block because I had always lived an unpredictable life and couldn't plan. I wanted to get off the couch and be adventurous. It was up to me to open the doors, create opportunities, use my imagination to live the life I was destined to live and fulfill my fortune cookie fortune by visiting exotic places.

I had to maintain my fitness, to get stronger and stronger all by myself. I had already watched other friends with CF do this by attending The Transplant Games of America. The games were competitive athletic events designed to offer transplant patients all levels of competition. I was unsure of how fit I could become, and I wondered if I could ever be a successful swimmer again. I had not been a big exerciser since my miracle days of swimming championships. So, the first step forward was to get fit and become stronger with the games as my goal. I would gather all the strength, confidence, and will I could muster and get my ass to the gym—no more couch potato.

chapter seventeen

Grateful

At this post-transplant time, with all of the deep breaths and tears of relief, our family felt the most significant emotion: gratitude. We were a part of a miracle. We witnessed our loved one's life being saved, watching Anna muster her strength to make it through successfully. Our hearts were full, and every day began with "Thank you!"

It became important for Anna to thank those whose most crucial decision made the miracle possible: the donor family. Organ recipients like Anna are offered the opportunity to write to their donor's family, thanking them for their gift of life. The donor family is also allowed to write to the recipient. Their identities are anonymous and unknown to each other. The letters are passed by the social workers who safeguard the identities and contents of the letters. If a recipient sends a letter, it is up to the donor family to decide if they want to respond. There are no expectations. For whatever reasons, some respond in kind, and others do not.

Some donor families become active in Donate Life organizations, raising awareness of the need for more organ donors. There are thousands of people at any one time waiting on the transplant lists for organs to be offered, and not all who need organs receive them in time to spare their lives. For many donor families, being involved with the transplant community gives them a connection to the lost loved one and the understanding that they made a significant difference in the lives of others. It is healing and hopeful for them. Other donor families wish to stay silent in their grief.

This is an act that most transplant recipients consider, but not all follow through with letters. Anna needed to express her gratitude and took the opportunity to write to her donor family twice. They never responded, but she was grateful to have shared how their gift saved her life. She felt it was essential to let them know that she would never forget her donor, always honoring her with all she did. Here is her first letter.

Anna - *Dear Donor Family,*

My life changed nine months ago when I received a double lung transplant at Stanford Hospital. I received "the call" that they had lungs for me on November 21, 2010. The transplant took place on November 22. I had spent 119 days on the transplant list. I was not told much about my donor except that she is a female. I am so grateful for this gift of life that I wanted to contact you to let you know how much this selfless gift has changed my life.

Today, I woke up early and put on my running shoes. I ventured to the park where I have walked to maintain my health with cystic fibrosis (CF). Today was different. Today, I was able to RUN. Ever since my transplant, I have been working on getting stronger and increasing my endurance and strength. Today was a miraculous day. I ran an entire mile without stopping. I have never in my life done this. When I had my CF lungs, even when I was fairly healthy as a child, I could not run more than a few feet without having to stop and cough so hard I would turn purple. It was so uncomfortable for me that I ended up really disliking exercise, ESPECIALLY running.

It was just so hard for me that I ended up avoiding it. Growing up in school, we had to "run the mile" for P.E. class. Well, I always was allowed to do an adapted version because of my CF, and I just walked. This was literally the first time I have ever run a mile in my thirty years!!! When I came around the park to the bleachers where I started my mile, I took a deep breath, felt the energy, love, and generosity of my sweet donor, and I just began to cry. The gift that your family has given me is something that is indescribable.

I have been able to do the simple things in life with ease that were so difficult before my transplant, but today I was overcome by the magnitude of how different my life is now, and I just had to let you know how thankful I am. I feel that it is so important for me to take care of this precious gift you have given me. I take very good care of my body and make sure to follow the doctors' protocol, take my anti-rejection meds religiously, eat well, and also try to enjoy myself. I don't want to miss out on any moment of this borrowed time. I have immense gratitude to your family and my donor.

I have always been very involved in the CF community and have helped to organize a weeklong retreat every year. One evening of the week, we have a memorial service for those we have lost from cystic fibrosis and who were involved in the community. This year when I attended the memorial, I made a special card for my donor and lit a candle in her honor. I had your family in my heart that day (and every day), but I brought you with me and shared my gratitude that because of you, I was able to return this year after being so sick the year before. It is because of you that my family, my parents, my sister, my boyfriend, and my friends still have me in their lives. I am so sorry for your loss, and I can't imagine the pain that you must be going through as you are trying to put the pieces back together. I think about it often, and with each new experience, I remember that you are having new experiences without your loved one.

Please know that I never have taken this gift for granted. I think about your family all the time, and with each day, I send thoughts and prayers to you that you will find peace. This is difficult to reconcile, but I want to live vibrantly in order for your daughter, sister, aunt, friend, or mother to live on in me.

My life and experiences have changed so drastically that everything I do feels new and exciting. It truly is like being reborn. Every time I try something, I "talk" to my lungs, and

I feel like I am sharing each of these experiences with her. One really strange thing that has happened to me since the transplant is that I never feel alone. I used to spend a lot of time feeling lonely before the transplant. Now, I feel like I always have a friend with me, encouraging me, supporting me, whispering YOU CAN DO IT in my ear. When I breathe, I breathe for both of us. I truly feel she is with me all the time. I am living for her; she lives on through me.

I plan to have an extraordinary life in this second chapter, thanks to my sweet donor. I plan to bring her with me wherever I go, and will take her to places that I have never seen, do things I have never done, and spread my wings in a way I was never able to before. I dedicate my life to her memory and hope that it brings you peace to know what a wonderful gift you gave to a young woman who didn't have a chance to explore this life without the help of your loved one.

With immense gratitude,

Anna

For a number of months after our transplant marathon, I realized that this path of mothering put me through my paces on an uphill climb. Gradually, I started to find my feet again as my grief poured out and the healing grace of gratitude comforted me. I needed silence and being alone, but for Anna, her new life was just beginning.

Anna *- My life was changing very quickly. I was more me than I ever thought I could be. I could not sit still, and there was not enough time for sitting anymore. My life was about sitting still for my treatments and sitting because I was too tired. But no more. Other changes were also brewing inside of me. I had no idea how significant my personal growth would be or what form it would take, but I knew I needed to break through all that had been holding me back.*

Finally, the day that I had been waiting for arrived. It was one of those momentous breakthrough moments. I had set a goal for myself long before the transplant happened to prove to myself that my transplant was the miracle of my dreams. It was a simple task to be done but so profound for me. I went for a real swim and was joined by my wonderful friend Isa, a fellow CFer and transplant recipient. I was so thankful she could join me as I described how each stroke felt and how amazing it was to be in the water again.

I got in the clear blue pool water for the first time, and it was warm! I was so thankful. My first underwater breath was surreal and so easy. I was amazed how my body remembered how to be in the water. I had not tried swimming laps for years and had not been in a pool for about two years since I was on oxygen. This was a long-awaited moment. I had been talking about it with Steve, my rehab transplant buddy, throughout our program. We fantasized about swimming on the same relay team in the transplant games, so there was a lot of buildup to this moment.

I tried all the strokes. Freestyle was as easy as I could remember. Breaststroke, I still sucked at. Backstroke was relaxing, and the stroke I loved the most, the butterfly, I remembered how. The incredible thing was that I used to count breaths between strokes and could only go for three strokes in freestyle. On this first trial, I noticed I was continuing past 3, 4, 5, 6, 7. Then I had to tell myself, "You gotta remember, you need more air!" I just had so much in my lungs!

When I tried the butterfly, I wasn't trying to desperately take a breath every stroke. My swimming strategy changed as I developed my strokes with my new breath. I felt liberated and invigorated by the swim. It was great to swim hard, be out of breath, and take big, deep breaths in my new lungs. When I was up around thirty laps, I knew I needed to stop swimming as I didn't want to hurt myself by doing too much too fast. It was incredible to feel that I needed to stop myself instead of being so exhausted that I had to drag myself out of the pool. It was a *momentous day shared and witnessed with such a close friend, and it helped to develop my confidence and courage to move to the next level of swim training.*

At this point, I had my seven-month post-transplant clinic visit. My strength and improvement were obvious and showed up as a PFT of 94% FEV1. I could not remember when I had lungs with that vital capacity since I was a very young child. All I could think of was, "Holy crap!" It was nothing less than awesome. My swimming ability improved weekly, and I attended the transplant boot camp at the Stanford track and started yoga. I also was ice skating, fishing, boating, hiking, biking, couponing, and cooking. My involvement also included becoming a board member for the Richie's Spirit Foundation and planning the CFRI teen and adult retreat. I was so active and doing everything I wanted to do. Was this a life of normal? It was so full, and I was thrilled. I felt like I was making up for so much lost time.

My next milestone was to turn thirty years old. I was never directly told that I was to only live to a nonspecific age below thirty. Still, having CF and having friends with CF, I have always known I would not become an old lady. I always dreamed of thirty, but I was never sure I would get there. This birthday would have been very different if I had not received my beautiful lungs. I tried to find the words to express my feelings about this birthday. Still, instead, only tears welled up in my eyes with goosebumps on my arms when thinking about what was and what would become of my life.

When I look back on the past year, the only way to describe many of my experiences is a year from hell. However, there were so many perfect moments within the struggles. For one, I met the Dalai Lama, and I am speechless about how profoundly important this was for me. Other memories included everyone's support and caring. The loyalty and dedication of so many was unwavering. The time I spent with my family, their care, and support, especially in the hospital with my dad, was worth every pain

I endured. The caring visits from my doctors, the whole transplant team, and their excitement when I got my Christmas miracle to go home. The loving calls and check-ins from the doctors and medical staff who had seen me since I was a child, through my adolescence, and into the end of my life with CF lungs. My most wonderful surgeon, whose kindness and smile lifted me each day he visited. I was so fortunate to have the exceptional nurses who helped me through. My fabulous dietician was such a sweet friend and so supportive. I can't forget the most amazing respiratory therapist, who cheered me on like no one else. And I will never forget the most wonderful doctor who called me a peach. There was so much love given to me during my greatest struggle.

What is so bizarre is that these things are what I remember most about the entire experience. I remember the love, compassion, and strength everyone gave me. I remember my banana bunch poster with all the kind faces and everyone who came to visit with their shirts. My CF friends, who have helped me through my entire journey with CF, and all my transplant friends, who, just by walking in the door, gave me hope that my life would turn out alright. My healthy friends had to endure seeing me in such a state, but did so anyway because they love me. It truly is love that lifts us.

All of this has inspired me to want to give and give to others. I want to help them and provide them with hope that they can get through rough times. This core belief in me is why I studied psychology. It is why I pursued my graduate degree. But it isn't education that allows us to provide hope and love and help others be strong. That simply comes from the heart. Through my education, I learned a lot about human existence, how the mind works, and how messed up we as humans can get. Still, there is something innate that my education didn't teach me. The biggest life lesson is that to give love is to receive love. I want to share all that was given to me.

In the next decade of my life, my purpose is to love. To love me, to love my partner, to love my family, to love my pets, to love my donor, to love my friends, to love my caretakers, to love my community, to love strangers, to love life. I hope that by doing this, I will enable others to reach their potential. The most powerful medicine is love.

I couldn't be happier at thirty. I feel like I have the world at my fingertips. I just hope the world is ready for me! And I hope that I am ready for the world!

PART THREE

Living the Gift

a story of love

"You are not your circumstances. You are your possibilities. If you know that, you can do anything."

Oprah Winfrey, *O Magazine*, January 2007

chapter eighteen

A Movie Star with Gold Medals

A door into a much larger world than Anna ever imagined opened in the summer of 2011 with the premier of the documentary film *The Power of Two*. She and John arrived at the theater in Los Angeles to all its pomp and circumstance, including well-known movie stars. It was only eight months since her transplant, and her journey as a transplant recipient was to be witnessed on the screen, opening hearts and making her a movie star.

The opportunity for this unlikely experience began in fall 2009 when our friends, Ana Stenzel and Isa Stenzel Byrnes, began filming *The Power of Two*, a documentary movie companion to their book. The book was a memoir of their lives being identical twins with cystic fibrosis and receiving lung transplants. The film was loosely based on the book, being more concerned about the current lives of Ana and Isa as advocates for organ donation. Because they were half Japanese, the movie was partially filmed in Japan, highlighting Japanese cultural concerns and controversies regarding organ transplantation.

At the start of the filming, I was invited to travel with the twins and the film crew to Tokyo. It was then that I was given the fateful fortune as I threw sticks in a sacred temple that foretold, "Your request will be granted. The patient gets well soon."

As part of the trip, I attended a musical fundraiser for cystic fibrosis on a university campus in Sendai. On stage with Ana, Isa, and other Japanese CF family members, I unfurled and presented a string of brightly colored, hand-decorated flags. I had the honor to be a CFRI ambassador. The healing/peace/prayer flags were made under my direction by members of our CFRI community as an offering of friendship to CF families in Japan. It was an unusual opportunity to connect to this group. CF is rare in Asian populations, and because of this, these families are isolated. This was a way for all of us to feel part of our worldwide community and a great honor for me.

It was months after I returned to the U.S. that Anna's health worsened, and she was listed for her transplant. At that same time, a story of hope and courage was being captured by *The Power of Two* film crew, and Anna's real-life experience was included. The film director asked Anna if she would be in the evolving story as the face of someone waiting for a lung transplant. Anna never wanted to be depicted as a sick person, but when asked if she would share this intimate time of her life, she knew she should, telling me, "I want to help others and make something good from this terrible state I am in. I am going to say yes and will let my guard down."

As if part of the script for the movie, Anna got her call for new lungs on the very day of the final wrap of filming. Nothing past that day could be included in the film. It was another one of those serendipitous miracles that made us feel our experience was orchestrated in some magical way. Because her surgery came precisely that day, the film ended with the message, "After 119 days of waiting, Anna Modlin received her lungs." It was a miracle on top of a miracle that felt surreal and the best way to end a film about the wonder of organ transplantation. And miraculously for our family, our Anna's journey was to be shared in theaters around the country.

Anna - I was still so vulnerable and in recovery. My face was swollen from prednisone, a common side effect for all transplant patients but annoying. I was in a movie star culture, and it was just little old me. The film began with images from Ana and Isa's visit to the transplant games in Japan. The film was fantastic and received a warm and loud response from the audience. I was invited to go on stage with Ana, Isa, Andrew, and Marc, the director. I guess I was a movie star? What a surreal experience for me—to have just been through the most challenging experience of my life as the sickest I had ever been, and to see it on the screen with the note I was successful in getting my miracle, and then to be applauded and loved and cared for by all of these strangers in the land of movies. Too much! Incredible! And, holy crap!

The grace of this experience continued for several months. The Northern California premiere was in San Francisco at the Castro Theater. It was there that I knew many people in the audience. So many people from our community came to see the film and support us. Again, we went on stage to the loving applause of a mix of strangers and, this time, caring friends. The support was beyond measure and all like a dream. I was invited to other openings across the U.S., traveling to San Diego, New Mexico, Florida, and Atlanta, Georgia. I also was able to be with an audience of medical students in the north Bay Area who learned from the film about transplantation's effects. I did this for a few years and loved this part of sharing the film the most.

Ana and Isa traveled to many more openings than I did. Still, when I was with them, it was filled with excitement and helped me develop my confidence and courage to be a part of the world and a face for organ donation and transplantation. When we got on stage after the film, we sat in a panel to answer questions and share even more about our experiences.

I was often asked, "So now, are you going to have a baby?" What? I could not understand why I was repeatedly asked this. I had never seen myself as a mother of a child because I never thought I would live long enough to be one. Also, being pregnant can be rough on the body, and I had to reserve all the good health and energy I had to simply survive. I asked my mom about these questions, and she thought it was a natural question to ask and told me, "To those people, having a child is a part of having a normal and healthy life that no one should miss out on. They do not understand your situation, but it seems like an obvious question for the general public." I got the explanation, but it stumped me at the same time.

The film continued to be shown nationwide at film festivals, winning various documentary film awards. I loved being included in introducing the film to the public and was invited to a few openings, including one in Santa Fe, where Anna and I traveled together. We stayed in a beautiful southwestern-style adobe home with Ana, Isa, and their mom, Hatsuko.

It was such a fun getaway with no sounds of cystic fibrosis anywhere to be heard. Our daughters were freed from the CPT, air compressors, and other reminders of their past breathlessness by their transplant miracles. We ate downtown in restaurants, walked through the art galleries, and viewed the street vendors' Indian wares. We were doing something together that a mom and a thirty-year-old daughter should be able to do. It was amazing.

Our trip to Santa Fe included visiting El Santuerro de Chimayo, considered the Lourdes of North America. Its dirt is thought to be sacred, and it is one of the most visited healing sanctuaries in America. It has been so as far back as before the missionaries when only the Pueblo peoples lived in the area. Ana Stenzel suggested we visit, which was an experience that all three—Isa, Ana, and Anna—wanted.

Hatsuko and I were in this extraordinary place with our daughters, who already had received miracles and were glad to receive more if the land's energy and the spirits' wishes made that so. Ana was not feeling well at the time, and making this healing pilgrimage was most important to her. We entered the inner sanctuary with reverence and could feel the prayers of the thousands of people who had visited the site. Moments such as these were precious to both Hatsuko and me.

The film continued to be shown the next year and was used as a teaching tool in medical schools. Even though Anna loved participating, time was precious. Her focus changed to prepare for The Transplant Games of America. They were to be held late in July 2012 in Grand Rapids, Michigan. Unfortunately, her training was interrupted when she was struck with two bowel obstructions in two weeks. She went to the ER for one, returned home three and a half days later, and quickly ended up in the hospital for another week.

Finally, her training, which was on a bowel obstruction hiatus, began in earnest. Preparing and rebuilding muscles after such medical challenges was very tough. After the first week of training, she returned to the hospital disappointed with yet a third bowel blockage. CF was still wreaking havoc in her gut.

Anna was upset, to say the least, and demanded that the transplant team get the GI team on board and try to figure out what was wrong. After starting a new drug, Amitiza, she stayed out of the hospital for another two weeks with no signs of discomfort. Other than that, her lungs felt fantastic, and she was determined Michigan would happen.

Anna - The events I entered in Michigan were the fifty-yard backstroke, freestyle, and butterfly, along with the 100-yard freestyle and medley relay to swim with Ana and Isa. I practiced my butterfly for most of my training.

During this time, I returned to my old neighborhood pool, where my record was posted from when I was six years old. I was faster at six years old than I was then! I swam the twenty-five-yard butterfly twenty-four years previous in 21.56 seconds. I thought it would be motivational to see, but it turned out to depress me. I rallied and focused on what I could do, because I only had about six weeks more to train. I focused on what I had, not what I did not.

It is hard to gain the muscle needed that quickly, so I did what I could by swimming every day, looking up some good workouts, calling up my old coaching skills, doing drills, kick-boarding, and swimming different intervals to help me gain speed and muscle. My competitive spirit was intact and engaged. I was going to do my best and prayed I would stay out of the hospital.

Being part of the games for the first time, I was introduced to my new community of incredible people who were like me in such a significant way. Most of them had an existential struggle to save their lives, threatened with falling off the edge, whether needing a new heart, kidney, liver, or lungs. There were others, too, whose suffering was ended through tissue donations like cornea and bone marrow transplants. We all depended on the generous gesture of donors to gift us an organ or tissue.

The games were a celebration of our lives. We came from a place near death and suffering to new lives filled with hope and promise. By coming together at this semi-annual grand national party, the gathering of thousands was an expression of joy, love, gratitude, and the profound spirit of living. My mom came with me for the experience and to be my cheerleader. We were part of the NorCal team of transplant recipients, family members, and donor families.

The games began at a large stadium with a parade of transplant athletes from each state of the United States. The U.S. is one of many countries that organizes games such as these. There are other games throughout the world too. Every other year, one of the countries hosts a World Games where participants represent their countries in a grand event of united nations celebrating joy and cooperation. It is a phenomenal healing event that is, unfortunately, little known to most people.

These events show why the medical world offers transplants to save the lives of worthy and fortunate souls. Anna and I wished everyone who had already been lost and those on the list waiting for their lifesaving gift could be there. You feel the joy and relief of the fellow recipients who worked hard for their friendly competitions, to feel alive, to express their profound gratitude, and to make the world better. They were heroes with the greatest of spirits. We had never been to such a joyous party with so many honored guests.

After the opening ceremony, the games began. They were organized by different sports and athletic venues. There was a competition at differing levels so anyone could participate. At the national games, no one was denied a way to play. Some of the athletes were more serious competitors than others. Still, everyone wanted to show their stuff, and everyone wanted to cheer for their fellow teammates and, beyond state boundaries, cheer for everyone present at the joy fest.

Anna - I was ready to dive into my competition. I deserved to be there. I'd had my struggles with my bowel blockages and training, but I was ready, very ready. I remembered the sweet taste of victory when I was just a child and won my swimming races. I wanted to feel that again. I did not know if I would. I was curious to know who would be challenging me at these games. I was a new lung recipient. This was a position of vulnerability. We competed against all other recipients: lung, heart, liver, kidney, or tissue. We were all on the same playing field. I was representing my team from northern California and swimming against some team members. The excitement was high. We all just wanted to do our best and stood in the stands, cheering on our teammates.

It was my moment. I had my own story and relationship with the pool. Only my mom and I knew what this meant and how it would affect my life story. I was a champion kid swimmer. I loved the pool, but my disease took that away very early on. At the time, I lost my nerve and knew I would never have a chance again to succeed like I had. But I was wrong. I was here preparing to climb on the diving blocks, waiting for the starting gun. My toes were at the edge of the block, my body aligned with my dive, and I knew exactly what to do.

With the starting gun, I flew through the air and into that clear blue pool. My attention was on the technique my body knew so well. I could breathe. I could breathe. I could breathe as I lifted my arms in rhythmic strokes. Fifty yards to swim. At the end of the first twenty-five yards was a flip turn, and I rose up, my arms pushing the water away and behind me. I touched the side. I made it, and not only that, I won. I won. I won.

In the stands, I was out of my mind with excitement. As Anna swam, I yelled at the top of my lungs, "Go, Anna, go, go, Anna, go, go, Anna, go!" just as we did when she was a small child on the Greenmeadow swim team. It was as if we were in a time warp. That moment in time healed so much that it went backward, forward, and around again in our hearts. When her race was over, and she won, I plopped down on the bench and wept tears of happiness, pride, sadness over lost time, and incredulity. After Anna hugged her teammates, she climbed into the stands, reaching out to me. It just took our breath away, as they say! She swept the field and won five gold medals. Little Anna was reawakened.

At those first games, we also met donor families with harrowing stories who showed us their grief, the pain of their losses, and their love and gratitude for their children to have a legacy of such profound generosity. They saw the lives of the ones they loved in the recipients. It sustained them and gave meaning to their losses. The donor families were in high honor at the games, and they were also allowed to participate in a few of the competitions.

Among the donor families, we met a woman in her fifties with dark hair, a medium build, and a warm and loving smile. She lost her son in an accident, and his organs were donated. She and her younger daughter were at the games with a heart transplant recipient. Together, they competed in ballroom dancing. Her partner was a tall, slim, dark-haired, handsome man about thirty-five years old and the recipient of this donor mom's son's heart. They found each other after the transplant and became very close. It was like out of a storybook as they embraced each other and danced the waltz across the floor. This donor mom was dancing with her son's heart beating inside of her partner. Miracles like this were part of the overall magic.

When the games are done, the athletes gather for a closing ceremony. It is an eventful and emotional week of competition, fun, friendship-making, and self-reflection. The state team that won the most competitive points is acknowledged and has the privilege of caring for a high-point trophy until the next games. Certain athletes are chosen to be the athletes of the year. They are selected for their competitive success, participation in various events, and cooperative spirit.

The final ceremony also inspires everyone to return to other games, whether in the United States or the World Games in another country. The state chosen as the next host is announced, and an invitation to the World Games for the following year's competition is made.

Sitting in seats surrounded by our NorCal teammates in a grand auditorium, Anna had five precious gold medals hung with ribbons around her neck. Clearly, this was a new home for her and where her star would shine. We were all hovering above our seats with the magical lift of love, courage, and miracles we had just been a part of. The stage lit up to show an invitation for the next World Games in Durban, South Africa.

On the film screen were dramatic images skimming the top of ocean waters toward a mountain peak, flying over canyons with rivers and waterfalls, lions in the bush, ancient tribal rock paintings, warriors dancing and drumming, ocean waves and surfers, and a cosmopolitan city.

A deep male African voice with an accent from a far-off

land called to the audience. "Take a journey to the place that gave birth to all humankind where the sky is so vast, even a thousand hills are not too many. A place of such beauty even God has a wind on it…"

And then, at a pause of this hypnotic description, we were called and inspired by African women's voices singing and trilling to beating drums before the male voice began again to say,

"This is KwaZulu-Natal, home of the Zulu kingdom."

Another melodic African woman's voice led to a young woman on the screen representing the South African transplant team who invited us by saying, "I received my second birth in January 2008, when I received a double lung transplant. I participated in the World Transplant Games 2009 in Australia. We're very excited to be in Sweden now, and we can't wait to have you all in Durban in 2013."

Looking over at Anna, I could see she was stunned, moved, shaken, and probably hypnotized by the invitation to the World Games. An internal earthquake had just awakened another part of her. She told me that she knew the young woman from South Africa was like her, and it was CF that caused her to have a lung transplant. You could hear it in her telltale CF-sounding voice, characteristic of others with CF. Anna and this other young woman even looked alike. She knew she had to get to know her. She had to go to those games. I saw her heart leaping from her chest when she called out, "Yes, please!"

chapter nineteen

A Renewed Life and Africa!

Anna was fully immersed in her new life and getting stronger. For me, the identity of being a mother actively involved with her daughter's healthcare for thirty years was still hard to shake. I knew deep in my bones how to rise to Anna's emergencies, but I was still unsure about who I was without those occasional jolts of adrenaline. It was time for me to move forward. I wanted to begin something new but had to let the process work out inside me. I had always pursued my personal interests as best I could and wore many hats, but now, I found that I was not inspired in my creative life. Taking walks on vineyard trails filled my days with many inward inquiries.

I was a mosaic artist with a wonderful garage art studio at our vineyard home. Even though it had been over a year since we were launched by the transplant, my problem was I did not know what to do, create, make, or envision. Every day, I went into my studio and simply sat for a time. I could not get any inspiration for months, even when placing materials in front of me. My creative mind was exhausted and just needed to rest.

In the first few months during this period, I also did a lot of crying. It seemed so strange that I had so much sadness after all we had been through and then becoming victorious. Why wasn't I just ecstatically happy? I could cry so easily. Finally, after a longer time than I expected, a cloud lifted; I came to terms with the loss of identity I was grieving and began to relax into a new me. The new me was still the same woman, but now I was me with some of that grief of the years before emptied out. The stored-up sadness and concerns that could not be expressed for many years caused me to be the strong one, the mother rock always there. I was now softening. This was good.

I could now make plans as the demands on my schedule were so much less. Anna became so independent that I could do many things I never could without worrying that dates would have to be canceled because she was in crisis and I had to run to her side. There was more time and less worry in my life.

After these many months, I had a breakthrough into my new, untethered, creative life in our favorite place in the country, Murphys, where we lived part-time. Walking up to my friend Sue's house with tile nippers, mastic spreading knives, and dishes to break into mosaic pieces, I was wanting to begin anew. She offered me the opportunity to begin my mosaics again in the company of friends. Working on a homemade backyard pizza oven with a red spiral and chili topknot design opened a new personal era and path for my artwork. I loved the community feel of creating outdoor mosaics with my dear friends, Sue and Peggy.

During this healing time I also sought an outlet for my interest in helping others with their grief and discovered SoulCollage®. This healing art process uses intuition to select vibrant images from magazines and one's imagination to create a meaningful visual collage. Called the SoulCollage® three Is: images, intuition, and imagination, this combination is magical. With an intention to understand one's personal life, this artful process can generate many "ah-ha" moments. Learning about this simple process using just scissors and glue with an internal focus seemed brilliant and was perfect for me. When I first tried exploring my new identity with this newly discovered technique, I found a lot of personal healing.

One of my first collaged cards depicted the troubling emotional dichotomy I had as the caregiver of my mother wanting to die and my daughter wanting to live. The collaged images clearly showed how I was split in two, with a candle that ushered in light and then, just as purposefully, a light to be blown out. A colored sky could be either a sunrise or a sunset. Seeing what that looked like revealed a greater understanding of why I had so much grief to release. I was, as they say, hooked on the magic of this process. I became a certified facilitator and had a powerful tool to offer others in many settings, including hospice with bereaved clients and CF adults at their annual retreats.

My creative life took off. We built a new studio for me nestled in the pine and oaks of the Sierra foothills. My first project was organizing and constructing a mosaiced wall to reflect on the losses and hope of a community hit by wildfire. The Butte Fire consumed 500 homes very near our country house. The mosaic shrine, called "Pieces," included items from the burned-out homes of the survivors. In my studio, my mosaic partner, Anne Cook, and I lovingly washed each item as sacred objects from someone's life. *Pieces* became a memorial shrine for the community and for us as artists to grieve our own losses. Our hearts grew as we placed the sacred items on the wall, and survivors came to tell us their harrowing stories.

I was making a mark as an artist with mosaics and the power of art and creativity for healing a community along with SoulCollage® for individuals. I was living the life I had always dreamt of that had been out of reach due to being an active caregiver for my daughter. My life was filled with gratitude, fulfillment, and spiritual grace, and it was a big difference from the constant caregiving when Anna was so ill. The miracle of transplant had liberated me, too, with its powerful transformation of healing and hope.

Time was moving on, Doug was settled at his job, which

offered him new ways to use his creativity, management style, and abilities. Sara was in medical school near where we lived. She was on her way to becoming an osteopathic physician. Anna was alive and full of dreams to fulfill. Nothing could be better.

Even so, Doug and I knew every day, every week, every month of Anna's life was a gift and bonus. The stability we experienced was temporary as all of life was. Only 50% of lung transplant patients lived more than five years with their transplants. We saw other recipients we knew in our community not survive, but Anna was thriving. It was thrilling, and we knew Anna was determined to do everything she could to take care of herself and extend her life past any expectations. That was her way. She also made goals for her life that not long before were unrealistic and now were amazingly possible. Her life became the reason transplant is called a miracle. Her active involvement in the transplant games made the miracle all the more incredible.

My life was busy in these exciting and new ways, yet I stayed involved with Anna, loving our new times together and attending the transplant games. Going to these events with my miracle daughter was a joy and inspiration. Meeting others whose lives were saved, along with their families and donor families, was an honor. The games gave Anna extraordinary encouragement to reach beyond any perceived limitations she might have had. As a parent, it was thrilling to watch. She would not let anything stop her from living to the fullest as she prepared to attend her next challenge, the World Transplant Games in Durban, South Africa.

Anna - Just after I was listed for my new lungs, I attended the adult CF retreat while tethered by oxygen tubing with the hiss and blow of the compressor, creating oxygen to sustain me. The entire retreat gang gathered near my room to allow me to attend the daily group rap session more easily. We sat under the syca-more tree outside my door, its roots and grass cover creating a rough pillow under us.

The group facilitator asked us if we could go ANYWHERE, where would it be? Many people answered with places like Greece, Italy, and Europe. When it came my turn, my breathy, weak voice said, "Africa."

Everyone looked at me, quite stunned. How would I ever get to Africa? Looking at me with oxygen, needing constant treat-ments, and with the hope of a transplant, it would be too dan-gerous to fly that far. But little did everyone know that I made my intention that day, and it became a reality only three years later!

Without fear and with the promise of fulfilling her dream, Anna was headed for South Africa, but it took a while for Doug and me to decide to attend. What it came down to was how could we not? Our miracle daughter was competing on a world stage in swimming. Our little six-year-old champion swimmer who flew across the pool to win with her com-petitive spirit was at it again in her new adult life and now in Africa. We had to go. Doug found a research connection between the lab where he worked and a university in Durban to make this a working trip, vacation, and parent support trip.

We flew to South Africa via Dubai for an evening in a very exotic place before arriving at our final destination. Staying for the night in Dubai included evening walks in this modern city with tall avant-garde architecture built out to the shore-line. The Persian Gulf was extremely warm to the touch of my bare feet. The lapping water was clear, and the sand was white, but the air and ocean water heat strangely foreign. I was not a traveling adventurer. I was really a homebody, so this trip would never have happened without Anna's inspiration. She was taking us places and to experiences we would never have had without her.

After we arrived in Durban and before the games began, Doug and I went on a guided safari to see wild African animals at a nearby reserve. Not far off the road, standing tall in full color with its exotic beauty, there was an animal I had only seen in a zoo. As we drove with our guide into the park and turned a bend, a magnificent giraffe took my breath away. It was stunning, and my response was to tear up and cry. I could not believe I was in Africa. My good fortune was overwhelming me with gratitude. This was such delicious icing on the cake of Anna's miracle. Our trip took us down dirt roads throughout the park to see many groupings of these long-necked beauties. We watched as they ate from the tallest limbs of the trees.

Our skilled guide stopped the jeep while we looked for lions, telling us to stay still and quiet. Through his binoculars, we could see a pride of lions lounging on rocks, with one hanging sideways on a horizontal tree branch. We would not have seen what was camouflaged in the distance without the guide.

A few times during the second day we watched as a herd of elephants hiked along trails in the distance. Then at another point, we had to stop in the dirt road as not far ahead we saw the enormous backside of an elephant strolling along. They do not move quickly but are dangerous in size and visitors are warned not to startle them or come too close. If you do, they have the power to step on and crush your car.

Hunting for hours to find the elusive and endangered white rhino, we came upon one standing in an open field with its magnificent horn. Everywhere there were herds of antelope, zebras, and other hoofed animals constantly in danger of becoming someone's meal. When it was time for our meal, we barbequed outside our safari hut. As we ate our dinner, we watched hyenas arrive to find scraps and lick the grill. It was all thrilling.

Realizing this was an experience to see these wild animals

that no one should miss, I was taken to a place inside my soul, connecting me to a feeling of wonder. Our three days on safari were eye-opening for both of us. From our safari in the bush, we returned to the city of Durban to be welcomed with a banner strung across the entrance road announcing the World Transplant Games. It was a not-so-subtle reminder that we were there because of our transplant miracle. Anna and John arrived for the games a few days after us. Before they arrived, we continued our sightseeing trip, visiting areas around the city including a township where many poor South Africans live.

After arriving at the venue for the games, we stayed among the participants from around the world at a hotel on the east African coastline in Durban. Our hotel window looked out upon a blue sea and white sand beachfront with a long boardwalk to explore restaurants and shops on the other side of the world that we knew. In the cafeteria, we heard the voices of many languages and friendly people.

The opening ceremony was rich in color and vibrant in spirit. A parade of participants marched into a convention center carrying the flags of their countries in every color combination. These were people from all areas of the earth whose lives were saved by organ donation and transplantation and their families. Inside the athletes with those smiling faces of many colors were new hearts, kidneys, livers, lungs, corneas, and more!

Before this, I only thought of the miracle of organ transplantation being available in large, economically prosperous countries, but there were participants representing many little countries we had never heard of. They all were beaming, excited to be alive, and part of the event to show that transplant is a spectacular miracle and worthwhile intervention to save lives. These were ambassadors of goodwill. For those of us attending the event, we were offered a warm connection between peoples of the earth.

Anna *- Attending the transplant games in South Africa was an absolute dream destination and a dream of a competition. I was going to see what I could do on the world stage. I trained hard. I fundraised hard and organized a once-in-a-lifetime trip because this was my one shot to go to South Africa. I told everyone who knew me I was on the road to this fantastic competition and journey to South Africa, my first international trip since my transplant.*

I was introduced to a woman named Alice through a mutual friend on Facebook. She lived in South Africa, and it turned out she was the face on the screen I saw back at the closing ceremonies when I learned of this fantastic adventure. We became quick friends. Our lives were so similar in so many ways. We looked alike, our partners looked alike, we had three cats, CF and lung transplants, and a younger sister. The list went on and on and on. It was official: she was my South African doppelganger. Our friendship bond happened quickly and grew strong. It was so exciting to meet each other in person at the games.

Doug and I were also able to meet Alice and her husband. The parallels in the lives of the two young women were uncanny. The doppelganger miracle became part of the magic of traveling so far yet feeling connected. Alice and Anna were both competing but in different sports. They could only get together between competitions, but their attraction to each other was powerful and promised a long, deep friendship.

Anna's swimming competition was in a large pavilion. The air in the pool area was filled with the familiar smell of chlorine and the anticipation of the athletes. The women's team from the U.S. found each other at warm-ups, supporting each other with good luck wishes. I had met some of them at the games in Michigan, and it was fun to witness them again now all on the same team against some stiff competition.

Anna was excited and nervous. She could see the qualifying times of her competitors, and there was a woman from

England who would be formidable. Doug and I sat in the stands, cheering on the Americans in an athletic competition like no other. Our Anna was a star. We had gone from bedside supporters rooting for her to be able to breathe to supporters in the stands cheering her on to win. It was a remarkable transformation, and our hearts were exploding. I know we were not the only ones having this experience. You could see it on all the faces in the stands and hear it in the shouts of encouragement. This was an unusual group of people with a common bond: miracles. The ones they loved were alive.

Anna won two golds, one silver, and joining in on the four-women relay with her amazing butterfly, won bronze. Breaking through a stalemate of the past, the American women's relay team placed for the first time. Her team was ecstatic, and they wrapped American flags around themselves, accepting their medals at poolside. It was a stunning and ecstatically happy day.

Doug and I returned to our home in California after a final excursion to a rural village with Anna and John. But there was more to do in this exotic place before Anna and John returned.

Anna - As I believed this to be a once-in-a-lifetime trip to South Africa, I packed in the adventures after the Games. First, I wanted to swim with sharks, so I did off the coast of Durban. It sounds a lot more glamorous than it is. The freezing water nips at your breath and attempts to steal it away as you slip into a cage submerged below. The splash of "chum," pieces of dead bloody fish, being thrown in the water was something I had not thought about before and was a bit disgusting. Still, it was amazing to see these spinner sharks swim by. It was even more impressive on the boat, watching the spinner sharks jump in the air, making 360-degree spins before entering the water again with a big flopping splash.

We also took a rural village tour and were welcomed with homemade food from ingredients we had purchased at the market on the way. They also offered us their "Zulu beer," which we were unsure of, but we had a glass in the name of respect. John and I took on this adventure with excitement to be introduced to the Zulu nation outside of the city of Durban. We also went to a fantastic animal sanctuary where we stayed on the beautiful native land of the cheetahs and servals. We got to pet and roll around with a cheetah. Being so close to touch and learn about these felines was just incredible.

Next, we joined a safari game drive, seeing the white rhino, giraffe, water buffalo, elephant, and lion. It was incredible. There isn't a proper word to describe the enjoyment this brought me. I breathed in the smell of Africa with its fresh air, smoke from small local fires, and freshly brewed rooibos tea. It is a subtle, unique smell.

The sunsets of South Africa created the most incredible sky. It feels like you have been whisked into a watercolor painting, where the purples, blues, and pinks sink into each other, creating an exotic rainbow of colors in the sky. It is so amazing to watch the colors dance on the horizon. I was entranced by the singing, the voices and clicks, the kindness and beauty of South Africa. I could not have asked for more. It lived up to every expectation I had. But seeing it once just wasn't enough.

After Anna returned home from her first trip to South Africa, she again planned her coming year around her swimming training for the next games. The games were addicting, and many of the participants returned year after year. This was her plan, but she still had a taste of Africa and wanted more of that continent. She made her wish to return and let us know, but I passed it off as a whim. She had just had the fantastic opportunity to go via the games. It was rare and unique for anyone to go to Africa one time, and going a second time would be even more unusual, or that was how I looked at it. Traveling there was expensive and difficult, but Anna wanted to spend more time with Alice and have her as a guide.

A few months later, I got a phone call. "Mom, I have to

tell you. I was watching the local news, and a sweepstakes was advertised to win a trip to South Africa. I wrote down the instructions and decided to enter."

As things went with Anna, I was not surprised she would try and enter the contest. I wished her well and said, "You never know. If you are meant to go again, then you will."

A few days later, Anna called me again with the news, "Mom! I won! I won the contest for a trip to Cape Town, South Africa!"

And what was I to say but a big "OMG!" Anna's power of manifestation was on and hot!

Anna and John met Alice and her husband, Chris, in Cape Town at the tip of Africa, and their friendship was cemented forever. This second trip was a gift from the universe, a random TV show, and part of Anna's magic that had infected us since the beginning of her life. But traveling twice to Africa was also not enough for her. She and John went again for a third time.

Anna - We made the pilgrimage to the beautiful country of South Africa three times between 2013 and 2016. Within this time, I saw the Big Five (lion, leopard, buffalo, rhino, and elephant) and most places that a tourist could visit, having spent almost a total of three months in the country.

We traveled and stayed with Alice and her husband on our third trip. Being with South Africans, we had insider information on how to see Krueger National Park in the most amazing way and drove ourselves on a safari together. We had accommodations right in the middle of the park, sipping Amarula and gin and tonics and watching the wildlife go by.

We drove all day and into the night, seeing a pride of lions and cubs being nourished by their most recent kill, a karate-kicking giraffe, and an incredible encounter with a male elephant in Musk. We stood so still as to not upset him while he walked past our car less than a foot away. I was gifted some of the most incredible adventures with my friend, Alice, that I will never forget, including walking around Table Mountain, hiking at the beautiful Tsitsikamma, and visiting elephants at the Knysna reserve. I had the most romantic love affair with South Africa in those three years. A piece of my heart will always be there.

After seeing Alice and Chris on that third and final trip, Anna and John had an opportunity to walk with the lions in another game reserve. Anna's unique connection to felines—cats of all shapes and sizes—made it an obvious opportunity she could not pass up. We saw the photos of her in the open area with a guide walking in a sanctuary with African lions. What a match those lions had and an opportunity for them to walk with our Anna. She embodied power, leadership, and courage that is attributed to the lion. She was a lioness walking with a lion.

Alice and Chris visited America to meet with Anna and John and see California. It was a comfortable friendship with such an unlikely chance to meet and see each other so many times. Both Anna and Alice were miracles and shared a sense of adventure and the courage to live their gifted lives to the fullest. Not long after, Alice fell into a dangerous period of organ rejection. After a few months, she became the first successful lung transplant patient to receive a second transplant in South Africa. Her precious life was saved once again. She is thriving.

The good fortune and miracles of Anna's life continued to astound me. That voice that spoke to me at the beginning of this journey told the truth: "If she lives a short life, there will be blessings; if she lives a long life, there will be blessings. They are both the same." It was true. Blessings and miracles were abundant.

The serendipities of meeting Alice, traveling to South Africa so many times, and the physical realities of how Anna's life changed from a very sick young woman to a brave, strong woman leading her life as she saw fit was incredibly moving beyond words.

I have used poetry when I have needed to express what stirs inside me, even if there may be no words. At this time of her life, there was no way to express having no words other than writing a poem.

There Are No Words

Saw my daughter today
and there are no words
It has happened before
For the past over two years
I hear the tale of her daily life now
We look at each other, and there are no words
There simply are no words
But we thought of one, reincarnation
It is like that
One life of chronic illness, creeping disability,
rigorous schedules of health care,
short breath, dependency, oxygen tanks...
And then the gift
From an anonymous gift giver
Lungs without disease
Lungs that breathe
Lungs that are taking her into this other life
Exercise, her past word of pain, difficulty and "it is too hard"
Has become her strength, goal, love and inspiration,
taking her to of all unbelievable places, South Africa
And with the help and support of so many
There are no words
Just new life
There are no words

Especially for a mother who nursed her in that other life
Especially for a mother who witnesses this reincarnation
There are no words
Just an endless hug

Robin Modlin, 2012

chapter twenty

Embrace

With the big changes in my life due to Anna's transplant and feeling the fullness of a renewed life, I wanted to find a way to give back to our community. I imagined a weekend retreat for CF moms to get away from their family activities in the company of other CF moms with presentations designed for personal healing. This was something that I needed for myself many years before, and because I was now freed up, I had the time to organize and implement it.

I also had a positive story to share with other mothers about our CF experience. Anna had lived past her expiration date with CF lungs and had a successful transplant. She was still with us, thriving and living an important story of hope and courage.

As we sat on my vineyard patio having tea, I presented my idea to CFRI's executive director, Sue Landgraf. Sue was also a mom with a daughter with CF and a dear friend. Her daughter had a liver transplant necessitated by CF when she was twelve. Only a few years later, after our meeting, her daughter would also have a lung transplant.

We discussed newly published articles about CF families and how caregiving for our children significantly affected mothers, causing anxiety and depression at a greater-than-expected frequency. This was so obvious to us, and we understood it well. Managing the care of children with cystic fibrosis can be so overwhelming that many mothers become depressed. This can cause a decline in adherence to their child's health routines. In these families, poor outcomes for the children and strife in family relationships were concerning.

A new large-scale study known as TIDES, The International Depression/Anxiety Epidemiological Study, was being widely discussed. It evaluated 1,000 mothers and 182 fathers of children with CF for depression and anxiety. Thirty percent of mothers met the clinical criteria for depression, which was double the rate in the average population. It also found that fifty-five percent of the children's primary caregivers, whether mothers or fathers, were anxious. The parents felt isolated and stressed by their many challenges. The study suggested that mothers did not get enough support from their spouses and carried the greatest burden.

As a result, it was recommended that healthcare providers give more attention to the emotional well-being of the parents, particularly mothers, by providing screenings for anxiety and depression and offering interventions when needed. The study stressed the need for more of this type of guidance for parents as it would likely improve the children's health and their adherence to medications and treatments. The researchers also found that parents struggling in the most challenging times of the disease were resilient and frequently made stronger because of their experience.

We wanted our program for CF mothers to address these issues and provide examples of positive coping skills while acknowledging their courage and resilience. First, we needed funding. Various medical equipment and pharmaceutical companies provided the funds for our proposed retreats as the problem of depression among mothers was becoming more widely known.

Evaluating the retreats using questionnaires to measure their effectiveness showed the program's impact on the moms. The participants were asked about their self-awareness, level of anxiety and depression when they arrived and following the retreat, and if they learned any new strategies for coping. The results over the years have been overwhelmingly positive.

The weekend before Mother's Day in May 2015 was our first CFRI mother's retreat held in Menlo Park at a beautiful Catholic retreat center called Vallombrosa. As the Friday evening program opened, my friend, a mother of an adult son with CF, Darlene, and I sat on folded chairs on a small stage in front of a large round room with red carpeting and a high peak in the ceiling. The room was known as the chapel. In our laps were scripts we read to an audience of thirty women.

I had known Darlene for about twenty years. She has a son, Joe, with CF. I invited her to share the stage with me to tell the stories of our children's diagnosis of cystic fibrosis. It was typical that many children were not properly diagnosed. The experience was commonly fraught with errors, misunderstandings, and misdiagnoses.

We took turns telling our stories and how that moment of truth that our children had the disease became a doorway. We were forced to step into an unwanted and scary world. It was at that moment when we learned about the dangers to our children's health and their prognosis for a very short life that our world as we had known it crumbled. Our dreams, expectations, and hearts were broken, and we had to pick up the pieces. We became mothers who had to sharpen our advocacy skills, build our courage, and find ourselves. We both began to feel a growing maternal fierceness that would not let anything get in the way of us doing all we needed to save our children.

The women who sat before us all had children with the same disease and had gone through that same portal. Still, their children were of all ages, from newborn into adulthood, and had varied levels of illness. A few who came had already lost their children. They came from different areas of the country for support and a community.

After Darlene and I told our diagnosis stories, we invited each of the women to pair up with another mom they did not know to tell their stories. In this way, the room became a chapel filled with sacred doorways, open hearts, spirit connections, and hands touching each other. Tears cleansed the group.

We gathered the mothers into a circle where Darlene and I took turns reading a poem, setting the tone for the weekend and our ritual bonding. Every year, this adopted poem, "The Invitation," by Oriah Mountain Dreamer, is read aloud as if it is our creed. To personalize the poem for our group, we added a last paragraph.

> And for my sisters, you mothers of CF children,
> I want to know if you accept and embrace this journey,
> our journey, the CF journey...
> You have been invited to meet this most difficult
> of challenges.
> I want to know if you can be honest and true,
> reaching out to each other, reaching into yourself
> as you meet the pain and sorrow
> and the joy and the blessings of having these very
> perfect children.

After reading this powerful poem, we celebrated being together in sisterhood with a ritual of sharing purple shawl-like scarves placed on each other's necks. Thirty women stood silently in a circle as the scarves were placed over their heads one after the other.

That first night opened hearts and felt like magic because of the honesty, the listening ears, the ritual of community, and the caring friendships. Love, acceptance, and healing were palpable with each breath we took. This group of women needed a place and a way to recognize the difficult path a mother never wishes to step upon. They needed a community to witness their pain and joy as mothers. The maternal journey started with the birth of their children. Still, in the diagnosis, they were initiated to being a mother in ways they never knew they would have to be. I called this gathering of women Embrace.

Embrace has become an annual event, and a core of mothers return every year. The format has remained the same. We believe that addressing our grief and why we are there from the start with openness and honesty is the most healing. We have created an environment of trust and acceptance for what is going on for each mom. Some arrive with a lot of stress, and just by being with other moms who get it, they are helped and feel heard. They can cry when needed and express their pride and joy about their children. Everyone knows the stress of the responsibility and what is at stake with all our children's lives being threatened by the disease.

The Embrace program also features the personal stories of the mothers in our community. We highlight one or two of our mothers' stories each year by inviting them to create a presentation for the program. The mothers also learn practical advice and have questions answered by moms who may be more experienced.

Two other essential parts of the program are writing and art workshops. The result is a personal expression of the inner life of each mother. These artworks have become part of the integration of our themes and something they take home to remind them of what they have awakened to in the retreat.

On Saturday evening and after dinner, the chapel is transformed to hold a circle of drums. Entering the round room where the night before they were initiated into the sisterhood, each mother chooses a seat and a drum and is led by a professional to an experience of release and joy. The room is filled with a syncopated rhythm that is loud and grounding. Our drum circle magically creates a greater connection with ourselves and generates a group heartbeat.

The practice of drumming in a group has been documented as healing for individuals and bonding for groups. It is a crucial part of the healing for our gathering. Fully energized by the drumming, the mothers gather for a party and time together to share friendships. Sunday morning offers workshops in yoga or Pilates, mindfulness, or other healing exercises. By the end of the weekend, we are bonded, have learned more about self-care from each other, and have been restored.

I started Embrace with the support of my CF mom friends, especially Sue and Darlene, and later the next CFRI executive director, also a CF mom, Siri. They are women who have been inspired by their children with CF, allowing CF to open their hearts and lead them into their worlds of professionalism, inner growth, and greater meaning. My life has been rich with so many CF moms sharing their wisdom and care in my life. I see what the TIDES study also suggested—that these moms have grown in resilience with their challenges.

I am so grateful for the moms who have met the difficult challenges and grown as a sisterhood. Our community is filled with blessings and miracles. With Embrace, we can share this experience and how we have grown with other moms who are still struggling to find their voice.

Darlene: *"I believe that CF saved my life! I know that's an odd thing to say. However, I might have worked myself to death, had minimal time for my kids and mom, and spent the better part of twenty years beating myself up for not doing everything well or not doing more. Prior to CF, I was obsessed with perfection. After CF, I began to let go of trying to please others and trying desperately to look or seem great, like I had it all handled.*

Life with CF gave me new meaning, and I began looking at where meaning was missing. As Joe became more independent, I began to take better care of myself physically, emotionally, and spiritually. I noticed that there was a huge hole in my life. I had once been deeply spiritual and felt a new call to reclaim this part of my life. I trained as a coach and a spiritual director. I made a difficult and bold decision to begin new work in these fields

*rather than return to corporate work. I began to see myself dif-
ferently, to love myself, which expanded my ability to love others. I created new and deep friendships, ones I'd never had before.*

*It is clear to me that CF, a life-threatening, horribly dam-
aging illness, was one of my greatest gifts; the gift of letting go
of everything that had no meaning and replacing it with work,
people, and communities that meant everything."*

CF and our children changed our lives. Our children and
their challenges are our muse to create a life with meaning
and purpose we never thought we would have. For me, I was
growing by giving back to our community, developing more
as an artist, and watching in awe as Anna's life was transformed as her transplant gave her wings.

This Path

This path that you are sending me on
I have already walked for a number of miles
Met many other travelers going my way
Passed by many going another way
A direction was set out for me
No one asked me if this was the way I wanted to go
No map can be found
I round a bend and another twist
Another turn
Another unknown
Another and then another
This path you are sending me on
Sometimes I grip onto the edge of my seat
Afraid I may fly off
Sometimes I say, "Really?"
Always I am asked to accept and keep going
Stretching my skin and my mind
My heart is bruised and recovers

Grand sights are seen
Many losses are had
Sounds of birds and water and laughter give respite
Before the next bend
The next twist and turn
This path you are sending me on
Each step takes me further to a ground
Unknown until I get there
Trust, you say, trust...
But who are you that is steering my way
Looking into the mirror and into my eyes
A deep soul stirring wishes to know itself
I am you and you are me
Traveling in time and space so that we can be One.
You set out the way
I take the steps
Thinking I do not know the way
I am fooled
It was me all of the time carving out this path
Pointing the way to go.

Robin Modlin, 2018

chapter twenty-one

Meeting the Aussie

I t was a day she would never forget. Anna was training for the 2014 Houston Transplant Games. While training with her swim coach, she had her best time ever in butterfly and was so excited. Her hard work was paying off. Later, she saw Olympic Gold Medalist Michael Phelps swim at the Santa Clara International Swim Center. It was a day of dreams and inspiration three weeks before her competition. Then, in one of those split-second twists of fate, as she was getting out of her car and stepping off the curb wrong, she broke her foot.

Deciding everything was fine despite her foot turning purple and twice its size the next day, Anna was determined nothing would get in the way of the games. She was simply not going to accept she had seriously injured herself. I scooped her up as she writhed around on the floor in her denial and demanded she get an X-ray. Her fifth metatarsal was broken, but her dream still held. She bargained with the orthopedist, who decided to give her a chance to compete by giving her a bone stimulator. If she improved, he would give her the go-ahead to swim. I was available to attend the games with her and be her forever sidekick to help her get around while she wore a cumbersome boot and used a knee scooter.

Once again, we watched Anna push through an obstacle that would stop others. She could not waste the training, time, or her hopes, and she had heaps of gumption. She had to cancel out of her other land-locked competitions, but she was allowed to swim. At the side of the pool, Anna balanced on my arm as I moved with her to the starting blocks, where she hobbled up, took her aim, and swam for more golds. She did it again, swam her best with that broken foot, and added more medals to her collection.

Anna was living as though she was in control of her life as much as life would allow. She still struggled with bowel blockages, regulating her blood sugars, and dealing with the other parts of having CF. However, her indomitable spirit, guided by her discipline and determination, was winning. This affected her relationship at home with John. It became clear that her attitude, life, and relationship with John were changing.

They found each other when they were young, while Anna was disabled with her CF. John hung in and lived life on a low-key note with her. She did not have the energy to be physically active or adventurous even though she was bubbly and funny. John loved to ride bikes, so on the weekends, he would go on extended rides through the hills around the Bay Area for his getaways, but was perfectly happy when at home with Anna. Together, their life was mostly home-based while slowly and steadily Anna headed toward her transplant.

After Anna's transformation following the transplant, John just did not meet the energy level or have the personal inspiration to go at the same pace as Anna. Their relationship was not going well. Anna also never felt supported by his family. She wanted out. She was successful and powerful in her new life and felt that staying with John was holding her back. But it was hard to know how to get out of the relationship.

Over coffee and lunch, Anna and I talked about her problem. Even though she was strong, it was hard to see how she could maintain a full-time job to support herself independently if she left John. And she did not want to come back home and live with us. The transplant center recommended that patients not work full time as they wanted them to be primarily focused and diligent about their care. She was a full-time patient living a miracle life and wanted to treat herself with the utmost care.

Together, she and John owned their little house in Sunnyvale, but this was one of the most expensive areas of the U.S. Since John was a full-time engineer, he had the means for her to be at home, not working, but it became unbearable for her. She felt she was in a cage, unable to use her wings fully and with a man she no longer loved.

I heard her pain and understood, telling her she would find a way. It was a new and scary challenge. If she had passed away before her transplant, we would have viewed John as her savior for her to have had an adult life, and now, where that was true, her adult life was changing. She needed to find a new way to live. This was not easy. Wanting to offer advice, I thought I was being smart, telling her, "Anna, be careful you don't have an affair. Be honest and work this through with John until you are sure you want to leave the relationship and find a way out."

That advice, "Don't have an affair," rang in my head as a dumb mother thing to say. I knew life was messy, especially when relationships came to an end. It was not for me to tell her what to do. She was in her thirties, and I knew she would figure it out, but she was confused and felt stuck. Still, Anna continued with her personal athletic goals amid her failing relationship and in 2016 prepared for the Cleveland Transplant Games. Since I was once again going with Anna to the games, I invited a dear friend, Peggy, to come with us. She'd had a heart transplant in 2014. For Anna, those Cleveland games became the most fateful of them all, and for Peggy, they were a powerful gift of inspiration.

Peggy was in her sixties and had developed heart failure without warning. She had always been healthy and active. One spring day, I was with her when walking a favorite trail lined with California poppies and lupine and she had to stop and catch her breath. Her energy and exercise tolerance were not what they usually were. Peggy thought it might be her asthma that was causing her to be out of breath. After seeing her doctor, it was recommended that she see a cardiologist. I went with her for support.

I stood outside the physician's office when she came out. Heading straight for me with a look of shock, she said, "Robin, I cannot believe it. I have congestive heart failure. He said I may need a heart transplant." She then collapsed into my arms. It was quick, blunt, scary, and unexpected for Peggy.

My heart sank, but I told her, "Peggy, if that happens, I will be here for you. I have done this before. If you need a transplant, you will get through it." And that is how it happened. Within two years, she was listed for a heart. Her transplant was successful, and our friendship was forever deepened. Peggy became part of our transplant family. It seemed so strange and coincidental that I would have a friend who needed support in this way at that time. The need for a transplant is relatively rare and to have a close friend whom I could help was unique.

Because of Anna, Peggy knew of the transplant games and wanted to attend. She was also a swimmer and prepared for the adventure to be with us in Cleveland. Excited to be there, Peggy literally dove into the experience. The joy and spirit of the games were infectious, and she was caught in its spell. Like the others, she had nearly lost her life. She was saved by an anonymous donor and loved being a part of this beautiful celebration of life.

Peggy swam with the over-sixty-year-olds. My friend climbed on the swim blocks, looking like a champion to everyone on her team as she dove in. At the other end of the pool was the promise of a medal. Her son, Kevin, and I cheered as she finished her race and reached for the railing and pool steps. She was smiling ear to ear when she got out of the pool; the joy on her face was priceless.

Anna was Team NorCal's manager that year. She organized her team's group activities for the five days of the games, as well as participating in swimming, golf, and volleyball. Her accomplishments were once again extraordinary; she won seven gold medals. As the games ended, we gathered at the final closing ceremony, where it was announced that Anna was awarded the Female Athlete of the Year for the entire 2016 games. I knew she deserved the honor but was overwhelmed with the reality of who Anna had become and how important these games were for her and now for my dear friend, Peggy. Gratitude was overflowing, and praise came from everywhere for Anna.

That fateful week was recorded in our hearts as monumental and became even more so that evening for Anna. To celebrate her win, Anna went to the bar where the athletes gathered for a toast, drink, and friendly banter. I stayed behind. A contingent of Australian transplant athletes she'd met during her competitions was also at the bar. They all intrigued Anna, but one of them particularly caught her eye, Terry. He qualified to compete in the games due to corneal transplants and attended with his other Aussie friends for the fun of it all. Terry and Anna hit it off and sat for hours talking and exchanging contacts.

The next day, Anna, Peggy, and I readied to leave on a short road trip to drop Peggy off to see her son in Toronto and for us to see Niagara Falls. I could tell Anna was distracted in the car and spending a lot of time texting on her phone. After arriving in Niagara Falls, she told me that she had spent time with the Aussies the night before. They were going to Hawaii on their way home and had invited her to join them. They wanted to buy her a ticket.

Right there, I started to wonder, who do you meet in a bar who wants to buy you a ticket to Honolulu? She reassured me they were kind and loved doing things for people. Anna's love of adventure, allure, and attraction to this Aussie would not allow her to refuse this generous offer. Within a few days after returning home, Anna was on a plane again to Hawaii, and life was about to change dramatically once again.

Anna - He bounced with joy when he walked by with a smile from ear to ear. I noticed his energy, and it drew me in like a magnet. I was intrigued and interested in who this man was. I noticed his green and yellow camouflage shirt and red backpack. The shirt told me he was an Australian competitor at the games. It would at least be interesting to hear his accent. I wanted to chat with him. He seemed so kind and happy.

I ended up in the convenience shop at the stadium, and in walked this friendly face in the green and yellow. We struck up a conversation, just a few words of hello. I don't remember the details of exactly what was said. I don't know if we even introduced ourselves by name. We actually spoke longer as the cashier was having some difficulty. It is a memory I wouldn't usually keep, but meeting Terry that day changed the entire trajectory of my life.

During the rest of the week of the transplant games, Terry and I waved at each other or just said hello in passing. We never really had a serious conversation or spent any time chatting. We just kept missing each other. It wasn't until the last night after the games were over, the closing ceremony had happened, and I had been awarded the female athlete of the year that we finally found ourselves in the same place at the same time. We were both in the hotel bar, celebrating and having fun with our friends. I was immediately drawn to sit with him and his two other friends, one of whom I had gotten to know well throughout the week.

Terry and I spoke throughout the evening. We even ended up separating ourselves from the group. We got to know each other through drinks, jokes, and flirty comments. We were both enjoying the company of each other. It was so comfortable and easy to share and listen. We learned a lot about each other, and a friendship was definitively started that evening. However, since it was the last night that we were in the same city and he would be going back to Australia, I didn't give it too much consideration that we would be in each other's lives forever, other *than being the eternal Facebook friend.*

Terry ended up leaving a little early to join some friends elsewhere, and we said goodbye with a hug. I was amazed I'd met such a great person and looked forward to the messages I knew would come. However, I was not thinking of this as anything romantic, except I was probably crossing a line through my overt flirting and dirty jokes. That evening, we did become Facebook friends, and the next day, the messages began.

There were long streams of consciousness sent out on my phone. As we drove through Ohio, Pennsylvania, and New York, the messages kept coming, including cheeky responses and serious questions. It was a good combination of get-to-know-yous. Even through my trip to Niagara Falls and Toronto, the messages flowed. Until one evening, I was asked, "Will you meet me in Hawaii?"

As Terry returned to Australia, he was to stop in Hawaii for two nights. I said yes and booked my flight. A few heavy thoughts flooded my mind. What am I doing? Am I leading him on? Is he a crazy person? Am I a crazy person? Do I have bad intentions? Will I regret this?

My gut instinct told me I should just go, and I did. Fortunately, I also had a best friend who lives in Oahu and I could meet up with her, so I planned a fun, short Hawaii trip. I was beyond nervous about meeting Terry in Hawaii. I thought he was traveling with the large group of Australians he was at the transplant games with, but it turned out that he was only traveling with his sister on the way home.

I got to the hotel where I was to meet him just after they arrived. I could see him in the lobby from my friend's car. OH MY GOD, what am I doing? She dropped me off to spend the next forty-eight hours together. Who does this? I have never done anything like this before in my life. I followed my instinct and continued, trusting I was where I was supposed to be.

I booked a parasailing adventure for the next day, and that evening, we walked around downtown Honolulu, grabbed a burger, and then participated in a music trivia night, where we won second place together. Something felt serendipitous about that evening. I was where I was supposed to be. We walked on the beach in the moonlight, wandered around the city, and talked about every detail of our lives. I was drawn more and more into this man's world, one where he lived on the other side of the planet. What was happening?

It wasn't until the morning of the last day as we were walking from the hotel to have breakfast that I suddenly had a vision of me, Terry, and our child. It was on a sand beach with a little girl with long, blonde, curly hair. I could hear Terry say, "Go to Mummy," and I saw myself reach out to this little girl. Was I the mummy? How could this be? I had just been telling Terry that I can't have kids and also don't want kids. It was not a responsibility that I felt I could handle. Where in the world was this vision coming from? I didn't want it, but it was real. It felt like a vision of the future. How do I end up with a child? And with this Australian man? No way! I started to think I was certifiably insane. But this series of events changed my life forever.

chapter twenty-two
Australia? Really?

As usual, Anna's focus for the next year was to train for the games, but now she had friends in Australia. The convenient thing about Australia was it was summer when we had winter. Swim training in summer was much preferred for an outdoor swimmer like Anna. The inconvenient thing about this was Australia was on the other side of the world, yet that did not matter to Anna. The idea of summer swimming called to her. The adventure was far too alluring.

Clearly, by now, we understood that when Anna got an idea, there was no stopping her. She was smart, thought things through, and with her creative resourcefulness, she would find ways to make her visions become realities. As she had been for Africa, Anna was determined to go to Australia in January, February, and March of 2017. She had it all figured out. It made perfect sense to leave winter to be in summer and with friends to support her.

Getting nervous, Doug and I wondered what this fascination was with Australia. I knew she was having continued contact with her Aussie friends. Still, I was suspicious something else was going on with her. At the same time, Anna's struggles with what to do with her relationship with John continued. The pressure in her relationship was mounting.

After returning home from Hawaii and her time with the Aussies, Anna told me things had changed. "Mom, I recognize as I stand in my kitchen and look out the window that nothing seems to be mine anymore. A voice inside is telling me that I no longer belong. I can see a new door is opening."

Where she had been continually going in circles with her relationship, a new path was opening, and she could feel it. I understood, remembering when I had a similar feeling, sending my Washington boyfriend home before I met Doug.

Anna was in therapy to help her work through her confusion with her relationship and hoped she and John could have couples therapy, but John was not interested. He was in denial about what was happening between them. Their relationship was doomed to fail. This was especially clear as Anna openly told John she had made friends who lived in Australia and was planning a three-month-long trip to get away and evaluate their relationship. John did not protest.

The idea that Anna would go so far away to a place we knew nothing about was very unsettling. I had brief encounters with the Australians at the games. Still, I was never introduced and did not know who they were. With her trip positioned as part of the solution to her relationship problem, Doug and I were worried. I made a date for lunch with Anna in mid-November 2016 to clarify what was going on with this crazy idea that was only weeks away from happening.

We sat at a bistro table in a corner of a restaurant near her house, and questions were bursting in my head. I had to ask, "Anna, what are you doing? Are you just running away from John and not dealing with this?" She reassured me that her focus was swimming and the great opportunity to go to Australia.

I tried to give her the emotional space she needed without dealing with an interfering mother, but I could not hold back more questions. "Come on, Anna, who is this Terry you talk about? You seem to be constantly talking and texting, and he has been so helpful to you to make this trip."

Finally, she was honest with me. She was falling in love with him. Their brief meeting and short time together in Hawaii opened up a friendship she could not resist. It was true she wanted to train in an Australian summer, but that romantic notion was not all that was romantic. She was also going to see if this relationship with Terry that had grown over phone calls and texting while her relationship with John was crumbling was real. It just so happened it was in Australia!

Part of me had known, but now it was real. I panicked that Anna might decide she really was in love with Terry. I dared not think she might move there. I did not want to believe this was happening. I was afraid Anna was having a rebound relationship with Terry as it was clear that the relationship with John was over. Rebounds are not uncommon or necessarily bad, but this was to manifest in Australia, so far away. It was almost Thanksgiving, and we would be with Doug's elderly father for the holiday. I did not want to upset Doug by telling him. I was upset enough for both of us.

As the Christmas holiday neared, we planned our usual family get-together. Anna, John, Sara, and her boyfriend, Ian, came to our house for Christmas Eve and morning. Anna was planning to embark for Australia on December 31. Tensions and confusion were high. What did this all mean to all of us? After Christmas, we could discuss what was to come, the trip, what it was about, and how it impacted John.

We had folded John into our family life for fifteen years since they'd met. We loved and respected him for everything he had given Anna and for sticking with her through the transplant. Still, we could see how the foundation of their relationship had shifted. The possibility that Anna was falling in love with someone on the other side of the world was becoming more and more real.

We sent Anna off on her trip with a full awareness of our worry and concern for the distance she was traveling. It seemed John was letting her go, not fully in touch with what this might mean for their relationship. Yet, his lack of resistance was also a type of resignation that even he understood they no longer had the commitment to each other they once had. Their lives together were at a significant turning point, and John knew it.

During this time, Sara finished her years in an osteopathic medical school near our home. She had to decide on her next move to a family medicine residency and chose one in Maine. Both of my daughters were leaving for far-off reaches from California. I fully expected them both to come back, but feared they would not. My babies were flying far from the nest. Every mom goes through a kind of grief when having to let go. Yet I had been through so much with Anna's disease and transplant, it felt unfair that I had to deal with these extreme distances, too.

After two months in Australia, Anna and Terry called to tell us they were getting married. Terry wanted to begin getting to know each other through phone calls. Our daughter, who had sent us on a journey to beat death, welcome new life, and watch her thrive, was now stretching us to the limit again. This time, she was moving to the other side of the world and marrying a man we had never met. Friends who heard about this remarked how wonderful it was. Wonderful? Were they kidding? It was scary, complicated, and hard for me, Doug, and Sara to accept, mainly because it was happening so fast.

We wanted our newly borrowed time gifted from the transplant to be spent with Anna in this country near us. We had fought for her life. Now, she was leaving for the other side of the world. It may have been selfish on our part. Still, our need to have her close so we could touch her and know she had excellent medical care or come to her aid when needed was screaming, "Don't let her go!"

Friends would say, "She will be only a plane flight away!" True, but a sixteen-hour flight to Melbourne, Australia, is not the same as a fifty-minute flight to LA. It just was hard to assimilate in our minds. We should have been thrilled, but we had to catch up to take this ride with Anna.

The first plan for this extravaganza of a life change was for Anna to return home, finalize her breakup with John, and get her American affairs in order. A few months later, Terry would arrive so we could spend some time getting to know each other. In the fall of 2017, they would be married in Australia, where they were to live permanently. But quickly, that plan was tossed. Immigration laws were changing, and an immigration attorney warned them they should marry sooner. The new plan was the end of May, and we had to wait until then to meet Terry.

Anna returned to the U.S. quickly to say her final good-byes to John, split up their belongings, and gather her things for an enormous move. John did not resist and let her go with the mutual understanding that the relationship was over. John stayed behind in the house they owned together, and Anna was moving on, leaving many things behind that she simply could not take to the other side of the world.

Anna also attended Sara's graduation from medical school with us. The following day, she returned to Melbourne to finish the wedding arrangements before Doug, Sara, and I traveled to Australia to attend the wedding about two weeks later. It all happened in a flash. I could not believe it. Both of my daughters were leaving to fulfill their dreams in opposite directions that were halfway around the world from each other. It was a bit more than my mother heart could take.

So much of my adult life was about being a mother, and I was dedicated to these daughters. I loved being with them. Sara could not move farther than Maine while staying in the U.S., and Anna was going to the other side of the world where it was a different day and a different season. Really? I thought I would get to relax in my later years.

Anna planned her wedding with her very generous mother-in-law-to-be. It was all so bizarre for me. She was owning her decision and doing this for herself because it made the most sense to her. Like everything else in her life, Anna was in charge, had a vision, and knew how to make it materialize. We would just watch in wonder.

We arrived in Melbourne on a Friday with the wedding

set for Sunday. The season was spring at home, but there it was fall. We were reminded of this by the wind blowing fallen leaves in the streets and wearing coats when it should have been time to shed them. We had one day to get acquainted, including with Terry's family. This was really happening.

The wedding venue was in a downtown hotel. It was a room with a bar a few floors up with windows looking out at a city we did not know. It was romantic, with flowers, music, appetizers, and new, unfamiliar accents. Anna's creative taste was clearly an influence. With short notice, fifty people came to witness their wedding and wish them well, including a friend from Anna's childhood who had moved to Australia years before. Dressed informally in a tweed jacket and tie, Doug walked Anna down the aisle; she wore a stylish multi-length white gown. Sara, her bridesmaid, and I entered the room and ceremony together. It was sweet and lovely.

The wedding celebrant led the ceremony, talking of the miracle that Terry and Anna had found each other. Even though the physical distance was a challenge, their love was more important and could not be resisted. She went on to talk about marriage and having a family, and I just zoned out. Anna was never to have a child, nor had she ever wanted one. The wedding was fanciful, and I thought those comments were over the top, yet somehow it was right. We knew it and felt it. It just took a while to catch up to it. Anna was always steps ahead of us, but it was a few thousand miles this time. I was not yet in gear.

During the wedding, I was churning inside. It was so hard for me to be there and enjoy the moment. I needed to catch up to this surprise in Anna's life and develop trust. I knew I could get there, but I just needed a little time, and there was none of that. Being sensitive to this, Anna and Terry devised a "family moon" instead of a honeymoon. After the wedding, the five of us left for Port Douglas and the Great Barrier Reef. We went snorkeling, saw the sights, ate and laughed together, and quickly bonded with Terry. We all fell in love with him.

Our adventure into the Barrier Reef took us on a boat with a few other sightseers. We were given black wetsuits, face masks, fins, and snorkels. Like my trip to Africa, I could not believe I was in this iconic place. Jumping into the warm tropical waters, we plunged into a sea with endangered creatures. It was obvious the reef was not what it had been years before. Some of the coral had died in the reef, so the colors were not as vibrant. But swimming as parrotfish, angelfish, and clownfish surrounded me, I was in a magical place, and undeniably there were underwater colors everywhere. As we all looked for turtles, someone from our group spotted one. I swam over but missed it. Not seeing the teeming sea life I had expected, I was disappointed that this natural place was clearly impacted by climate change. Yet, we were again so lucky to have this opportunity to be there together.

We also had other Aussie experiences exploring the Daintree Rainforest with its infamous bird, the cassowary. It is not a friendly creature; in fact, it is the world's most dangerous bird to humans. As we walked in its territory, we were told to be careful and not threaten it. I wanted to see one with its bright blue head, top knot casque, and huge claws, but it was best we did not. From there, we tasted teas that are famous in Daintree. Another of our favorite stops was Kuranda, a little hippie village found after a long, winding road through the tropical forest. It had charm, delicious food, and fun shops. We laughed and loved being together the whole way through.

After that week, I wished I had that time before the wedding to enjoy the ceremony and celebration more, but that was how it happened. Our next task was to give them our love and acceptance, bless their marriage, and leave for home without our miracle daughter, who was now living permanently in Australia.

Not long before, there was no way this would have ever happened in any imaginary universe. When Anna was a child, we were blessed that she simply survived at the time of her diagnosis and hoped she might live to her early twenties. She went so far beyond that expectation. She defied her death at twenty-nine, was in a documentary film, was reborn as an accomplished athlete, went to Africa three times, met her doppelganger, fell in love with an Australian, and married and moved there when she was thirty-six! It was stunning and truly unbelievable, and Doug and I were spinning. I remember asking out loud when she was a child when we experienced the extraordinary with her, "Who are you?" That question was never more relevant.

chapter twenty-three

Two Ends of the Earth

It felt like I lived in the center of two ends of the earth with each daughter on opposite sides because that was actually what was happening. They both settled into their attractive new homes, and Doug and I prepared ourselves for a life with a lot of variety. We would be traveling to the East Coast and Maine and then over the Pacific Ocean into the southern hemisphere to Melbourne, Australia, while also living in two homes in California and buying a perfect teardrop camper to enjoy outings with friends in 2017.

Our little trailer was named Rosie with a license plate that said "65 Rosie." Named because we had both just turned sixty-five, and for its rose red trim. But it was also a take-off on "65 roses." This was the nickname for cystic fibrosis that came from a child who could not pronounce cystic fibrosis, so said sixty-five roses. Our Rosie said to us, and there was no denying it; we were forever on a journey due to our life with CF. No grass was growing under our feet. We were figuring it out and living in a style we never expected. Needless to say, we were proud and in awe of both of our daughters and how they were living their dreams, and we had to live ours too.

Even though they were living permanently in Australia, Anna and Terry still wanted to be involved with the Transplant Games in America and planned to attend in Salt Lake City, Utah, in 2018. The year before, in a dance studio in Melbourne, they enrolled in ballroom dancing lessons as preparation for competing in the games as a dancing couple.

Doug came with me to those games in Utah to meet up

with our Aussies. Dressed in ballroom attire, they arrived for the ballroom dancing competition and again stole our hearts. Watching them dance as newlyweds whose romance story began at the previous games was magic. Anna was beaming and strong for her other swimming events, winning even more medals for her cache.

After a quick trip to see Sara and Ian in Maine, Anna and Terry returned to Australia. Next, they quickly went from participating in the U.S. Games in Salt Lake City to entering even more competitions at the Australian Transplant Games on the Gold Coast. Anna was a new athlete on the team, entering her regular swimming events and other competitions for fun. I wished I could have been there. It was the first of her games I had missed. She did not disappoint her new Aussie teammates. Anna flew down the lanes with her signature butterfly, backstroke, and freestyle. She and Terry swam with two other men in a relay and won a hard-fought relay together.

Once again, as when she was a little girl, she swam with the boys! I heard there was a buzz in the crowd about Anna, the new team member. By the end of the games, Anna had done it again and won Female Athlete of the Year for Team Victoria. She had won two top honors in two countries. I wonder if this has ever been done before by any transplant participant.

The idea of miracles happening repeatedly in Anna's life inspired us. We witnessed her hard work and intention for these accomplishments. They did not drop in her lap (except sometimes, like winning her trip to South Africa). Anna worked for it. Her transplant was the miracle that gave her these possibilities. She was the one who seized them with a hunger and passion to know life and what she was capable of.

Gradually, my grumpiness about Anna being down under started to give way to acceptance. We could either complain about the distance and difficulty getting there or we could get on board. We decided to visit Anna and Terry at least once per year and hoped they could do the same coming our way. When we did make it there, we made frequent trips to Bunnings, the Aussie version of Home Depot, for fix-up items to help prepare their new home and garden. Doug developed a reputation as the forever chief odd job maintenance worker and miracle fixer of mechanical and electrical problems. Anna and I also swept the "Op shops," the Aussie name for thrift stores for curios and treasures.

Many elements of Anna being in this new country, including her medical care, started to make sense. We knew she would never have considered the move if her medical care was not up to par with what she had at Stanford. The lung transplant center at The Alfred in Melbourne has an international reputation for its excellent care and longevity of its patients.

The climate in the Melbourne area was much like northern California and was comfortable. We were used to eucalyptus mixed into our forests in the Bay Area, so it did not look like a totally foreign place. English with a particular accent and new slang made understanding what was said hard to decipher at times, but it was English. What was most different was the architecture and residential neighborhoods built more of brick and concrete composites than our American homes, which were mostly made of wood. Australia had its unique beauty, and enjoying being there for our visits became easy.

We also missed Sara and were committed to visiting her at least once per year. Travel to Maine was shorter than to Australia, but it was not easy either. We took the red eye to Boston, a small Cape Air plane north to Augusta, Maine, then a short drive to her home in a quaint historic town. The houses were typical of New England, with old front porches, some with columns, old interesting doors, and yards with no fences. The gardens were lush with roses, lilies, daisies, cosmos, and black-eyed Susans.

The small town, founded in the 1700s, sits on the edge of

the Kennebec River. We would walk in the pastoral Vaughn Woods down the street from their house or go downtown and sit on Adirondack chairs lined up on a viewing deck to watch the sturgeon jump from the depths of the river. Sara was living in this idyllic place as a medical resident at the local hospital. While visiting, Doug had a fisherman's paradise at his disposal, and I loved walking the neighborhood and exploring the antique stores. Sara and Ian took us on adventures to the inner countryside, coastal Maine, and Quebec. I could see myself living there, but not Doug, who was not interested in the cold winters.

Three years after moving to Maine, Sara and Ian were married. They returned to California in November 2019 for a short time to have a small ceremony with family and a few longtime friends in a picturesque 1800s bright yellow school house near our second home and country house in the Sierra foothills, Murphys.

Sara was in her fourth year of residency and very pregnant. Standing in a white dress and leather boots with her tall, red-haired Ian under an old and stately oak, taking their vows, she was beautiful. The wedding celebrant was a dear friend from medical school. We enjoyed a delicious dinner of roasted autumn vegetables and meats, local and Napa wines, and danced to a live band. It was intimate and warm, just how Sara wanted it to be. Both of my daughters had lovely autumn weddings. Still, one was in a city in May in the southern hemisphere, and the other in the country in November in the northern hemisphere. And very happily, we were to have our first grandchild soon after, in January 2020.

With all her heart, Anna hoped to come and be a part of Sara's wedding. Her arrangements for a flight for both her and Terry were made long in advance, but she became ill and could not travel. Difficulty in travel became a sad problem for her. This time, though, she had become very ill and was in and out of the hospital for a severe fungal infection. We all were very concerned as the days and weeks went by. There was no improvement, and she lost significant lung function. Her team discussed a second lung transplant, which was not a likely option because of the fungal infection. Following Sara's wedding, Doug and I had to make another travel plan.

I was committed to being with Sara for the birth of her first child in January and could not go to Anna's bedside, but Doug could. We decided he would leave for Australia first in early January. Then, I would go in February after the baby arrived and Sara was recovering. Sara had a three-month leave from her residency to be able to have her baby.

At the end of December, we were invited to a New Year's meal at our friends Andrew and Isa's house before leaving to each end of the earth. It was Japanese-style with sushi, and shared with a few other friends. Before we ate, we went around the table in a gratitude ritual, offering wishes and prayers for our world, family, friends, and ourselves. When my turn came, I reminded everyone that Anna was very ill and struggling in Australia. We held hands, bowed our heads, and sent positive energy and thoughts of healing to her.

Shortly after sending those thoughts, my phone rang. It was Anna. "Mom, I had to call and tell you I just had the most amazing experience. I was able to get out of the hospital to go with Terry for a walk. As we walked through a grove of eucalyptus, a blue budgie parakeet flew from the trees, landed on my head, and would not leave. It stayed with me for about ten minutes. I have a picture I will send to you. It was magic, and I know it was special, and something important was happening."

Surprised, I told her that, coincidentally, we had just held her in our thoughts, sending good vibes and healing. She thought that must have been why the budgie arrived. It was to give her hope and inspire her that she would get better. I shared this with the group, and we celebrated that Anna felt our good wishes and sent her more.

That evening, after returning home, I thought about Anna's

experience while looking at the photo with the blue bird perched on her head. I started to feel chills of magic and heard bells and whistles go off in my mind. The blue budgie answered a question I held close to me for over thirty years since we had been with Lama Gangha. He had given Anna a small coin purse with blue parakeets on the front, and since that day, I wondered about its significance.

Could this have been a spiritual visitation from Anna's healer, Lama Gangha? Did he give that gift to her as a clue and premonition for a time to come when he would visit again when we needed it most? It was an irresistible thought that I shared with Anna. "Anna, I have something for you that I have saved since our time with Lama Gangha. It is the small change purse that you used to play with. It has blue budgie parakeets on it. Do you remember? I think Lama Gangha came to you to give you blessings and help you get well. I will have Dad bring it to you when he comes."

In response, Anna thought about my fanciful realization. Because when the bird landed on her head, it felt like a magical moment that came from another place; she was receptive and agreed. "Mom, yes. That is a good explanation. I don't have a better one. It must have been Lama Gangha. I cannot wait to get it from Dad."

We knew Anna's medical care team was as worried as we were about how she would recover from the dangerous fungal infection that had infiltrated her lungs. We all thought we were headed in a very dicey direction with her health and braced ourselves. The most amazing thing was from the day when the blue budgie appeared; she started to get better.

Before he left for Australia, Doug did some research on her fungal infection and the toxic nature of a drug that was being used to combat it. After a discussion with Anna's physician about the drug, it was decided to stop it for fear it could cause harm.

A few days later, Doug arrived in Melbourne. He had

reserved a small apartment near the hospital to be with Anna as much as possible, but things had changed quickly. Upon an X-ray, the fungal balls and nodules in her lungs were disappearing. Anna was suddenly on the road to getting better and was being released from the hospital. Wondering what it was that did it and whether the stopping of the toxic antifungal was a key, Doug happily canceled his reservation for the apartment.

Upon deciding to release Anna from the hospital, the physicians agreed that they could not explain how or why she was recovering. There was no obvious reason for her sudden turnaround. They saw her amazing improvement, increased lung function, and better blood values, and said they would just accept what was happening without knowing why. Things changed so much that the difficult conversations that Terry and Doug had expected to have about what was next for Anna were not needed. Gladly, we moved on, and hope for her future returned.

In mid-December while in the middle of this crisis and fear of losing Anna, we learned another miracle was about to visit them. The vision of the child that Anna and Terry held in their hearts was about to be born out. The magical reality of a child for Anna and a grandchild for us was to manifest in the months to come. That child needed Anna to be her mother. We could not lose Anna to this fungal infection. The fear that she might not survive sent Anna into what she said was among her darkest of days. She desperately needed a miracle and the magic of that blue budgie perched on her head. Loving the idea that it carried a surreal explanation and had delivered whatever she needed to get well, it was another of her unexpected miracles and "a highly improbable or extraordinary event, development, or accomplishment that brought very welcome consequences."

She never shared her magical budgie experience with her doctors, but kept it close to her heart and only shared it with friends. As the months moved on, Anna continued to get better and finally fully kicked the infection. Her healing and recovery became legendary among the multidisciplinary teams caring for her. Since then, her husband Terry has placed the blue budgie coin purse in her go-to-the-hospital bag whenever she has had to be admitted.

The blue budgie story is in our family archive as a legendary tale that gives hope, magic, and smiles. Again, Anna was alive because of unexplainable circumstances that felt like a miracle.

On the other end of the earth in Maine, Sara, Ian, and I were relieved that Anna was in recovery and we could focus on the birth of their daughter, Freyja. I was a lucky mother to be able to be with Sara and Ian while she was in labor and gave birth to our first granddaughter on a cold and snowy January night. I called her my snow fairy. Holding her in my arms was a gift as I walked through that door of grandparenthood. I wanted to share this moment with Doug. There seemed to be so much magic in our lives with Anna recovering, Freyja being born, and the new possibility of a second Aussie grandchild on the way.

After Anna was settled, Doug returned to California with a renewed hope she would heal from her latest scary infection. Wanting to meet Freyja, he jumped on another plane to Maine for a few days and had the opportunity to hold his first granddaughter. It was beautiful for us to be together with this gorgeous baby and our new stage of grandparenthood. As it turned out, we had no idea something sinister like a pandemic was lurking in the world and would prevent us from visiting again until Freyja was well over a year old.

As our life was about all the ever-moving parts of being in one place or another, I returned to California for another flight to Melbourne to see Anna as we had previously planned. In this never-stay-still life, I was desperate to see Anna and be in her new house in Point Cook. We were still worried about the fungal infection as it was not yet all gone. Once again, I was on a plane and landed at the Melbourne airport sixteen hours later.

While walking in Melbourne with tourist shops and cafés, Anna and I stopped for a coffee. I ordered a flat white with almond milk and Anna, a regular latte. We came to a place with picnic tables to sit, and when I did, tears overcame me. I knew I just needed to cry. "What's wrong, Mom?" Anna asked.

All I could respond with were more tears. I just simply had to cry. Anna looked quite disturbed to have a blubbering mother. "I cannot go on, Anna, until I let this out. I was so scared I would lose you, and Australia is so far away." And I kept crying.

Finally, Anna told me, "Mom, you have to get over it. You have to accept this." The jag of tears finally finished, and I dusted myself off, and we went on.

Thank goodness the door to her future did not close, as 2020 was a year that would be very big and full of changes for Anna and Terry and the rest of the world.

chapter twenty-four

Becoming Bubbles, Becoming Mummy

In her early pregnancy, Sara asked me what I wanted to be called as a grandmother. I did not know and went online researching grandmother names. My mom was Grammy to the girls. I wanted something different, fun, and less traditional than just Grandma.

I talked with Sara on the phone about my research. "I cannot believe some of the names that women take as grandmothers, Sara. I have not yet figured it out. I have read that some have even called themselves Bubbles. I think it is a sort of Jewish Bubbe name."

We laughed about Bubbles when she said to me, "Mom, that is it. You are Bubbles!" I could not dissuade her. She was determined that was to be my name. I decided, why not? If it made my beautiful Sara happy, then that is what it would be. Excited about my new identity, we were waiting for the arrival of our first grandchild only a plane flight away in Maine.

Next, we had to decide what Doug's name was, and Grandpa Doug did not sound right either. After some banter, Doug's position at the Lab came up as he was Chief of Engineering. That was it. He was Chief. We were to be known as Bubbles and Chief. What made these names stick was they made us smile. We were suffering the distance in miles between us, so names that were a bit humorous helped the edge of loneliness.

From early in their childhoods, I always imagined that Sara

would be the one who would make us grandparents. I understood that Anna could never have a child. When Anna met Terry, she told me about her mystical vision of a young child with curly blonde hair calling to her from Australia. At the time I could only shake my head. I never could allow myself to believe she would have a child. But, within a year after their marriage, I discovered they were serious about this.

Anna never thought she wanted to risk having a child, but finding Terry changed all of that. Moving to Australia gave her a new life. She was not surrounded by memories of her sick past. No one knew her in the life she had growing up. She was now Anna Lark Holyoak, happily married, and they wanted a child together. Anna felt she could be an at-home mom. It was too difficult for her to create a career in her new life, as so much time had to be spent caring for her health. Being Mum would become her work and her life.

Anna talked about being a mother with her Aussie friend Kate who had a transplant and a child. Kate encouraged her, saying it was hard, but if she could do it, Anna could too. It grew increasingly important to Anna to make her vision real and for her and Terry to have someone to share their dreams with.

Adoption was not an option in Australia due to her health, so they explored surrogacy. It can be very difficult to find the right surrogate. Referred to as unicorns, surrogates are rare and precious. In Australia, surrogacy has to be altruistic. Parents-to-be are not allowed to pay for a surrogate, making it even harder to find one.

It was complicated for me to get on board. As I worked on my mosaics and talked with my friends about it, I ruminated for a long time. I was simply worried. Taking the leap of accepting Anna being a mom seemed impossible for me because it took so much for her to simply be and take care of herself. Having a baby meant the baby would have to become the center of her world, and I was so used to her being the center of all of our worlds. I felt she had no idea what she was getting into. For sure, she didn't, and the truth is no woman does until that baby arrives.

There was a point when Anna had another talk with me, saying, "Mom, you have to stop thinking I am going to die. I am alive, and I am living. I am going to continue to live. I am going to have a child, and I need your positive support."

She hit the nail on the head, and I had internal work to do. It was true that since she was first diagnosed, I believed she was going to die. I did not know when it would be, but I was preparing, always. I needed to make a shift in my beliefs for myself and for Anna. I had to change my outlook that, truly, Anna was living. The overwhelming evidence was there. She was alive! I knew it but parts of my heart had not fully taken the leap of faith that this would continue. She was going to have a child, and it had nothing to do with me. It was between her and her husband. She was making a choice for herself, like she did to move to Australia. Anna owned her life. I would be a grandmother called Bubbles to her child if the surrogacy was successful. I had to let go and accept.

My struggle to see Anna simply living every day in all of her choices was a direct result of my trauma so many years previous. I created a way to protect my heart and mind as a young mom by wanting to be always prepared for her death. That is what happens in trauma. We develop strategies to cope. Those strategies are sticky, attaching with a tight grip that may not serve us later. Even though we just had reason to fear the outcome of her recent illness, she did not die, she survived, and her belief in her life was strong.

It was not easy, but I paid attention to letting go. I let myself be more in the moment than in the future I feared. As I did, I could feel the gripping layer of protection soften around my heart that had been there since the beginning of our CF journey. I am still learning to wiggle and loosen those belief tentacles. I have always collected the blessings of her short or long life, but I still have had to accept more of the messiness of the unknowable about her life. Standing in the middle of it is uncomfortable and scary. I knew that if I could just allow more of the unknown to be present without my tight grip, I would be freer to just be with Anna and her having a child.

Of course, my greatest fear was that CF and the complications of transplant would end Anna's life, leaving her child without a mother. I had to make this real possibility fluid in my mind and heart and be present one day at a time. Projecting fear into the future for my grandbaby to come was not productive for any of us. I needed faith and allowed the unknowable to sit more comfortably inside my heart, accepting and grateful for all we had been given.

__Anna__ - Soon after I met Terry, I had a vision, as clear as day, that I would be a mother of a little girl with curly blonde hair. This wasn't the dream I longed for, but my abrupt, strange out-of-place vision confused me and surprised me. It didn't take long to realize that if I was to make a life in Australia, away from all that I knew and all those that I loved, I needed to create a new life with roots and a new family, my own family.

Terry and I discussed ways to become parents together. I always assumed adoption would be my option if I ever did become a mother. However, adoption in Australia was not an option for us, as a variety of factors were stacked against us. The next option was surrogacy. We researched and learned that despite the common myth that surrogacy in Australia was illegal, it, in fact, was not and was completely legal if a potential surrogate altruistically offered you the opportunity.

There were so many legalities of how to approach the topic. You could not "advertise," and you could not pay. It had to be completely altruistic on behalf of the surrogate. The other issue was you were not legally allowed to ask anyone to be your surrogate. It had to be an offer from the potential surrogate to you. These are some pretty extreme rules around the issue that must be thought through and delicately approached. However, once we learned more about how it all worked, we learned the ways to navigate the process.

Terry and I decided the only way we would be able to really get into this world of surrogacy was to dive in by attending a weekend conference in Sydney where we could meet others who were also in their surrogacy journey. Arriving excited and eager to learn, we heard this was often a place where intended parents and surrogates met in person on their way to developing a journey together. Attending this conference was probably the most overwhelming experience of our lives. Hearing the stories of struggle, refinancing houses, failed IVF, medical problems, legal paperwork, overseas surrogacy, and many other experiences and potential pitfalls was so intense.

Terry and I walked out of the first day like zombies looking at each other with blank stares, white as ghosts, and with a deep fear of the future instilled in us. I remember Terry attempting to calculate the potential cost from some of what we had heard, and he looked like a cartoon character with dollar signs in his eyes.

The process was daunting, from the start of IVF, creating embryos, passing all the testing involved, and then finding a surrogate who was the right fit. We were so discouraged by the end, and we didn't think it would be possible for us to ever figure out this journey to parenthood. However, we trudged on despite the pure exhaustion and loss of hope.

Letting people know that we were attending the conference was our opportunity to announce that we were embarking on the surrogacy process and that we would be looking for a surrogate. The wording had to be just right, but it was common for people to share their needs with their families and friend communities. Often, friends or family would take the announcement as an opportunity to find out more or "offer" to look into being your surrogate.

My post on Facebook: "We are embarking on a huge journey

as a couple and looking to grow our family. Because of my transplant, we are learning about surrogacy to help us have a child.
We have come to Sydney for the big Families through Surrogacy
Conference to learn the options out here and in other countries.
This is the beginning of our journey... We want to be open and
share as this is a journey of support and love, and hope for our
future dreams. The love and generosity of someone will change
our lives for the better."

I made this post in the taxi on the way back to the airport
to return to Melbourne. Within the next couple of hours, we had
eighty-one messages of support and love. Following this post, we
also had four women offer to help us. It was a roller coaster ride.

Two of the offers were ruled out because their doctors were
not supportive for the sake of their health, and the other two
had life circumstances that didn't allow them to go forward. We
couldn't believe that we had such a reaction from one Facebook
post! Despite the interest, we still did not have a viable option for
a surrogate. We did learn at the conference that being involved in
the surrogacy Facebook community was often a place of resource
and accessibility to women who wanted to become surrogates. It
was a place with strict rules of how to meet and introduce your
story, but also a place to get support and be "exposed" as someone who needed a generous woman's help.

I had a few conversations with potential surrogates. It felt a
little like online dating. We had started to lose hope in ever finding someone in Australia, but continued on, as we had a lot of
steps in the process to get through. We had time to find someone.

With two rounds of IVF, we, fortunately, created five
embryos that were frozen and ready for when we did find our
surrogate. Still, we had many medical appointments to complete with a genetic counselor, doctors, nurses, counselors, blood
draws, surgeries, recovery time, financial consultation, and all
the many steps that go into the IVF process. Trudging through it
all, we were accepted into the surrogacy program at Melbourne
IVF, and yet we had not found our surrogate.

Feeling we had to expand our search, we looked at the idea of sending our embryos to Canada and finding a surrogate there. That is when one fateful post in search of others who had done just that changed the trajectory of our journey. A woman named Michelle saw my post and commented that she was in Melbourne and looking to become a surrogate, and since we were relatively close, we should chat. Things moved quickly from there. We sent many Facebook messages and quickly decided to meet for coffee.

I learned she was a police detective, her husband was also a police officer, and they had four kids. She was done having kids for herself but always thought she could help another person by having a child for them. We stayed at the coffee shop for hours until she finally realized how late it was and that she needed to pick up her older kids from school. Our relationship was off to a great start. It all flowed quite naturally from there. Soon after, we were officially a surrogacy team, the Lehmanns and the Holyoaks.

Our mission was to create an amazing little human. The process took us just under two years to complete. Looking back, it wasn't long, but while going through the process, the time felt drawn out and as if the end result would never arrive. Despite creating the embryos before we met Michelle, we still had to proceed down the road of bureaucracy and many hurdles with caution, compassion, honesty, a little luck, magic, and miracles.

We participated in counseling sessions, psych evaluations, medical appointments, legal agreements, and standing before a patient review panel. We did it all while feeling amazed and grateful that Michelle, with the support of her husband, Damian, continued to want to help us every step of the way.

After our patient review panel approval, we were finally given the green light to go forward with the embryo transfer. The process was so strange. Terry and I met Michelle at the clinic to medically inseminate her with our embryo. We were in the room watching the embryologist suck the embryo up into a long tube that was then passed to the doctor and then quickly inserted into Michelle. Boom, done. We were now what is affectionately called PUPO (pregnant until proven otherwise).

Michelle and I share a belief in the value of acupuncture and many spiritual things. After the embryo transfer, we headed down the street for a treatment of acupuncture. We both had a session. It has been shown that acupuncture is extremely supportive during the IVF process, enhancing the body's acceptance of embryos. We wanted to do whatever we could to support Michelle in keeping our little embryo safe and growing. It would require two weeks, fourteen days, a fortnight to know the results. That doesn't usually seem like a long period of time, especially since the whole process took just under two years, but waiting those fourteen days (20,160 minutes) until we got the blood results to know if Michelle was pregnant felt like an eternity.

We found out on December 8, 2019, that, indeed, our little embryo had stuck, and we were pregnant with the little miracle of life who was to be known as Zoe in nine months! She was due on August 12, 2020. It was two days later that I ended up in the hospital for what we thought could have been a possible ending to my life story. But fortunately, the miracles continued, and it was not the ending. Not even close. My health recovered, and quite a lot of my lung function returned. I had a goal. I had a purpose. I was going to be a mama.

When I arrived by myself in Australia in February 2020 after being with Sara for the birth of Freyja, Anna was recovering from the threat to her life due to the fungal infection. She was still healing and getting stronger. We talked about the magic of the blue budgie's appearance to lighten our emotions. It made us smile and feel hopeful, remembering our earlier times with Lama Gangha.

The passing health crisis with the dangerous fungal infection was most intense at the time because we had learned just before that their surrogate, Michelle, was pregnant. My greatest fear of potential loss concerning a future grandbaby losing her mum made a poignant appearance. But the threat to Anna and Terry's dream of becoming parents together was quickly disappearing.

Climbing out of that hole of potential devastating loss, we shifted with Anna's lead and started to prepare for the baby one day at a time. Right after arriving in Melbourne, I went with Anna and her mother-in-law and other grandmother-to-be, Rhonda, to a baby exposition at a downtown conference center. Rhonda was over the moon that they were to have a child, and I was relieved that Anna had her nearby. I felt lost not being the grandmother and mother for Anna to rely on, but so grateful she had Rhonda.

Together we looked at the prams, cloth diapers, diaper bags, and all of the gear that Anna wanted to start her mummy journey. I was so glad that I could be there and buy her a few things. Rhonda was extraordinarily generous, loving her new role. My favorite purchase for the little one was a darling chair upholstered in a pink fabric with woodland animals and flowers, perfect for a toddler to sit in.

I had just witnessed the birth of my snow fairy, Freyja, in Maine. I knew I would not have that same chance with Michelle, but we planned for me to come later in August and be with them as Mom and Bubbles, along with Rhonda as Nana.

They were going to have a girl. Anna's vision was being realized, but the baby needed a name. Terry, Anna, and I visited one of their favorite restaurants downtown and discussed names to consider. There were likes and dislikes between our appetizers, wine, main dishes, and dessert. By the end of dinner, they both agreed on one. It was Terry's favorite. It was Zoe. Anna picked up her phone and looked up the meaning of Zoe. It was from the Greek and meant "life." It was perfect. Zoe was life. Sharing that table and conversation was an honor for Bubbles.

I returned home on a Qantas flight with the talk of a pandemic in the news. While on the plane, I heard the attendants discuss whether they should wear masks. It was eerie. I was fully expecting to return to Australia when our little Zoe was to arrive later in August, but just a few weeks later, a worldwide pandemic was declared.

At the time, it seemed the pandemic would not last long. Doug could not go to work, so we considered ourselves lucky and got to stay in our country nest getaway in a little town in the foothills of the Sierra. As time passed, the way to work for Doug and so many people to keep the world going was telecommuting. Doug was the Chief Electrical Engineer working from the kitchen counter. Who would have ever thought that possible?

I snuggled into our retreat from the world and went to the grocery store to get our supplies once per week at 6 a.m., fully masked with nitrile gloves to limit my exposure. When the groceries came home through the garage, I would wash them all before putting them away. We were part of this weird and crazy new life.

We were the lucky ones. We had a remote home to stay away from people and the virus as best we could. Doug's highly professional job could continue online through Zoom. This was true for our son-in-law, Ian, as well. Sara got a short extension for her maternal leave. Still, she would have to resume seeing patients at the hospital. Because she had a young baby at home, she did not have to see Covid patients. Still, after work, she would strip and shower before taking her baby in her arms, hoping the virus did not find a way to tag along with her.

But for Terry, he had to stop working. This caused painful anxiety for him. He was secure in his work for a family business; still, in Australia, especially in Victoria, everything shut down more and longer than anywhere in the world. Thankfully, the government provided a stipend to all its working citizens.

At the beginning of the shutdown, Anna and Terry were expectant parents. They could not leave their house but for groceries. Anna's transplant and her immune suppression made her very vulnerable to Covid-19. It was frightening and emotionally very difficult for them and us, who worried about them from the other side of the world.

We all thought this would be over quickly until we saw the statistics of people dying and the political turmoil. Expecting the intense search for a vaccine would go well into the future, we had to accept that we were stuck and could not fly to our daughters or see our grandbabies. It tore at our hearts. Anna was going to have to become a mom on her own. I would not be able to be there.

What was amazing for Anna and Terry was that the pandemic created a cocoon for them to be first-time parents. They were home together all day, every day, for months on end. This meant that Anna had the total support of her husband to raise Zoe. She was not alone. They became a powerful team. That gave me such solace since I could not be there to help. Anna had total support from Terry. It was one of those silver linings that comes with terrible storm clouds.

The loss of being together and missing the milestones of the babies' births and growth, including the first birthdays, caused many tears. We also missed Sara's graduation from her family medicine residency and saw it on Zoom. Still, there was something else besides losing in-person time with our daughters and grandchildren. Doug and I found peace in living full-time in the foothills with our trees, the birds, the creek, and a simpler life.

After breakfast, Doug would open his laptop and sit at the kitchen counter with his coffee, conducting meetings. After my morning coffee, I would go outside to my art studio for a day of work on my mosaics. There were no interruptions but for the tugs on our heartstrings and the underlying discomfort that a virus lurked somewhere.

I was filled with the enjoyment of having time to dedicate myself to producing new art. I completed a mosaic on a concrete block wall in front of my studio, a commission for a large mirror for a friend, and learned how to do glass-on-glass flowers. A woman in England started a new Facebook page with the gift of tutorials for anyone who wanted to learn her techniques to create flowers out of stained glass mosaiced on mirror. It was a way to create more beauty in a world rocked by fear. I loved every moment I spent in that studio.

We were all surprised by the quick approval of a vaccine and got ours as soon as possible. This was what we saw as the only way out of our isolation. In April 2021, we could travel again to Maine, reuniting with Sara, Ian, and Freyja with relief and happy tears.

It wasn't until May of 2022 that we were able to get to Australia, rush into the arms of Anna and Terry, and meet Zoe, who was already twenty-one months old. It was also the first time I hugged my incredible daughter who was unbelievably known as a mother called Mum. It was, of course, another miracle. We all survived our first and hopefully last worldwide pandemic.

chapter twenty-five

Who Could Ever Have Imagined?

Sitting on the kitchen floor in front of the pantry at Anna's house, I was at eye level with Zoe. She had her pink fairy wings on and was not yet two years old. We had only spent time together while I was an image known as Bubbles on the screen in the cell phone box. Our separation was due to the pandemic that kept her locked away and me unable to fly to Australia. It was an easy start to our new in-person relationship, and it was so delicious that now I got to hug her and have her near me.

As we made friends, she sat on my lap, and I hoped that one day, she and her cousin Freyja would meet. Noticing her short curly hair, just like Anna's at her age, I marveled that my dear daughter had a daughter herself. My mind repeated over and over, "Never in my wildest dreams..."

I watched as Anna was Mummy (an Aussie Mommy), preparing breakfast with healthful and varied foods similar to how I had cared for her. Zoe was almost the same age as Anna was when she came home from the hospital after her diagnosis of CF. How time had gone by. As Zoe ate her breakfast, she proved to be Anna's daughter with her healthy appetite and love of food.

During our visit and after meeting Zoe for the first time, we knew we had to do our best to grow our connection and be part of Zoe's life even though we lived thousands of miles away. This was our fourth visit to Australia, and having her in our lives made us feel connected to the country in a more profound and personal way.

Outside Anna's door and at the end of the street, a barrier fence held a sign announcing "Final Releases," and it caught Doug's eye. The last lots for residential buildings in her neighborhood were for sale. We looked at the land lots, schemed, and discussed ways to buy one to build a home just around the corner, fulfilling our promise to stay well connected.

When Anna first told us about her interest in Australia, I warned her, "We are NOT going to Australia. This is our home here in California!" I was serious and scared at the time, and maybe I thought if I said that, she would come to her senses and not go there. But it became clear it was her destiny. Now, what was happening to us?

Before we got together to scheme a way to buy a lot around the corner, Anna was already dreaming of investing in a property. It was part of her undying love of real estate. Even though we lived so far away from each other, we decided this might be a project we could share. Doug and I joined with Anna and Terry to buy a lot and build a house. We could use the house when we visited, but it would be theirs and part of a legacy for Zoe. Again, it was something we never thought we would do and another unexpected adventure with Anna.

We chose a builder, and Anna and I designed the house to be built. It would take about two years before completion. The land lots still needed to be prepared with infrastructure before the house would be built. This opportunity to make a plan and to have a comfortable way to be in our Aussie family's lives enticed us. Life was continually presenting unexpected changes and experiences. Our project would build on our Aussie future with Anna fully living, and we wanted to live alongside her, Terry, and our sweet Zoe (at least part of the time). Who could ever have imagined?

When Anna was about fifteen, she and I attended a country harvest fair at Hidden Villa, not far from our home. There was a booth for a psychic among the arts and crafts. "Oooo, let's go there, Mom, and have a reading!" she implored me. Always game for these fun adventures with her, I agreed. These types of experiences were a part of our ever-continued quest to find magic.

The young woman psychic used cards for our reading. "You two have a special bond as mother and daughter," she told us. "The cards tell me you will be traveling worldwide together and doing some work with children." She emphasized, "You will do important things together, maybe write a book, but mostly, traveling."

After asking her to clarify more about travel to far-off places, we walked away from her booth laughing. "Well, that psychic was way off," we agreed. Never in our wildest dreams were we traveling anywhere else in the world. We both knew what the other thought, even if we did not say it directly. Anna would never be able to travel like that. Besides, CF would rob her of her life before any opportunity to do so. The idea of going to other countries and spending time together in that way was a ridiculous pipe dream.

We will always remember that reading and our reaction to it. It never made sense until the miracle that would come years later changed everything. In retrospect, her prediction was accurate in many ways. Still, we were not privy to the future like that woman at the little harvest fair seemed to be.

What the psychic could never tell us about were the intimate details. The how and why, the trials, and the life and death challenges it would take to get to this point. We became world travelers with a child, our Zoe, to love and raise. Only Anna, Sara, Doug, and I know what it has been like to get here. We have grown and matured and are wounded warriors with coping skills that emerged out of our traumas due to CF and transplant.

For Doug and myself, our lives have never been simple. It is now very complicated to have our own lives as an artist and retired scientist/engineer while being active parents and grandparents not living near our children. Still, for now, we are doing the best we can.

To gain perspective, I sometimes reflect on our ancestry to understand the constant conundrum of inconvenience and travel distance with our daughters. We are direct descendants of many courageous people with unimaginable lives, making risky choices to move, travel, escape danger, and live a life no one else has lived. I might think our lives are not so different, but in these modern times, it is quite a bit easier to meet these life challenges. It is true, too, that everyone alive today has similar ancestors who have struggled and triumphed. We all come from courage and survival.

But who would have ever imagined when Anna was first diagnosed with what appeared to be truly insurmountable odds that she would live into her forties on the other side of the world, become a full Australian citizen, marry an Aussie, and be the mother of a child? The answer is no one in their right mind unless they were that psychic at the harvest fair. Anna's life is a testament to her miraculous spirit and the evolution of medicine and life for humans on this planet.

Also, with the spirit of adventure, moving long distances, and living without sunken roots, Sara, Ian, and Freyja returned to their two-bedroom yellow cottage in Napa, California, in autumn of 2021. Arriving with suitcases of clothing but leaving their household items behind, they came to see if they wanted to relocate permanently. Their hearts were still attached to their quaint New England home in Hollowell, Maine, but they felt it was too hard to be far from family. Sara was newly pregnant again and started her California medical career while her tummy grew. At the end of May 2022, our third granddaughter, Maeve, was born.

Not long after, in August 2022, our Australians traveled to California for a stay and to finally reunite our family with three granddaughters. Sara, her new baby, and Freyja excitedly waited for us as we drove home from the airport with our Aussies. As soon as we arrived at our Livermore home, Anna jumped out of the car, running to the side door, where joy burst out. The sisters grabbed each other, falling to the floor in an unending embrace. They had not seen each other for four years. The two little girl cousins, Freyja and Zoe, saw each other for the first time not on FaceTime, and immediately hugged and held hands. It was a beautiful climax to the end of a painful separation created by the far distance and the pandemic.

Our house was instantly full with six adults, a new baby, and two two-year-olds. The children were mini copies of their mommies but with different personalities. We all had to learn each other's needs and cope with a sweltering summer. Climate change offered us temperatures over 110 degrees in Livermore, so we escaped to the coast where we could better survive. It was a full and poignant three weeks that I could never have imagined as a young mom with a sick child with CF. Miraculously, I was grandmother Bubbles to three granddaughters and had both of my daughters and their husbands with me.

The night before Anna, Terry, and Zoe were to return to Australia, Anna became very ill with a fever and felt she could not get out of bed by the morning. Our grand reunion was rudely interrupted by that unwanted guest of severe illness who slipped in without us noticing.

As Sara and I watched, Anna tried to sit up, but then collapsed into what we feared was a seizure. After coming to, Anna told us she had never felt so terrible and wanted an ambulance, an unusual and alarming request. Sitting on the bed surrounded by half-packed suitcases, Sara assessed her condition, assuring her we could get to the ER without an ambulance.

Sara and I drove Anna to the ER at Stanford Hospital, about fifty minutes away. Chief and the daddies stayed behind to take care of the children.

When first admitted, Anna went in and out of consciousness and was considered for the ICU. After tests, she was diagnosed with parainfluenza and severe sepsis, requiring many lines of saline and multiple antibiotics. It was not clear how the sepsis that ran through her body came about. It is something that can just happen in immune-suppressed patients like her. Thank goodness it struck before they left for the airport. Anna spent a week in the hospital. It was terrifying to see her so sick so quickly, but once again, she miraculously recovered after receiving care at a highly specialized hospital.

Anna needed to stay two more weeks to complete her IV therapy at our home. After one week, Terry and Zoe were ready to leave. We went downtown for a final dinner to celebrate her recovery and our month together. It was a beautiful and warm September evening. We ate pizza outside near a public square as Native American dancers and drummers gathered.

In what seemed spontaneous to us but was a planned event, a performance began with traditional Native American dances, haunting drumbeats, and the drummers' songs. We were mesmerized, and the girls loved it. Joining in, Zoe, Freyja, and I sat in a circle of drums, beating the skins, and, to end the evening, joined in a circle dance. I held the girls' hands as we stepped in unison to celebrate the importance of family and community. We were thrilled to participate in this spontaneous, magical, and deeply meaningful event to top off our family time together. It was another blessing of spirit, perfect for us and very unexpected.

The evening's gifts were especially precious to Anna since Terry and Zoe would leave the following day. It felt even more magical for Anna, watching Zoe as she took to the drumming while patting her little two-year-old hand over her heart.

After this beautiful experience, Anna reminded me of when she was little and before Sara was born; my ancestral interests and spiritual seeking led us to a powerful Native American medicine circle. Tara, the medicine woman of the group, did a healing ritual for Anna (one of her many healing experiences as a child).

Not long ago, a friend, Denice, reminded me that we also had a fire ceremony to rid us of something from our lives. I brought a nebulizer and tubing to our ritual representing Anna's disease. The group supported my prayer that the burden of Anna's lung disease be lifted from her as it burned in the fire and drumming and ancient chants filled our ears. As a witness to what happened that night of the ceremony, Denice feels Anna's life of transplant demonstrated the fruitful blessing of that seemingly impossible prayer.

Later, Tara painted a drum with Anna's medicine animal. On the drum was a coyote howling at the moon. The coyote spirit represents survival, adaptability, tenacity, resourcefulness, and cleverness. She has always had a coyote by her side.

This experience of native healing was a part of my search for my spiritual path. I shared my lifelong quest with Anna and Sara while they were growing up, exposing them to many ways of perceiving spirituality. Through all of our harrowing and magical experiences, both of my daughters have also explored their inner lives and spirituality through Buddhism, meditation, yoga, books, podcasts, teachers, psychics, and their Jewish ancestry. They also know their life is a spiritual journey and have a strong interest in finding meaning and understanding their lives, believing the fundamental source to all life is love and compassion.

I have watched them become mothers, and I have attained the great position of Bubbles, the grandmother to support them and love my granddaughters. They both are wonderful mothers with deep spirits and kind natures. I see myself in them and them in me. Since becoming a mother, when Anna and I have visited, she says, "Oh, of course, that is why I am the way I am. I am so much like you, Mom." What a joy that brings to my heart.

In May and June 2023, during our visit to Australia about

eight months after our reunion ended and Anna recovered and flew home, we once again witnessed Anna still in the clutches of CF. Rough and troubling punches to Anna's gut as digestive blockages were much too frequent. They were wearing on her spirit and preyed upon our hearts. The tremendous challenge of being a mum, keeping her life organized, and all of the continual problems due to CF and immune suppression were clearly taking a toll.

The many traumas of infection and hospitalizations have exhausted her. She has lived long past her original life expectancy with her lung transplant miracle. It is tough to continue to battle for good health with CF not leaving her alone, yet she does. She keeps going. Her life has given her enduring inspiration with the magic and miracle of Zoe. This special child carried in the womb of a unicorn surrogate to be Anna and Terry's child has brought her purpose. Watching her daughter as she plays fills Anna with an elixir of joy that melts the hard stuff into the background.

After one month on this trip, Doug returned to California, but I stayed an extra two weeks. Near the end of my visit, I sat up in bed at 3:30 a.m. and could not sleep. Earlier in the evening, shortly after Zoe went to bed, Terry had taken Anna to the hospital for the second time since we'd arrived. The evil ghost of intestinal pain had started to haunt her early in the afternoon. By evening, it had knocked her off of her feet. I held her, kissed her sweet head, and helped her get in the car for yet another terrible onslaught of pain. It is hard to accept that her body still has to endure this cruel, rude chronic illness taking even more from her. It feels so unfair.

My precious daughter needs more miracles, and I need to stop aging. I am not done being her mother. Our future days are uncertain, and I need to be flexible at this time of my slowing. I cannot just stop and fold into my instinct for retreating in my older age. We are now in our seventies, squeezing life from its tube. Juggling two daughters and three granddaughters with my one heart and one body requires agility. I resist having to go here and there and want to gather them all under my apron at the same time and same place, but life still points in different directions. I need faith that I will always find a way to be me, Robin, Mom, and Bubbles in the best ways possible as I follow this path.

The sadness, pain, and chronic sorrow of the potential loss of my daughter has stopped me in my tracks for forty years. I feel a familiar rush of worry at the arrival of every storm that announces yet another threat. It grabs my heart. Meanwhile, we have learned not to have the storm be our focus. Doug and I are busy with our lives, engaged, lifting up, seeing the light, touching love, admiring beauty, and loving life.

Anna has gone into therapy for her trauma due to her continual hospitalizations. She is trying to heal and work through the pain that has been the price for her extraordinary life. The number of times she has had to enter the hospital in Melbourne and the mounting number of problems associated with being immune-suppressed has made her more vulnerable. She is learning about honoring all her feelings, acceptance, gratitude, and continuing to move forward. It is tough. Even so, sitting together in her kitchen having breakfast during our visit, Anna told me, "Mom, I am just an ordinary person sitting here eating my oatmeal."

My response was, "Anna, you are not an ordinary person. You have the courage of a lion with the tenacity, determination, will, spirit, intuition, power, and love of an extraordinary person. And besides, who could ever have imagined your life?"

Reflecting on how she made it through her most recent difficult times, Anna told me, "Mom, I am brave because I chose to go into the darkness with only a flashlight to find my path. There is no already paved yellow brick road. I find my way with my choices and effort to create miracles. I find rainbows in the rain and stars in the night sky with my gratitude."

The query, who could ever have imagined long ago what has happened in our lives as a result of an intrepid CF warrior living with us as our daughter, leads one to the next question: what more is there to come? We simply do not know, but we step forward with love, courage, and the hope for more miracles.

chapter twenty-six

My Spiritual Training Ground

Whraen I was twenty-six years old, just recently married, and with no children or any hint about my future life, I made a fateful prayer. Kneeling beside my bed dressed in its lemon-yellow comforter, I had made preparations for a serious yet sacred moment. On my bedside table was a lit candle, a small vase of white and purple cosmos picked from my little garden, and a floating string of fragrant smoke rising from a stick of incense standing tall in a small bowl of rice. With the mood set and being alone in my house, I completed an assignment exploring the experience of prayer.

"I pray that my life will be deep and rich and bring me what I need to grow and know my spiritual self."

My intentions were sincere. The words moved through my mind toward an inward and unknown place where prayers are heard. They resonated within me long after rising from my knees. Said so many years ago, the prayer was not to anyone specific, to God, or any other beings. It was a prayer of deep personal commitment concerning my relationship with my life, how I would meet it, and what I wanted from it.

During my parental journey, I understood the axiom, "*Be careful what you ask for.*" If we sincerely ask or pray for something like a rich and deep life, that doesn't mean that everything will be wonderful and full of constant happiness if it comes to pass. It does mean that when we are offered opportunities for deeper understanding, there will also be trials.

Only when experienced together will we deepen and enrich our lives. As it turned out, Doug and I had a child with cystic fibrosis and all of its terrible trials to love, learn, and grow.

Understanding early on that opportunities and trials, or the meaningful and the challenging, are usually found together helped me grow and find stability in times of deep crisis as a mother of a child with a life-limiting illness. This idea has been a key to recovery following harrowing moments and medical challenges. The dichotomy of experience now makes sense to me because I have seen that we are stretched to grow when life gets hard. There is always a healing morsel, a blessing to be discovered if we look for it. My life has become rich and deep, and I have had what I needed to grow and learn about my spiritual self through the ups and downs of being Anna's mom.

Being part of a community of other families who had similar trials was also integral to the richness and gifts CF offered us. We made lifelong friendships with people with similar experiences that were tough and unasked for. We needed each other. There were so many incredible people who were touched by this disease that terrified us. We were filled with a richness and intimacy we could never find in relationships outside this rare world. The challenge of CF deepened them, and knowing them deepened us. It was spiritual grace and a gift.

This is what I always wanted for my life, for it to have a significant richness. I did not know that my desire for that depth of meaning would include all the hard parts this disease would offer. Still, it did, and the challenges became the training ground for my spiritual life.

I now know my early exploration of my inner world and what I asked for in my prayer laid the groundwork, took me by the hand, and led me to meet the trials, obstacles, broken hearts, lessons, adventures, and joys of being Anna's mom. My life unfolded as it was meant to. I witnessed love, courage, and miracles in surprising ways. These primary experiences led me to find my precious teacher, Lama Gangha, the magic of Sai Baba's vibhuti, and the perspective of becoming a miracle collector. All of the specific challenges and sufferings were not asked for. Still, life with Anna and CF has been rich with the stuff of life and the ripening of my request of the heart.

I was plunged into a journey of self-discovery proven to be the most profound teacher. When asked, would you want a different life without CF so central in it? At first, I would say yes. I would wish the pain and sorrow, trials and tribulations, fears and bouts with death to be gone from the brow of both of my daughters and me and Doug. But it has been our life, rich and deep with extraordinary gifts, and I, then, would have to say no. This is what I asked for. I want to live authentically and fully, however it is to be.

I have learned that spirituality is quite simple. In the beginning of my quest to understand my inner life and what it means to be spiritual, I had opportunities for spiritual practice. I first learned meditation in college. It opened me to the understanding and experience that an inner world could be accessed. I studied Eastern religions in my graduate program. I met Tibetan lamas and became a student of its chanting, mantras, and exotic practices. Still, I have realized that a spiritual life is much simpler than I assumed as a young woman.

A spiritual life is a life of authenticity, acceptance of life as it is, and being kind and compassionate. I believe this is what the practices and spiritual teachers teach. In the terrible storms where pain and sadness reside, a knowing that there is also light, magic, and miracles to be found also grows with life's experiences. This has been the fruit of the path as it has unfolded for me as Anna's mom.

I know, too, that it is important to allow yourself to feel those storms where compassion grows, realizing there will always be another. That is the way human life is. But knowing you can choose not to dwell in the pain is also essential. You can shift your focus to beauty and collect blessings. I do believe this is the simple yet profound teaching of the Dalai Lama.

When Anna and I met him while she waited for her transplant, he gave a talk to a room full of heartbroken parents and very ill children. He wanted us all to know that despite the terrible reality of illness and suffering, we were also fortunate. We should never forget to be grateful. There is always a positive way to view one's life.

He let us know we were fortunate to receive care at a major hospital with the most modern technology, and we were lucky to have people who loved us. This was his message to parents who felt deep pain in their hearts. And this is what I have learned, too, being Anna's mom. The spiritual path I was searching for was always under my feet. It is found in gratitude.

This does take practice, though. My experience of CF gave me the ground for this practice and inner work. I grew to be grateful for what my life has offered me. I learned this is the true meaning of the voice I heard when Anna was first diagnosed. "If she has a short life, there will be blessings. If she has a long life, there will be blessings. They are both the same." Storms will always come. What you need is right in front of you. There is nowhere else to go. Just look. Blessings will always be there. That is faith, as I understand it.

Because CF is life-threatening, I pondered countless times what it would be like if Anna passed on. I knew that Anna did not want me to dwell on this idea. I did not focus on this all the time, but a mother of a CF child cannot let go of this future possibility as hard as we try.

Since her childhood, I have wondered what her memorial service would be like and have written many eulogies in my mind. These ponderings might come up while in the shower as the water washed the worry and doubt down the drain, and I would need to cry. Or, I could be walking in a beautiful place with trees and life all around, but still, I thought of her passing. I might also be just sitting at the kitchen counter with a cup of tea, and a script would be written in my mind of what I would say to the mourners who came to say goodbye to Anna. I always had to be prepared for that day. It was my way of practicing acceptance.

Others who do not have to deal with this type of diagnosis do not have the same in-your-face experience of mortality. They have other storms they have to weather. When you have to live with death's invitation on your shoulder, there is always a pain in your heart, but there are benefits. There is so much to appreciate and be grateful for. When confronted in this way, you prioritize what is most important and realize you don't want the little stuff to ruin your day. There is just not enough time for that. If you deal with the reality well, you may see something in your day as brighter than before with a growing gratitude for the now. This is what we learned from the Dalai Lama.

There has not been a day without thinking about whether Anna would have a long or short life, but I have always known I will find blessings no matter what. Through the years, I looked for them, and Anna did too. Something as simple as a flower blooming on a particular day or a fortune in a fortune cookie telling us things would be OK were all part of the magic and blessings in our lives. And now I can hug my darling granddaughter Zoe and feel the life that is so real. Anna is living. She is not dying. We are living together, and it is miraculous.

It was time to leave after a six-week visit to Australia in the spring/summer (southern hemisphere fall/winter) of 2023. Anna had to be hospitalized twice during the visit, and leaving was so hard. Before I walked out the door, Zoe and I played a make-believe game of feeding zoo animals. She cried as I got in the car, and tears filled my eyes as I told her, "Bubbles will come back."

I wish it wasn't this way with my coming and going, my arrival in Australia, my departure, my arrival in California, and going here and there. In the car driving to the Melbourne airport, I heard myself say, I wish. What is a wish, I wonder. It says things should not be as they are. A wish is empty, really. I wished it was all different forty-one years ago when Anna was diagnosed with CF. Then, my inner voice reminded me, "If she lives a short life, there will be blessings; if she lives a long life, there will be blessings; they are both the same."

My thoughts bounced out into the car. "The only thing we can do when we wish for our lives to be different, not so painful, and pushing us to our edges is to collect the promised blessings. We are forever miracle collectors with boxes and shelves filled and stacked in our memories. They are what sustain us, Anna."

While telling Anna about this, she began to cry as she drove the car on the Melbourne freeway. "Mom, that struck me. There is something about what you said that is important. I see how I am a collector of so many things and why, including all my thrift shop treasure finding and art collecting. People may look at my life and only see my struggles and how hard it is, and yet I have my collections of joy and miracles. I have made sure of that. I do not focus on the hard. I keep collecting."

Anna's wonderful collections are in plain view in her home, including reminders about her many travels held in tiny medicine vials. Each one holds sand from some far edge of the earth she has traveled. There is pink sand from the Bahamas, white sand from Dubai, orange sand from the Arabian desert, black sand from Hawaii, and more from the tip of South Africa, the coast of Maine, and at least forty others. It makes one wonder how this woman born with a devastating lung disease, living many years of disability followed by a lung transplant, could have filled her life with so many adventures.

As she continued to drive me to my flight, she told me, "The other day, when Dad asked me to tell him about my sand collection, it meant so much. I was filled with joy sharing the stories of each one. Every small vial has a story, a memory of a blessing, and the miracles that gave me my life. I collect what is important, what I value, the love, the relationships, and the experiences."

Resisting and wishing for something different will not reveal the blessings in the messiness of our circumstances. If a wish for my life to be different came true, those blessings I hold dear that gave comfort and inspiration would never have appeared. They are the precious gifts in our miracle collections. With each day, one foot in front of the other, we are still collecting. We do it all of the time.

While in Australia during this last visit, Anna and I walked at Campbell's Cove, where she has a rustic blue beach shack with bigger-than-life, enormous paintings of a white cockatoo with its yellow top knot, a pink and grey galah, a superb blue fairy wren, and most importantly, a blue budgie on its doors. They are artistic renderings of Aussie beauty, nature, and spirit. It was a pleasant winter day with clear skies and no wind. The clear crystal water shimmered as the light beams danced on the floor at the ocean's edge, bouncing off the rocks, seaweed, and pieces of sea glass. Anna said, "I don't know why I love the sea glass so much."

I answered, "It is because the sea glass appears to you as a treasure. You know how to find treasure in your life, Anna. That is what we do together."

As we walked and continued to find shore treasures, I promised in my heart that I, as Bubbles, would also show Zoe, Freyja, and Maeve how to be miracle collectors too.

Robin and Anna under the moon at Campbell's Cove, Australia, 2022.

Afterword

In telling the story about our family's cystic fibrosis journey, it is important to address the most recent advances in research and treatment, as they have been dramatic and life-changing for so many with the disease. The gene that causes cystic fibrosis was discovered in 1989. Since then, researchers have identified over two thousand mutations that can affect the cystic fibrosis transmembrane conductance regulator (CFTR) protein by disrupting normal chloride channel function in the cells of patients with CF.

The most common mutation is called F508del. About 90% of CF patients have one or two copies of this mutation. Another 10% of patients have two copies of less frequently found mutations in five categories. This variety means that there is more than one way that the chloride channel in the cell can be interrupted to cause the disease. The solution to correct these different mechanisms is a complicated problem. Aside from finding a way to correct the defective CFTR gene in all cell types (which is very difficult to do), each targeted solution needs to be different, and each alone would not work for 100% of patients. Knowing this, researchers eventually focused on the most common mutation, F508del, looking for a way to correct the chloride channel function to help most patients. The story about how this came about with a private pharmaceutical company, Vertex, and the strong support of the National Cystic Fibrosis Foundation is remarkable. It demonstrates the power of advocacy in the CF community.

After many ups and downs and successes, Trikafta® was approved by the FDA in 2019, providing a miraculous treatment for 90% of patients with at least one copy of F508del. As more and more patients have gained access to this costly combination of three modulator drugs, the evidence of its effectiveness has shown remarkable improvement in lung function, ability to gain weight, overall wellness, and life expectancy. The CF community considers Trikafta® a dream come true treatment even though a few patients have not tolerated it well.

Anna does not have a copy of F508del. Her genes are much less common, being N1303K and R553X. Her chance for a drug like this to save her lungs is long past, as she had her lung transplant in 2010. She and nearly all of the other 10% have not benefited from the miracle of Trikafta®. Still, Anna suffers from other CF problems, including bowel obstructions, weight gain, sinus infections, liver involvement, and CF-related diabetes. A modulator could still help her even as a transplanted patient. Research and the hunt for a cure for all patients with CF is not done. This also raises issues of equity access to medical treatment for all sufferers of CF worldwide. Equity is compromised by stereotypes, geographical location, political environments, research funding, and other biases.

The word is out that this miraculous treatment is dramatically changing the lives of many people with CF, elevating their life expectancy to near average for the general population. This has caused a dangerous drop in gift giving because people wrongly think the cure is found and all problems are solved. It is excruciating for the 10% to continue to wait for their cure, and they are screaming not to be forgotten. More funds must be raised for continued research, so no one is left behind.

As of this writing, in the summer of 2023, a recent paper giving a hint of hope for Anna was published about a case study in Israel of eight patients sharing one of her mutations, N1303K (the third most common worldwide). It showed that a trial of Trikafta® increased lung function and weight gain, among other changes. This is considered an off-label use for the drug as it targets a different mutation not yet approved by the FDA, making it not covered by insurance and unavailable for her. The cost of Trikafta® is over $300,000 per year per patient. It is an exorbitant cost. Other rare mutations will likely be found to benefit from modulator drugs, so their effectiveness and who can be helped until more targeted drugs are found is still evolving. With each discovery, the company that manufactures it, Vertex in the case of Trikafta®, has to request FDA approval.

Strong advocacy for this specific cohort of N1303K patients, representing 1.5% of the total CF population, estimated to be 2,885 patients worldwide, is needed to make it accessible. Approval for use is important for Anna and others like her waiting for relief. As Doug says, it is a double whammy for Anna. She has worked so hard to get to where she is; now that there may be some help with Trikafta®, she still has to wait.

The fight for the lives of those with CF is not over. The total number of patients, comprising the 10% not eligible for modulator treatment, is estimated to be over 7,000 patients worldwide. Awareness of the prevalence of CF in Asian countries continues to increase, making accurate estimates of how many patients there are worldwide difficult. We need the public to know that not all suffering from this disease is gone. It's not even close! There is much more to be done. Research dollars and patient advocacy are still required. One day, we hope to see something like Trikafta® for the many desperately waiting patients like Anna. When that happens, it will be another miracle lessening her CF-related problems so she can live her healthier, best life in Australia with Terry and as Mummy to Zoe. She deserves it.

Research to find a cure for everyone stretches beyond modulator drugs into stem cells, gene therapy, mRNA therapy, and gene redesigning with technology like CRISPR-Cas9. CFRI has funded efforts on several of these fronts. Many laboratories nationwide are looking for novel therapies to increase the arsenal of treatments and potential cures.

The care of transplant patients also continues to evolve. Every year, more is understood, surgical practices improved, and rejection is managed, extending lives even longer. If Anna's lungs fail sometime in the near future due to rejection or extreme loss of lung function and her health is stable enough, she will have a chance at a second transplant to give her more time with her Terry and Zoe.

For future patients who need transplants, there is currently research to build personal organs from stem cells that are no longer considered science fiction. Lung regeneration with stem cells is still years away, but it may someday revolutionize transplantation. But for now, awareness of the need for donated organs is crucial. More than 100,000 people in the U.S. are waiting for organs of all types. Everyone, including readers of this memoir, can sign up as a potential organ donor. Usually, this can be done when applying for a driver's license.

Advocacy, increased awareness of organ donation, and support for scientific research into lung transplantation and CF treatments will make this world a better place. It means that more families will have their loved ones in their lives longer, and those who are recipients will have the chance to live their own miraculous lives.

For more information:

Cystic Fibrosis Research Institute, CFRI
1731 Embarcadero Road
Suite 210
Palo Alto, CA 94303
650-665-7576
www.cfri.org

Donate Life America
5516 Falmouth Street
Suite 302
Richmond, VA 23230
804-377-3580
www.donatelife.net

The Cystic Fibrosis Foundation
4550 Montgomery Ave.
Suite 1100N
Bethesda, MD 20824
800-344-4823
www.cff.org

Transplant Games of America
1595 Galbraith Ave. SE
Suite 500
Grand Rapids, MI 49546
616-356-2331
www.transplantgamesofamerica.org

Acknowledgments

Thank you can never be said enough. I also have to include gratitude for the sun beginning to rise, encouraging me to get up and open my computer, the coffee sitting beside me on my table, the sounds of the birds as they awaken, bringing me joy and reminders of how there is always magic in our lives. And then there are those wonderful people who encouraged my writing.

Thank you, Sue Dougherty, my sister, for being one of those who always said the story needed to be told, for reading some of the manuscripts, and for approving my portrayal of our mom, whom we loved so much. Thank you to Doug, my husband, with whom I held hands on this journey, and who witnessed the countless hours I spent writing and rewriting and supported the effort. I am always grateful for my friend Sue King, whose happy spirit and loving way made me feel I was doing the right thing in relentlessly pursuing this project, and also Gail Bunge, who listened with understanding to the complications of motherhood when a child has unique challenges.

Thank you to my dear Peggy Kraft, a dedicated friend and brilliant, well-read woman who took the time to read the manuscript more than once. And a huge thank you to Sue Landgraf, a fellow CF mom and dear friend who read every word many times over, giving me extraordinary support. Bouncing ideas together helped me to see the wholeness of my story. Her understanding of how it is as a CF mom was so important to let me know I was sharing enough so that she could feel it and it was true.

And thank you to Wendy von Oech, my friend who was

with me from the beginning of my journey. You have always been a guiding light for me. Your writings inspire me, and your editing help was a joy.

Thank you to Dr. David Weill, Anna's transplant physician whom I contacted when the muse first tapped on my shoulder. I told him Anna's story needed to be told and asked for his support. He said he also wanted to hear more about the experience of the parents and families of lung transplant patients, which felt like permission for me to tell my side of the story.

And a special thank you to Dr. Richard Moss, who also agreed to read the story and offer feedback. He has been in our lives since before Anna was born and witnessed her miraculous recoveries and extraordinary accomplishments. I am forever grateful he was her specialist and always consulted with us about everything!

Thank you, Anna and Sara, for being my incredible daughters, living this challenging and miraculous life with me as your mom, and giving me three granddaughters! Anna, you brought your wisdom, insight, courage, and intrepid spirit to meet the extreme challenges of your genetic illness. You continue to fill our lives with immense joy and the opportunity for growth. Sara, you were always there for all of us, even as a child. You stepped up, and with your kind nature facing this difficult disease as a sister, you grew and deepened and have so much to offer. Your dad and I are so proud of you both. And, of course, thank you to Anna's donor and her family, whose gift of life created miracles for all of us.

I am so grateful to you all for supporting my effort and helping me to stay on task. Thank you to my incredible CFRI community and my Embrace sisters. Having you in my life has made it complete and rich with cherished lifelong companionships. And thank you to our dearest Anabel Stenzel and Isabel Stenzel Byrnes, whose love and friendship made our journey as a family filled with love and laughter. They are no longer here with us, but are forever in our hearts. Isabel's passion for writing and telling stories encouraged me to write *Love, Courage, and Miracles.*

About Atmosphere Press

Founded in 2015, Atmosphere Press was built on the principles of Honesty, Transparency, Professionalism, Kindness, and Making Your Book Awesome. As an ethical and author-friendly hybrid press, we stay true to that founding mission today.

If you're a reader, enter our giveaway for a free book here:

SCAN TO ENTER
BOOK GIVEAWAY

If you're a writer, submit your manuscript for consideration here:

SCAN TO SUBMIT
MANUSCRIPT

And always feel free to visit Atmosphere Press and our authors online at atmospherepress.com. See you there soon!

About the Author

ROBIN MODLIN lives with her husband—and little dog, Jack—in two places: the beautiful northern California foothills town of Murphys and alongside the vineyards of Livermore, CA. As an emerging author, Robin writes with an introspective point of view influenced by her interest in psychology, spirituality, and creativity. She has a Master's in East-West Psychology from the California Institute of Integral Studies and is a first-place winner of participatory arts by the Society for the Arts in Healthcare. As an artist, Robin currently creates individual and community mosaics and facilitates SoulCollage® workshops. The mother of two daughters, one with cystic fibrosis (CF) and a lung transplant, Robin founded Embrace, a retreat for mothers of children with CF, and was inspired to write about her life journey in her first book, *Love, Courage, and Miracles.*